Apache Spark 2.x for Java Developers

Explore data at scale using the Java APIs of
Apache Spark 2.x

Sourav Gulati
Sumit Kumar

BIRMINGHAM - MUMBAI

Apache Spark 2.x for Java Developers

First published: July 2017

Production reference: 1250717

Published by Packt Publishing Ltd.
Livery Place
35 Livery Street
Birmingham
B3 2PB, UK.
ISBN 978-1-78712-649-7

www.packtpub.com

Credits

Authors
Sourav Gulati
Sumit Kumar

Copy Editor
Safis Editing

Reviewer
Prashant Verma

Project Coordinator
Nidhi Joshi

Commissioning Editor
Amey Varangaonkar

Proofreader
Safis Editing

Acquisition Editor
Shweta Pant

Indexer
Tejal Daruwale Soni

Content Development Editor
Mayur Pawanikar

Graphics
Tania Dutta

Technical Editor
Karan Thakkar

Production Coordinator
Arvindkumar Gupta

Each chapter is dedicated to a topic and includes an illustrative case study that covers state-of-the-art Java-based tools and software. Each chapter is self-contained, providing great flexibility of usage. The accompanying website provides the source code and data. This is truly a gem for both students and big data architects/developers, who can experiment first-hand the methods just learned, or can deepen their understanding of the methods by applying them to real-world scenarios.

As I was reading the various chapters of the book, I was reminded of the passion and enthusiasm of Sumit and Sourav have for distributed frameworks. They have communicated the concepts described in the book with clarity and with the same passion. I am positive that you, as reader, will feel the same. I will certainly keep this book as a personal resource for the solutions I implement, and strongly recommend it to my fellow architects.

Sumit Gupta

Director of Engineering, Big Data, Sapient Global Markets

Foreword

Sumit Kumar and Sourav Gulati are technology evangelists with deep experience in envisioning and implementing solutions, as well as complex problems dealing with large and high-velocity data. Every time I talk to them about any complex problem statement, they have provided an innovative and scalable solution.

I have over 17 years of experience in the IT industry, specializing in envisioning, architecting and implementing various enterprise solutions revolving around a variety of business domains, such as hospitality, healthcare, risk management, and insurance.

I have known Sumit and Sourav for 5 years as developers/architects who have worked closely with me implementing various complex big data solutions. From their college days, they were inclined toward exploring/implementing distributed systems. As if implementing solutions around big data systems were not enough, they also started sharing their knowledge and experience with the big data community. They have actively contributed to various blogs and tech talks, and in no circumstances do they pass up on any opportunity to help their fellow technologists.

Knowing Sumit and Sourav, I am not surprised that they have started authoring a book on Spark and I am writing foreword for their book - *Apache Spark 2.x for Java Developers*.

Their passion for technology has again resulted in the terrific book you now have in your hands.

This book is the product of Sumit's and Sourav's deep knowledge and extensive implementation experience in Spark for solving real problems that deal with large, fast and diverse data.

Several books on distributed systems exist, but Sumit's and Sourav's book closes a substantial gap between theory and practice. Their book offers comprehensive, detailed, and innovative techniques for leveraging Spark and its extensions/API for implementing big data solutions. This book is a precious resource for practitioners envisioning big data solutions for enterprises, as well as for undergraduate and graduate students keen to master the Spark and its extensions using its Java API.

This book starts with an introduction to Spark and then covers the overall architecture and concepts such as RDD, transformation, and partitioning. It also discuss in detail various Spark extensions, such as Spark Streaming, MLlib, Spark SQL, and GraphX.

About the Authors

Sourav Gulati is associated with software industry for more than 7 years. He started his career with Unix/Linux and Java and then moved towards big data and NoSQL World. He has worked on various big data projects. He has recently started a technical blog called *Technical Learning* as well. Apart from IT world, he loves to read about mythology.

Sumit Kumar is a developer with industry insights in telecom and banking. At different junctures, he has worked as a Java and SQL developer, but it is shell scripting that he finds both challenging and satisfying at the same time. Currently, he delivers big data projects focused on batch/near-real-time analytics and the distributed indexed querying system. Besides IT, he takes a keen interest in human and ecological issues.

About the Reviewer

Prashant Verma started his IT carrier in 2011 as a Java developer in Ericsson working in telecom domain. After couple of years of JAVA EE experience, he moved into Big Data domain, and has worked on almost all the popular big data technologies, such as Hadoop, Spark, Flume, Mongo, Cassandra,etc. He has also played with Scala. Currently, He works with QA Infotech as Lead Data Enginner, working on solving e-Learning problems using analytics and machine learning.

Prashant has also worked on *Apache Spark 2.x for Java Developers, Packt* as a Technical Reviewer.

I want to thank Packt Publishing for giving me the chance to review the book as well as my employer and my family for their patience while I was busy working on this book.

www.PacktPub.com

For support files and downloads related to your book, please visit www.PacktPub.com.

Did you know that Packt offers eBook versions of every book published, with PDF and ePub files available? You can upgrade to the eBook version at www.PacktPub.com and as a print book customer, you are entitled to a discount on the eBook copy. Get in touch with us at service@packtpub.com for more details.

At www.PacktPub.com, you can also read a collection of free technical articles, sign up for a range of free newsletters and receive exclusive discounts and offers on Packt books and eBooks.

https://www.packtpub.com/mapt

Get the most in-demand software skills with Mapt. Mapt gives you full access to all Packt books and video courses, as well as industry-leading tools to help you plan your personal development and advance your career.

Why subscribe?

- Fully searchable across every book published by Packt
- Copy and paste, print, and bookmark content
- On demand and accessible via a web browser

Customer Feedback

Thanks for purchasing this Packt book. At Packt, quality is at the heart of our editorial process. To help us improve, please leave us an honest review on this book's Amazon page at `https://www.amazon.com/dp/1787126498`.

If you'd like to join our team of regular reviewers, you can e-mail us at `customerreviews@packtpub.com`. We award our regular reviewers with free eBooks and videos in exchange for their valuable feedback. Help us be relentless in improving our products!

Table of Contents

Preface

Apache Spark is the buzzword in the big data industry right now, especially with the increasing need for real-time streaming and data processing. While Spark is built on Scala, the Spark Java API exposes all the features of Spark available in the Scala version for Java developers. This book will show you how you can implement various functionalities of the Apache Spark framework in Java without stepping out of your comfort zone.

The book starts with an introduction to the Apache Spark 2.x ecosystem, followed by explaining how to install and configure Spark, and refreshes the concepts of Java that will be useful to you when consuming Apache Spark's APIs. You will explore RDD and its associated common Action and Transformation Java APIs, set up a production-like clustered environment, and work with Spark SQL. Moving on, you will perform near-real-time processing with Spark Streaming, machine learning analytics with Spark MLlib, and graph processing with GraphX, all using various Java packages.

By the end of the book, you will have a solid foundation in implementing the components of the Spark framework in Java to build fast, real-time applications.

What this book covers

Chapter 1, *Introduction to Spark*, covers the history of big data, its dimensions, and basic concepts of Hadoop and Spark.

Chapter 2, *Revisiting Java*, refreshes the concepts of core Java and will focus on the newer feature of Java 8 that will be leveraged while developing Spark applications.

Chapter 3, *Let Us Spark*, serves the purpose of providing an instruction set so that the reader becomes familiar with installing Apache Spark in standalone mode along with its dependencies.

Chapter 4, *Understanding the Spark Programming Model*, makes progress by explaining the word count problem in Apache Spark using Java and simultaneously setting up an IDE.

Chapter 5, *Working with Data and Storage*, teaches you how to read/store data in Spark from/to different storage systems.

`Chapter 6`, *Spark on Cluster*, discusses the cluster setup process and some popular cluster managers available with Spark in detail. After this chapter, you will be able to execute Spark jobs effectively in distributed mode.

`Chapter 7`, *Spark Programming Model – Advanced*, covers partitioning concepts in RDD along with advanced transformations and actions in Spark.

`Chapter 8`, *Working with Spark SQL*, discusses Spark SQL and its related concepts such as dataframe, dataset, and UDF. We will also discuss SqlContext and the newly introduced SparkSession.

`Chapter 9`, *Near-Real-Time Processing with Spark Streaming*, covers the internals of Spark Streaming, reading streams of data in Spark from various data sources with examples, and newer extensions of stream processing in Spark known as structured streaming.

`Chapter 10`, *Machine Learning Analytics with Spark MLlib*, focuses on introducing the concepts of machine learning and then moves on towards its implementation using Apache Spark Mllib libraries. We also discuss some real-world problems using Spark Mllib.

`Chapter 11`, *Learning Spark GraphX*, looks into another module of Spark, GraphX; we will discover types of GraphX RDD and various operations associated with them. We will also discuss the use cases of GraphX implementation.

What you need for this book

If you want to set up Spark on your local machine, then you can follow the instructions mentioned in `Chapter 3`, *Let Us Spark*.

Who this book is for

If you are a Java developer interested in learning to use the popular Apache Spark framework, this book is the resource you need to get started. Apache Spark developers who are looking to build enterprise-grade applications in Java will also find this book very useful.

Conventions

In this book, you will find a number of text styles that distinguish between different kinds of information. Here are some examples of these styles and an explanation of their meaning. Code words in text, database table names, folder names, filenames, file extensions, pathnames, dummy URLs, user input, and Twitter handles are shown as follows: "The mode function was not implemented in the numpy package.". Any command-line input or output is written as follows:

```
>>> import numpy as np
>>> from scipy import stats
>>> data = np.array([4,5,1,2,7,2,6,9,3])
# Calculate Mean
>>> dt_mean = np.mean(data) ;
print ("Mean :",round(dt_mean,2))
```

New terms and important words are shown in bold.

Warnings or important notes appear like this.

Tips and tricks appear like this.

Reader feedback

Feedback from our readers is always welcome. Let us know what you thought about this book-what you liked or disliked. Reader feedback is important for us as it helps us to develop titles that you will really get the most out of. To send us general feedback, simply email feedback@packtpub.com, and mention the book's title in the subject of your message. If there is a topic that you have expertise in and you are interested in either writing or contributing to a book, see our author guide at www.packtpub.com/authors.

Customer support

Now that you are the proud owner of a Packt book, we have a number of things to help you to get the most from your purchase.

Downloading the example code

You can download the example code files for this book from your account at `http://www.p acktpub.com`. If you purchased this book elsewhere, you can visit `http://www.packtpub.c om/support`and register to have the files e-mailed directly to you. You can download the code files by following these steps:

1. Log in or register to our website using your e-mail address and password.
2. Hover the mouse pointer on the **SUPPORT** tab at the top.
3. Click on **Code Downloads & Errata**.
4. Enter the name of the book in the **Search** box.
5. Select the book for which you're looking to download the code files.

5. Choose from the drop-down menu where you purchased this book from.
6. Click on **Code Download**.

Once the file is downloaded, please make sure that you unzip or extract the folder using the latest version of:

- WinRAR / 7-Zip for Windows
- Zipeg / iZip / UnRarX for Mac
- 7-Zip / PeaZip for Linux

The code bundle for the book is also hosted on GitHub at `https://github.com/PacktPubl ishing/Apache-Spark-2x-for-Java-Developers`. We also have other code bundles from our rich catalog of books and videos available at `https://github.com/PacktPublishing/`. Check them out!

Errata

Although we have taken care to ensure the accuracy of our content, mistakes do happen. If you find a mistake in one of our books-maybe a mistake in the text or the code-we would be grateful if you could report this to us. By doing so, you can save other readers from frustration and help us to improve subsequent versions of this book. If you find any errata, please report them by visiting `http://www.packtpub.com/submit-errata`, selecting your book, clicking on the **Errata Submission Form** link, and entering the details of your errata. Once your errata are verified, your submission will be accepted and the errata will be uploaded to our website or added to any list of existing errata under the Errata section of that title. To view the previously submitted errata, go to `https://www.packtpub.com/books/content/support`and enter the name of the book in the search field. The required information will appear under the **Errata** section.

Piracy

Piracy of copyrighted material on the Internet is an ongoing problem across all media. At Packt, we take the protection of our copyright and licenses very seriously. If you come across any illegal copies of our works in any form on the Internet, please provide us with the location address or website name immediately. Please contact us at `copyright@packtpub.com` with a link to the suspected pirated material. We appreciate your help in protecting our authors and our ability to bring you valuable content.

Questions

If you have a problem with any aspects of this book, you can contact us at `questions@packtpub.com`, and we will do our best to address it.

1
Introduction to Spark

"We call this the problem of big data."

Arguably, the first time big data was being talked about in a context we know now was in July, 1997. *Michael Cox* and *David Ellsworth*, scientists/researchers from NASA, described the problem they faced when processing humongous amounts of data with the traditional computers of that time. In the early 2000s, Lexis Nexis designed a proprietary system, which later went on to become the **High-Performance Computing Cluster** (**HPCC**), to address the growing need of processing data on a cluster. It was later open sourced in 2011.

It was an era of dot coms and Google was challenging the limits of the internet by crawling and indexing the entire internet. With the rate at which the internet was expanding, Google knew it would be difficult if not impossible to scale vertically to process data of that size. Distributed computing, though still in its infancy, caught Google's attention. They not only developed a distributed fault tolerant filesystem, **Google File System** (**GFS**), but also a distributed processing engine/system called **MapReduce**. It was then in 2003-2004 that Google released the white paper titled *The Google File System* by *Sanjay Ghemawat*, *Howard Gobioff*, and *Shun-Tak Leung*, and shortly thereafter they released another white paper titled *MapReduce: Simplified Data Processing on Large Clusters* by *Jeffrey Dean* and *Sanjay Ghemawat*.

Doug Cutting, an open source contributor, around the same time was looking for ways to make an open source search engine and like Google was failing to process the data at the internet scale. By 1999, Doug Cutting had developed **Lucene**, a Java library with the capability of text/web searching among other things. **Nutch**, an open source web crawler and data indexer built by Doug Cutting along with *Mike Cafarella*, was not scaling well. As luck would have it, Google's white paper caught Doug Cutting's attention. He began working on similar concepts calling them **Nutch Distributed File System** (**NDFS**) and **Nutch MapReduce**. By 2005, he was able to scale Nutch, which could index from 100 million pages to multi-billion pages using the distributed platform.

However, it wasn't just Doug Cutting but Yahoo! too who became interested in the development of the MapReduce computing framework to serve its processing capabilities. It is here that Doug Cutting refactored the distributed computing framework of Nutch and named it after his kid's elephant toy, Hadoop. By 2008, Yahoo! was using Hadoop in its production cluster to build its search index and metadata called web map. Despite being a direct competitor to Google, one distinct strategic difference that Yahoo! took while co-developing Hadoop was the nature in which the project was to be developed: they open sourced it. And the rest, as we know is history!

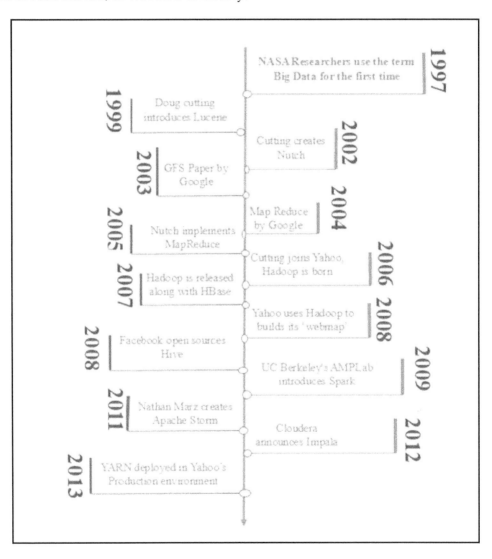

In this chapter, we will cover the following topics:

- What is big data?
- Why Apache Spark?
- RDD the first citizen of Spark
- Spark ecosystem -- Spark SQL, Spark Streaming, Milb, Graphx
- What's new in Spark 2.X?

Dimensions of big data

Big data can be best described by using its dimensions. Those dimensions are called the Vs of big data. To categorize a problem as a big data problem, it should lie in one or more of these dimensions.

The big data world started with three dimensions or 3Vs of big data, which are as follows:

- Volume
- Variety
- Velocity

Let us now take a look at each one in detail:

- **Volume**: The amount of data being generated in the world is increasing at an exponential rate. Let's take an example of social community websites such as Facebook or Twitter. They are dealing with billions of customers all around the world. So, to analyze the amount of data being generated, they need to find a solution out of the existing RDBMS world. Moreover, not only such big giants, but also other organizations, such as banks, telecom companies, and so on, are dealing with huge numbers of customers. Performing analytics on such a humongous amount of data is a big data problem. So, according to this dimension, if you are dealing with a high volume of data, which can't be handled by traditional database systems, then it's imperative to move to big data territory.

- **Variety**: There was a time when only structured data was meant to be processed. But, to keep yourself ahead of your competitor, you need to analyze every sort of data which can increase value. For example, which products on a portal are more popular than others? So, you are analyzing user clicks. Now, data from these various sources that you need to use to keep yourself ahead can be structured or unstructured. It can be XML, JSON, CSV, or even plain text. So, now the data that you may need to deal with can be of different varieties. So, if you have such an issue, realize that this is a big data problem.

- **Velocity**: Data is not only increasing in size but the rate at which it is arriving is also increasing rapidly. Take the example of Twitter: billions of users are tweeting at a time. Twitter has to handle such a high velocity of data in almost real time. Also, you can think of YouTube. A lot of videos are being uploaded or streamed from YouTube every minute. Even look at online portals of news channels; they are being updated every second or minute to cope up with incoming data of news from all over the world. So, this dimension of big data deals with a high velocity of data and helps to provide persistence or analyze the data in near real time so as to generate real value.

Then, with time, our 3D world changed to a 7D world, with the following newer dimensions:

- **Veracity**: The truthfulness and completeness of the data are equally important. Take an example of a machine learning algorithm that involves automated decision making based on the data it analyzes. If the data is not accurate, this system can be disastrous. An example of such a system can be predictive analytics based on the online shopping data of end users. Using the analytics, you want to send offers to users. If the data that is fed to such a system is inaccurate or incomplete, analytics will not be meaningful or beneficial for the system. So, as per this dimension, before processing/analyzing, data should be validated. Processing high volume or high velocity data can only be meaningful if the data is accurate and complete, so before processing the data, it should be validated as well.

- **Variability**: This dimension of big data mainly deals with natural language processing or sentiment analytics. In language, one word can have multiple usages based on the sentiments of the user. So, to find sentiments, you should be able to comprehend the exact meaning. Let's say your favorite football team is not playing well and you posted a sarcastic tweet saying "*What a great performance today by our team!!*" Now looking at this sentence, it seems you are loving the way your team is performing but in reality it is the opposite. So to analyze the sentiments, the system should be fed with lot of other information such as the statistics of the match, and so on. Another example, the sentence *This is too good to be true* is negative but it consists of all positive words. Semantic analytics or natural language processing can only be accurate if you can understand sentiments behind the data.

- **Value**: There is lot of cost involved in performing big data analytics: the cost of getting the data, the cost for arranging hardware on which this data is saved and be analyzed, the cost of employees and time that goes into these analytics. All these costs are justified if the analytics provide value to the organization. Think of a healthcare company performing analytics on e-commerce data. They may be able to perform the analytics by getting data from the internet but it does not have value for them. Also, performing analytics on data which is not accurate or complete is not of any value. On the contrary, it can be harmful, as the analytics performed are misleading. So, value becomes an important dimension of big data because valuable analytics can be useful.

- **Visualization**: Visualization is another important aspect of the analytics. No work can be useful until it is visualized in a proper manner. Let's say engineers of your company have performed real accurate analytics but the output of them are stored in some JSON files or even in databases. The business analyst of your company, not being hard core technical, is not able to understand the outcome of the analytics thoroughly as the outcome is not visualized in a proper manner. So the analytics, even though they are correct, cannot be of much value to your organization. On the other hand, if you have created proper graphs or charts or effective visualization on the outcome, it can be much easier to understand and can be really valuable. So, visualization is a really important aspect of big data analytics because things can only be highlighted if they are visible.

What makes Hadoop so revolutionary?

In a classical sense, if we are to talk of Hadoop then it comprises of two components: a storage layer called HDFS and a processing layer called MapReduce. Resource management task prior to Hadoop 2.X was done using the MapReduce framework of Hadoop itself. However, that changed with the introduction of YARN. In Hadoop 2.0, YARN was introduced as the third component of Hadoop to manage the resources of the Hadoop cluster and make it more MapReduce agnostic.

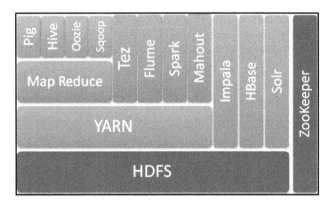

Defining HDFS

The **Hadoop Distributed File System** (**HDFS**), as the name suggests, is a distributed filesystem based on the lines of the Google File System written in Java. In practice, HDFS resembles closely any other UNIX filesystem with support for common file operations such as ls, cp, rm, du, cat, and so on. However what makes HDFS stand out, despite its simplicity, is its mechanism to handle node failure in the Hadoop cluster without effectively changing the search time for accessing stored files. The HDFS cluster consists of two major components: **DataNodes** and **NameNode**.

HDFS has a unique way of storing data on HDFS clusters (cheap commodity networked commodity computers). It splits the regular file in smaller chunks called blocks and then makes an exact number of copies of such chunks depending on the replication factor for that file. After that, it copies such chunks to different DataNodes of the cluster.

NameNode

The NameNode is responsible for managing the metadata of the HDFS cluster, such as lists of files and folders that exist in a cluster, the number of splits each file is divided into, and their replication and storage at different DataNodes. It also maintains and manages the namespace and file permission of all the files available in the HDFS cluster. Apart from bookkeeping, NameNode also has a supervisory role that keeps a watch on the replication factor of all the files and if some block goes missing, then it issue commands to replicate the missing block of data. It also generates reports to ascertain cluster health. It is important to note that all the communication for a supervisory task happens from DataNode to NameNode; that is, DataNode sends reports (block reports) to NameNode and it is then that NameNode responds to them by issuing different commands or instructions as the need may be.

HDFS I/O

An HDFS read operation from a client involves the following:

1. The client requests NameNode to determine where the actual data blocks are stored for a given file.
2. NameNode obliges by providing the block IDs and locations of the hosts (DataNode) where the data can be found.
3. The client contacts DataNode with the respective block IDs to fetch the data from DataNode while preserving the order of the block files.

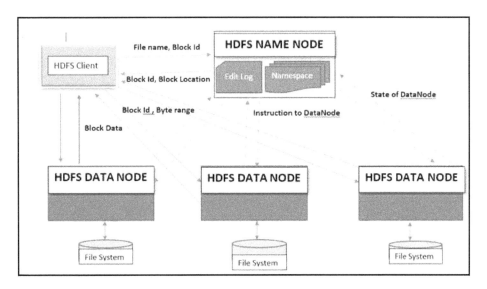

An HDFS write operation from a client involves the following:

1. The client contacts NameNode to update the namespace with the filename and verify the necessary permissions.
2. If the file exists, then NameNode throws an error; otherwise, it returns the client `FSDataOutputStream` which points to the data queue.
3. The data queue negotiates with the NameNode to allocate new blocks on suitable DataNodes.
4. The data is then copied to that DataNode, and, as per the replication strategy, the data is further copied from that DataNode to the rest of the DataNodes.
5. It's important to note that the data is never moved through the NameNode as it would caused a performance bottleneck.

YARN

The simplest way to understand **YARN (Yet Another Resource Manager)** is to think of it as an operating system on a cluster; provisioning resources, scheduling jobs and node maintenance. With Hadoop 2.x, the MapReduce model of processing the data and managing the cluster (Job Tracker/Task Tracker) was divided. While data processing was still left to MapReduce, the cluster's resource allocation (or rather, scheduling) task was assigned to a new component called YARN. Another objective that YARN met was that it made MapReduce one of the techniques to process the data rather than being the only technology to process data on HDFS, as was the case in Hadoop 1.x systems. This paradigm shift opened the floodgates for the development of interesting applications around Hadoop and a new ecosystem other than the classical MapReduce processing system evolved. It didn't take much time after that for Apache Spark to break the hegemony of classical MapReduce and become arguably the most popular processing framework for parallel computing as far as active development and adoption is concerned.

In order to serve multi-tenancy, fault tolerance, and resource isolation in YARN, it developed the following components to manage the cluster seamlessly:

- The **ResourceManager**: This negotiates resources for different compute programs on a Hadoop cluster while guaranteeing the following: resource isolation, data locality, fault tolerance, task prioritization, and effective cluster capacity utilization. A configurable scheduler allows Resource Manager the flexibility to schedule and prioritize different applications as per the requirements.

- **Tasks served by the RM while serving clients**: A client or APIs user can submit or terminate an application. The user can also gather statistics on submitted applications cluster, and queue information. RM also priorities ADMIN tasks over any other task to perform a clean up or maintenance activities on a cluster, such as refreshing the node-list, the queues' configuration, and so on.

- **Tasks served by RM while serving cluster nodes**: Provisioning and de-provisioning of new nodes forms an important task of RM. Each node sends a heartbeat at a configured interval, the default being 10 minutes. Any failure of a node in doing so is treated as a dead node. As a clean-up activity, all the supposedly running process, including containers, are marked as dead too.

- **Tasks served by the RM while serving the Application Master**: The RM registers a new the AM while terminating the successfully executed ones. Just like cluster nodes, if the heartbeat of an AM is not received within a preconfigured duration, the default value being 10 minutes, then the AM is marked dead and all the associated containers are also marked dead. But since YARN is reliable as far as the application execution is concerned, a new AM is rescheduled to try another execution on a new container until it reaches the retry configurable default count of four.

- **Scheduling and other miscellaneous tasks served by the RM**: RM maintains a list of running, submitted and executed applications along with its statistics such as execution time, status, and so on. The privileges of the user as well as of applications are maintained and compared while serving various requests of the user per application life cycle. The RM scheduler oversees the resource allocation for the application, such as memory allocation. Two common scheduling algorithms used in YARN are fair scheduling and capacity scheduling algorithms.

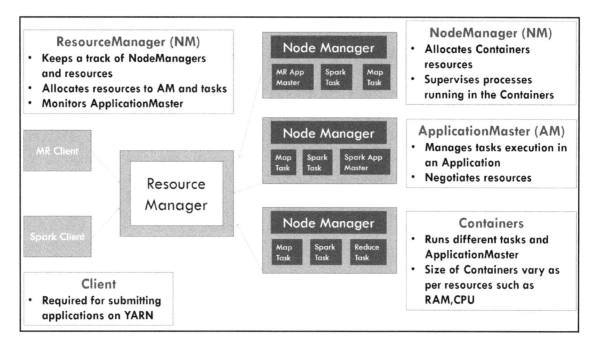

- **NodeManager**: An NM exist per node of the cluster on a slightly similar fashion as to what slave nodes are in the master slave architecture. When an NM starts, it sends the information to RM for its availability to share its resources for upcoming jobs. Then NM sends a periodic signal, also called a heartbeat, to RM informing it of its status as being alive in the cluster. Primarily, an NM is responsible for launching containers that have been requested by an AM with certain resource requirements such as memory, disk, and so on. Once the containers are up and running, the NM keeps a watch not on the status of the container's task but on the resource utilization of the container and kills it if the container starts utilizing more resources than it has been provisioned for. Apart from managing the life cycle of the container, the NM also keeps RM informed about the node's health.

- **ApplicationMaster**: An AM gets launched per submitted application and manages the life cycle of the submitted application. However, the first and foremost task an AM does is to negotiate resources from RM to launch task-specific containers at different nodes. Once containers are launched, the AM keeps track of all the container's task statuses. If any node goes down or the container gets killed because of using excess resources or otherwise, in such cases the AM renegotiates resources from RM and launches those pending tasks again. The AM also keeps reporting the status of the submitted application directly to the user and other such statistics to RM. ApplicationMaster implementation is framework specific and it is because of this reason that application/framework specific code is transferred to the AM and the AM that distributes it further. This important feature also makes YARN technology agnostic, as any framework can implement its ApplicationMaster and then utilize the resources of the YARN cluster seamlessly.

- **Containers**: A container in an abstract sense is a set of minimal resources such as CPU, RAM, Disk I/O, disk space, and so on, that are required to run a task independently on a node. The first container after submitting the job is launched by RM to host ApplicationMaster. It is the AM which then negotiates resources from RM in the form of containers, which then gets hosted in different nodes across the Hadoop cluster.

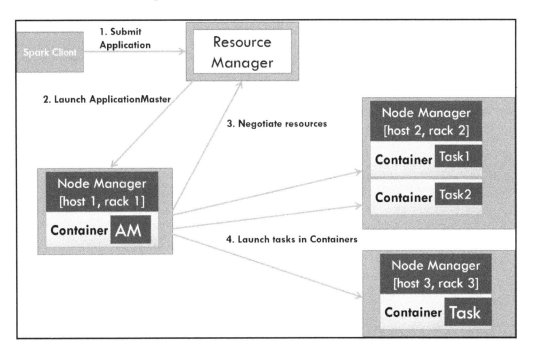

Processing the flow of application submission in YARN

The following steps follow the flow of application submission in YARN:

1. Using a client or APIs, the user submits the application; let's say a Spark job jar. ResourceManager, whose primary task is to gather and report all the applications running on the entire Hadoop cluster and available resources on respective Hadoop nodes, depending on the privileges of the user submitting the job, accepts the newly submitted task.

2. After this RM delegates the task to a scheduler, the scheduler then searches for a container which can host the application-specific Application Master. While the scheduler does take into consideration parameters such as availability of resources, task priority, data locality, and so on, before scheduling or launching an Application Master, it has no role in monitoring or restarting a failed job. It is the responsibility of RM to keep track of an AM and restart it in a new container if it fails.

3. Once the ApplicationMaster gets launched it becomes the prerogative of the AM to oversee the resources negotiation with RM for launching task-specific containers. Negotiations with RM are typically over:
   - The priority of the tasks at hand.
   - The number of containers to be launched to complete the tasks.
   - The resources needed to execute the tasks, such as RAM and CPU (since Hadoop 3.x).
   - The available nodes where job containers can be launched with the required resources.

   Depending on the priority and availability of resources the RM grants containers represented by the container ID and hostname of the node on which it can be launched.

4. The AM then requests the NM of the respective hosts to launch the containers with specific IDs and resource configuration. The NM then launches the containers but keeps a watch on the resources usage of the task. If, for example, the container starts utilizing more resources than it has been provisioned then that container is killed by the NM. This greatly improves the job isolation and fair sharing of resources guarantee that YARN provides as, otherwise, it would have impacted the execution of other containers. However, it is important to note that the job status and application status as a whole are managed by the AM. It falls in the domain of the AM to continuously monitor any delay or dead containers, simultaneously negotiating with RM to launch new containers to reassign the task of dead containers.

5. The containers executing on different nodes send application-specific statistics to the AM at specific intervals.

6. The AM also reports the status of the application directly to the client that submitted the specific application, in our case a Spark job.

7. The NM monitors the resources being utilized by all the containers on the respective nodes and keeps sending a periodic update to RM.

8. The AM sends periodic statistics such application status, task failure, and log information to RM.

Overview of MapReduce

Before delving deep into MapReduce implementation in Hadoop, let's first understand MapReduce as a concept in parallel computing and why it is a preferred way of computing. MapReduce comprises two mutually exclusive but dependent phases, each capable of running on two different machines or nodes:

- **Map**: In the Map phase, the transformation of the data takes place. It splits data into key value pairs by splitting it on a keyword.
  - Suppose we have a text file and we would want to do an analysis such as counting the total number of words or even the frequency with which the word has occurred in the text file. This is the classical word count problem of MapReduce. To address this problem, first we will have to identify the splitting keyword so that the data can be spilt and be converted into a key value pair.

Let's begin with *John Lennon's* song, *Imagine*.

Sample text:

```
Imagine there's no heaven
It's easy if you try
No hell below us
Above us only sky
Imagine all the people living for today
```

After running the Map phase on the sampled text and splitting it over <space>, it will get converted to a key value pair as shown here:

```
<imagine, 1> <there's, 1> <no, 1> <heaven, 1> <it's, 1> <easy, 1> <if, 1>
<you, 1> <try, 1> <no, 1> <hell, 1> <below, 1> <us, 1> <above, 1> <us, 1>
<only, 1> <sky, 1> <imagine, 1> <all, 1> <the, 1> <people, 1> <living, 1>
<for, 1> <today, 1>]
```

The key here represents the word and the value represents the count. Also it should be noted that we have converted all the keys to lowercase to reduce any further complexity arising out of matching case sensitive keys.

- **Reduce**: The Reduce phase deals with aggregation of the Map phase results and hence all the key value pairs are aggregated over the key.
  - So the Map output of the text would get aggregated as follows:

```
[<imagine, 2> <there's, 1> <no, 2> <heaven, 1> <it's, 1>
<easy, 1> <if, 1> <you, 1> <try, 1> <hell, 1> <below, 1>
<us, 2> <above, 1> <only, 1> <sky, 1>  <all, 1> <the, 1>
<people, 1> <living, 1> <for, 1> <today, 1>]
```

As we can see, both the Map and Reduce phases can be run exclusively and hence can use independent nodes in the cluster to process the data. This approach of separation of tasks into smaller units called Map and Reduce has revolutionized general purpose distributed/parallel computing, which we now know as MapReduce.

Apache Hadoop's MapReduce has been implemented pretty much the same way as discussed, except for adding extra features into how the data from the Map phase of each node gets transferred to their designated Reduce phase node.

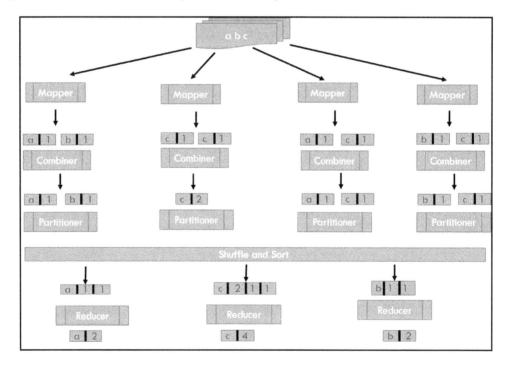

Hadoop's implementation of MapReduce enriches the Map and Reduce phases by adding a few more concrete steps in between to make it fault tolerant and truly distributed. We can describe MR jobs on YARN in five stages:

1. **Job Submission Stage**: When a client submits an MR job, the following things happen:
   - The RM is requested for an application ID
   - The input data location is checked and if present then the file split size is computed
   - The job's output location needs to exist as well

   If all the three conditions are met, then the MR job jar along with its configuration details of input split are copied to HDFS in a directory named the application ID provided by RM. Then the job is submitted to RM to launch a job-specific Application Master, `MRAppMaster`.

2. **MAP Stage:** Once RM receives the client's request for launching `MRAppMaster`, a call is made to the YARN scheduler for assigning a container. As per the resource availability, the container is granted and hence the `MRAppMaster` is launched at the designated node with provisioned resources. After this, `MRAppMaster` fetches input split information from the HDFS path that was submitted by the client and computes the number of mapper tasks that will be launched based on the splits. Depending on the number of mappers, it also calculates the required number of reducers as per the configuration, If `MRAppMaster` now finds the number of mapper, reducer and size of input files to be small enough to be run in the same JVM, then it goes ahead in doing so. Such tasks are called *Uber tasks*. However, in other scenarios, `MRAppMaster` negotiates container resources from RM for running these tasks, albeit mapper tasks have a higher order and priority. This is why Mapper tasks must finish before the sorting phase can start.

Data locality is another concern for containers hosting mappers, as local data nodes are preferred over rack locals, with the least preference being given to remote node hosted data. But when it comes to the Reduce phase no such preference of data locality exists for containers. Containers hosting function mappers first copy `mapReduce` JAR and configuration files locally and then launch a class called `YarnChild` in the JVM. The mapper then starts reading the input file, processes them by making key value pairs, and writes them in a circular buffer.

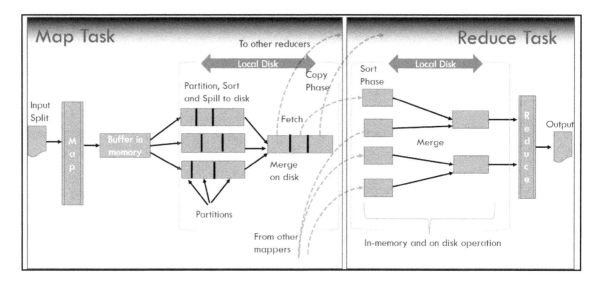

3. **Shuffle and Sort Phase**: Considering that circular buffers have a size constraint, after a certain percentage, the default being 80, a thread gets spawned which spills the data from the buffer. But, before copying the spilled data to disk, it is first partitioned with respect to its reducer and then the background thread also sorts the partitioned data on a key and if the combiner is mentioned it then combines the data too. This process optimizes the data once it is copied to its respective partitioned folder. This process is continued until all the data from circular buffer gets written to disk. A background thread again checks if the number of spilled files in each partition is within the range of the configurable parameter or else the files are merged and the combiner is run over them until it falls within the limit of the parameter.

A Map task keeps updating the status to ApplicationMaster for its entire life cycle. It is only when 5 percent of a Map task has been completed that the Reduce task starts. An auxiliary service in the NodeManager serving the Reduce task starts a Netty web server that makes a request to MRAppMaster for Mapper hosts having specific Mapper partitioned files. All the partitioned files that pertain to the Reducer are copied to their respective nodes in a similar fashion. Since multiple files get copied as data from various nodes representing that Reduce nods gets collected, a background thread merges the sorted map file and again sorts them and if the combiner is configured, then combines the result too.

4. **Reduce Stage:** It is important to note here that at this stage every input file of each reducer should have been sorted by key. This is the presumption with which the reducer starts processing these records and converts the key value pair into an aggregated list. Once the reducer has processed the data, it writes them to the output folder as was mentioned during the job submission.

5. **Clean-up Stage:** Each reducer sends a periodic update to `MRAppMaster` about the task completion. Once the Reduce task is over, the ApplicationMaster starts the clean-up activity. The submitted job status is changed from *running* to *successful*, and all the temporary and intermediate files and folders are deleted .The application statistics are archived to a job history server.

Why Apache Spark?

MapReduce is on its way to being a legacy. We've got Spark, says the man behind Apache Hadoop, *Doug Cutting*. MapReduce is an amazingly popular distributed framework but it comes with its fair amount of criticism as well. Since its inception, MapReduce has been built to run jobs in batch mode. Although it supports streaming, it's not very well suited for ad-hoc queries, machine learning, and so on. Apache Spark is a distributed in-memory computing framework, and somehow tries to address some of the major concern that surrounds MapReduce:

- **Performance**: A major bottleneck in MapReduce jobs are disk I/Os, and it is considerably visible during the shuffle and sort phase of MR, as data is written to disk. The guiding principal that Spark follows is simple: share the memory across the cluster and keep everything in memory as long as possible. This greatly enhances the performance of Spark jobs to the tune of 100X when compared to MR (as claimed by their developers).

- **Fault tolerance**: Both MR and Spark have different approaches in handling fault tolerance. The AM keeps a track of mappers and reducers while executing MR jobs. As and when these containers stop responding or fail upfront, the AM after requesting the RM, launches a separate JVM to run such tasks. While this approach achieves fault tolerance, it is both time and resource consuming. Apache Spark's approach of handling fault tolerance is different; it uses Resilient Distributed Datasets (RDD), a read only fault-tolerant parallel collection. RDD maintains the lineage graph so that whenever its partition gets lost it recovers the lost data by re-computing from the previous stage and thus making it more resilient.

- **DAG**: Chaining of MapReduce jobs is a difficult task and along with that it also has to deal with the burden of writing intermediate results on HDFS before the next job starts its execution. Spark is actually a **Directed Acyclic Graph** (**DAG**) engine, so chaining any number of job can easily be achieved. All the intermediate results are shared across memory, avoiding multiple disk I/O. Also these jobs are lazily evaluated and hence only those paths are processed which are explicitly called for computation. In Spark such triggers are called *actions*.

- **Data processing**: Spark (aka Spark Core) is not an isolated distributed compute framework. A whole lot of Spark modules have been built around Spark Core to make it more general purpose. RDD forms the main abstract in all these modules. With recent development dataframe and dataset have also been developed, which enriches RDD by providing it a schema and type safety. Nevertheless, the universality of RDD is ubiquitous across all the modules of Spark making it simple to use and it can easily be cross-referenced in different modules. Whether it is streaming, querying capability, machine learning, or graph processing, the same data can be referenced by RDD and can be interchangeably used. This is a unique appeal of RDD, which is lacking in MR, as different concept was required to handle machine learning jobs in **Apache Mahout** than was required in **Apache Giraph**.

- **Compatibility**: Spark has not been developed to keep only the YARN cluster in mind. It has amazing compatibility to run on Hadoop, Mesos, and even a standalone cluster mode. Similarly, Spark has not been built around HDFS and has a wide variety of acceptability as far as different filesystems are concerned. All Apache Spark does is provide compute capabilities while leaving the choice of choosing the cluster and filesystem to the use case being worked upon.

- **Spark APIs**: Spark APIs have wide coverage as far as functionality and programming languages are concerned. Spark's APIs have huge similarities with the Scala collection, the language in which Apache Spark has been majorly implemented. It is this richness of functional programming that makes Apache spark avoid much of the boilerplate code that eclipsed MR jobs. Unlike MR, which dealt with low level programming, Spark exposes APIs at a higher abstraction level with a scope of overriding any bare metal code if ever required.

RDD - the first citizen of Spark

The very first paper on *RDD Resilient Distributed Datasets: A Fault-Tolerant Abstraction for In-Memory Cluster Computing* described it as follows:

Resilient Distributed Datasets (**RDDs**), a distributed memory abstraction that lets programmers perform in-memory computations on large clusters in a fault-tolerant manner. As Spark is written in a functional programming paradigm, one of the key concepts of functional programming is immutable objects. Resilient Distributed Dataset is also an immutable dataset.

Formally, we can define an RDD as an immutable distributed collection of objects. It is the primary data type of Spark. It leverages cluster memory and is partitioned across the cluster.

The following is the logical representation of RDD:

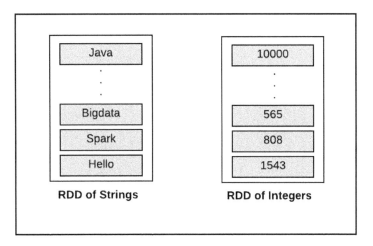

RDDs can consist of (key, value) pairs as well. The following is the logical representation of pair of RDDs:

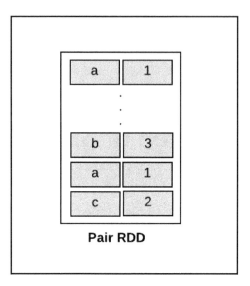

Pair RDD

Also, as mentioned, RDD can be partitioned across the cluster. So the following is the logical representation of partitioned RDDs in a cluster:

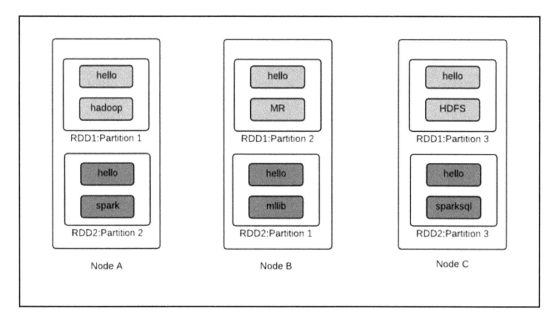

Operations on RDD

An RDD supports only two types of operations. One is called transformation and the other is called action. The following are the explanations of both of these:

- **Transformation:** If an operation on an RDD gives you another RDD, then it is a transformation. Consider you have an RDD of strings and want to filter out all values that start with *H* as follows:

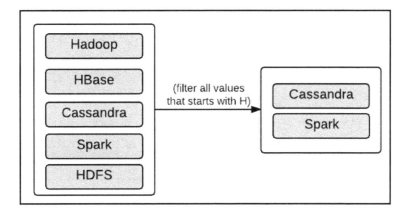

    So, a filter operation on an RDD will return another RDD with all the values that passes through the filter condition. So, a filter is an example of a transformation

- **Action:** If an operation on an RDD gives you a result other than an RDD, it is called an action: for example, the sum of all values in an RDD, or the count of all the values or retrieving all values of RDD in form of a list, and so on. The following is the logical representation of an action sum of an RDD:

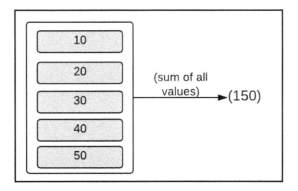

So, the rule is if after an operation on an RDD, you get an RDD then it is a transformation; otherwise, it is an action. We will discuss all the available transformations and actions that can be performed on an RDD, with the coding examples, in `Chapter 4`, *Understanding the Spark Programming Model* and `Chapter 7`, *Spark Programming Model - Advanced*.

Lazy evaluation

Another important thing to understand about RDD is **Lazy evaluation**. Spark creates a DAG, also called the lineage graph, of all the operations you perform on an RDD. Execution of the graph starts only when an action is performed on RDD. Let's consider an example of DAG operations on RDD:

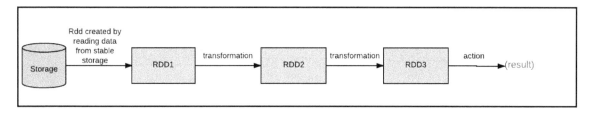

Here, first an RDD is calculated by reading data from a stable storage and two of the transformations are performed on the RDD and then finally an action is performed to get the result.

Look at the previous diagram; one would infer that **RDD1** will be created as soon as a Spark job finds the step to create it from the database and then it will find the transformation steps, so it will perform transformations. Then it finds an action and so it will run the given action to calculate the result. However, this is not true.

In reality, a Spark job will start creating DAG steps until it finds a step that asks it to perform action on RDD. When the job finds this step, it starts executing the DAG from the first vertex.

The following are the benefits of this approach:

- **Fault tolerance**: The lineage graph of the operations on an RDD, makes it fault tolerant. Since Spark is well aware of the steps it needs to perform to create an RDD, it can recalculate the RDD or its partitions in case of failure of the previous step instead of repeating the whole process again. For example, with DAG, if a partition of RDD is lost while processing, it can be calculated from **RDD2**, instead of repeating the process of calculating it from the database and performing two transformations. This gives a huge benefit of saving time and resources in case of failures.

- **Optimizing resource usage:** As Spark knows all the steps to be performed to calculate the end result in advance, it can leverage this information to use the cluster resources in a most optimized manner.

Benefits of RDD

Following are some benefits that Spark RDD model provides over Hadoop MapReduce Model:

- **Iterative processing**: One of the biggest issue, with MapReduce processing is the IO (Input/Output) involved. It really slows down the process of MapReduce if you are running iterative operations where you would basically chain MapReduce jobs to perform multiple aggregations.

  Consider running a MapReduce job that reads data from HDFS and performs some aggregation and writes the output back to HDFS. Now, mapper jobs will read data from HDFS and write the output to the local filesystem after completion and Reduce pulls that data and runs the reduce process on it. After which, it writes the output to HDFS (not considering the spill mechanism of mapper and reducer).

Now, let's say you want to perform another aggregation on the output data so you will execute another MapReduce job on the output data which will go through a similar I/O process. So the following is the logical representation of how iterative operations will run in MapReduce.

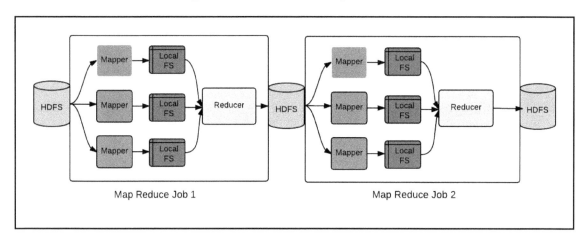

On the other hand, Spark will not perform such I/O in most of the cases for the job previously described. Data will be read from HDFS once and then Spark will perform in memory transformation on RDD for every iteration. The output of every step (that is, another RDD) will be stored in the distributed cluster memory. The following is the logical representation of the same job in Spark:

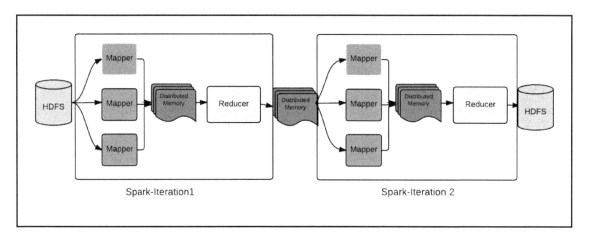

Now, here is a catch. What if the size of the intermediate results is more than the distributed memory size? In that case, Spark will spill that RDD to disk.

- **Interactive Processing**: Another benefit of the data structure of Spark over MapReduce or Hadoop can be seen when the user wants to run some ad-hoc queries on the data placed on some stable storage.

  Let's say you are trying to run some MapReduce jobs (or Hive queries) on the data to do some analysis. If you are running multiple queries on same input data, MapReduce will read the data from storage, let's say HDFS, every time you run the query. A logical representation of that can be as follows:

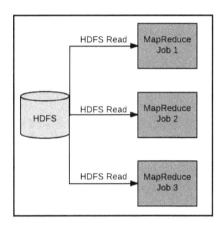

On the other hand, Spark provides a mechanism to persist an RDD in memory (different mechanisms of persisting RDD will be discussed later in `Chapter 4`, *Understanding the Spark Programming Model*). So, you can execute one job and save RDD in memory. Then, other analytics can be executed on the same RDD without reading the data from HDFS again. The following is the logical representation of that:

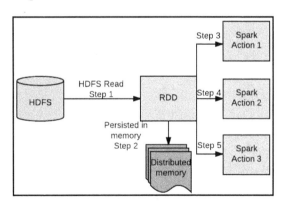

When a Spark job encounters *Spark Action 1*, it executes the DAG and calculates the RDD. Then the RDD will be persisted in memory and *Spark Action 1* will be performed on the RDD. Afterwards, *Spark Action 2* and *Spark Action 3* will be performed in the same RDD. So, this model helps to save lot of I/O from the stable storage in case of interactive processing.

Exploring the Spark ecosystem

Apache Spark is considered as the general purpose system in the big data world. It consists of a lot of libraries that help to perform various analytics on your data. It provides built-in libraries to perform batch analytics, perform real-time analytics, apply machine learning algorithms on your data, and much more.

The following are the various built-in libraries available in Spark:

- **Spark Core:** As its name says, the Spark Core library consists of all the core modules of Spark. It consists of the basics of the Spark model, including RDD and various transformation and actions that can be performed with it. Basically, all the batch analytics that can be performed with the Spark programming model using the MapReduce paradigm is the part of this library. It also helps to analyze different varieties of data.
- **Spark Streaming**: The Spark Streaming library consists of modules that help users to run near real-time streaming processing on the incoming data. It helps to handle the velocity part of the big data territory. It consists of a lot of modules that help to listen to various streaming sources and perform analytics in near real time on the data received from those sources.
- **Spark SQL**: The Spark SQL library helps to analyze structured data using the very popular SQL queries. It consists of a dataset library which helps to view the structured data in the form of a table and provides the capabilities of running SQL on top of it. The SQL library consists of a lot of functions which are available in SQL of RDBMS. It also provides an option to write your own function, called the **User Defined Function** (**UDF**).
- **MLlib**: Spark MLlib helps to apply various machine learning techniques on your data, leveraging the distributed and scalable capability of Spark. It consists of a lot of learning algorithms and utilities and provides algorithms for classification, regression, clustering, decomposition, collaborative filtering, and so on.
- **GraphX**: The Spark GraphX library provides APIs for graph-based computations. With the help of this library, the user can perform parallel computations on graph-based data. GraphX is the one of the fastest ways of performing graph-based computations.

- **Spark-R**: The Spark R library is used to run R scripts or commands on Spark Cluster. This helps to provide distributed environment for R scripts to execute. Spark comes with a shell called `sparkR` which can be used to run R scripts on Spark Cluster. Users which are more familiar with R, can use tool such as RStudio or Rshell and can execute R scripts which will run on the Spark cluster.

What's new in Spark 2.X?

- **Unified DataFrame and Dataset**: The Spark 2.X release has unified both the APIs. Now Dataframe is just a row in Dataset without any data type information implicitly attached.
- **SparkSession**: Prior to Spark 2.X, there were different entry points for different Spark jobs; that is, for Spark SQL we had `sqlContext` and if Hive features were also required then `HiveContext` was the entry point. With Spark 2.X this ambiguity has been removed and now we have one single entry point called `SparkSession`. However, it is to be noted that all the module-specific entry points are still very much around and have not been deprecated yet.
- **Catalog API**: Spark 2.X has introduced the Catalog API for accessing metadata information in Spark SQL. It can be seen as parallel to **Hcatalog** in Hive. It is a great step in unifying the metadata structure around Spark SQL so that the very same metadata can be exposed to non-Spark SQL applications. It is also helpful in debugging the temporary registered table in a Spark SQL session. Metadata of both `sqlContext` and `HiveContext` are available now, as the Catalog API can be accessed by `SparkSession`.
- **Structured streaming**: Structured streaming makes Spark SQL available in streaming job by continuously running the Spark SQL job and aggregating the updated results on a streaming datasets. The Dataframe and Dataset are available for operations in structured streaming along with the windowing function.
- **Whole-stage code generation**: The code generation engine has been modified to generate more performance-oriented code by avoiding virtual function dispatches, transfer of intermediate operation data to memory, and so on.
- **Accumulator API**: A new simpler and more performant Accumulator API has been added to the Spark 2.X release and the older API has been deprecated.
- A native SQL parser that supports both ANSI-SQL as well as Hive SQL has been introduced in the current Spark build.

- Hive-style bucketing support too has been added to the list of supported SQL functions in Spark SQL.
- Subquery support has been added in Spark SQL and supports other variations of the clause such as NOT IN, IN, EXISTS, and so on.
- Native CSV data source, based on the databricks implementation has been incorporated in Spark.
- The new `spark.ml` package which is based on Dataframe has been introduced with an objective to deprecate `spark.mllib` once the newly introduced package matures enough in features to replace the old package.
- Machine learning pipelines and models can now be persisted across all languages supported by Spark.

References

- http://www.evl.uic.edu/cavern/rg/20040525_renambot/Viz/parallel_volviz/paging_outofcore_viz97.pdf
- http://static.googleusercontent.com/media/research.google.com/en//archive/gfs-sosp2003.pdf
- http://static.googleusercontent.com/media/research.google.com/en//archive/mapreduce-osdi04.pdf
- *Mastering Apache Solr: A practical guide* to get to grips with *Apache Solr* by *Mr. Mathieu Nayrolles* [Page 6]
- https://web.archive.org/web/20051029085121/http:/weblogs.java.net/blog/tomwhite/archive/2005/09/mapreduce.html
- *Nutch: A Flexible and Scalable Open-Source Web Search Engine,* http://citeseerx.ist.psu.edu/viewdoc/download?doi=10.1.1.105.5978&rep=rep1&type=pdf
- https://developer.yahoo.com/blogs/hadoop/yahoo-launches-world-largest-hadoop-production-application-398.html
- http://data-informed.com/doug-cutting-reflects-on-hadoops-impact-future/

Summary

In this chapter, you learned about the history of Bigdata and its dimensions and basic concepts of Hadoop and Spark. After that, you were introduced to RDD, and you learned the basic concepts of the Spark RDD model. Then, you learned about the various components of the Spark Ecosystem and the newer features of Spark 2.x.

As this book focuses on implementing Spark Applications in Java, in the next chapter, we will refresh the concepts of core Java and focus on the newer feature of Java 8, which will be leveraged while developing Spark Applications.

2
Revisiting Java

This chapter is added as the refresher course of Java. In this chapter, we will discuss some concepts of Java that will be useful while creating applications in Apache Spark.

This book assumes that the reader is comfortable with the basics of Java. We will discuss useful Java concepts and mainly focus on *what is new in Java 8?* More importantly, we will touch upon on topics such as:

- Generics
- Interfaces
- Lambda expressions
- Streams

Why use Java for Spark?

With the rise in multi-core CPUs, Java could not keep up with the change in its design to utilize that extra power available to its disposal because of the complexity surrounding concurrency and immutability. We will discuss this in detail, later. First let's understand the importance and usability of Java in the Hadoop ecosystem. As MapReduce was gaining popularity, Google introduced a framework called **Flume Java** that helped in pipelining multiple MapReduce jobs. Flume Java consists of immutable parallel collections capable of performing lazily evaluated optimized chained operations. That might sound eerily similar to what Apache Spark does, but then even before Apache Spark and Java Flume, there was Cascading, which built an abstraction over MapReduce to simplify the way MapReduce tasks are developed, tested, and run. All these frameworks were majorly a Java implementation to simplify MapReduce pipelines among other things.

These abstractions were simple in fact, **Apache Crunch**, Apache's implementation of Flume Java, was so concise that a word count problem could be written in four-five lines of Java code. That is huge!

Nevertheless these Java implementations could never do away with the heavy I/O bound operations. And it was just then that Apache Spark was born, primarily written in Scala, which not only addressed the limitations of MapReduce, but also the verbosity of Java while developing a MapReduce Job without using any abstraction framework. In their paper, *Resilient Distributed Datasets: A Fault-Tolerant Abstraction for In-Memory Cluster Computing*, the authors state that:

> *"We chose Scala due to its combination of conciseness (which is convenient for interactive use) and efficiency (due to static typing). However, nothing about the RDD abstraction requires a functional language."*

Eventually the Java community realized that with time they would have to support functional programming to harness the capacity of cluster computing as vertical scaling of enterprise hardware was not the solution for applications being developed for the future. Java started releasing features around concurrency. Java 7 introduced the fork join framework to harness the capabilities of modern hardware; it also introduced an instruction set `invokedynamic`, which enabled method calls to be made at runtime. This single instruction set, change allowed dynamically typed language on the JVM. Java 8 beautifully utilized the concept of late binding in `invokedynamic` and developed entire Lambda expressions around it. It also released the Stream API, which can be thought of as a collection framework for functional programming in Java without actually storing the elements. Other notable changes in Java 8 are:

- Functional interfaces
- Default and static methods in interfaces
- New date and time API
- Scripting support

Apache Spark has added support for Java 8 and hence the difference in writing a code in Scala and Java is blurring with each release. The learning curve also matches its potential as one is left to learn only the Apache Spark API and not Scala as well. Another highlight of Apache Spark is Spark-SQL, which can come in handy if interactive and dynamic coding is required.

Generics

Generics were introduced in Java 1.5. Generics help the user to create the general purpose code that has abstract type in its definition. That abstract type can be replaced with any concrete type in the implementation.

For example, the list interface or its implementations, such as `ArrayList`, `LinkedList` and so on, are defined with generic type. Users can provide the concrete type such as `Integer`, `Long`, or `String` while implementing the list:

```
List<Integer> list1 =new ArrayList<Integer>();
List<String> list2 =new ArrayList<String>();
```

Here, `list1` is the list of integers and `list2` is the list of strings. With Java 7, the compiler can infer the type. So the preceding code can also be written as follows:

```
List<Integer> list1 =new ArrayList<>();
List<String> list2 =new ArrayList<>();
```

Another huge benefit of generic type is that it brings compile-time safety. Let's create a list without the use of generics:

```
List list =new ArrayList<>();
list.add(1);
list.add(2);
list.add("hello");
list.add("there");
```

Here, you can see that the list contains both integers and strings. If you retrieve an element of it, it will be of an object type by default:

```
Object object = list.get(0);
```

So the user has to specifically cast it to its correct type:

```
Integer object = (Integer)list.get(0);
```

This makes the code error prone. Because if casting is done correctly, it will throw `ClassCastException` at runtime. Let's create the same list with the use of generics:

```
List<Integer> listGeneric =new ArrayList<>();
listGeneric.add(1);
listGeneric.add(2);

listGeneric.add("hello"); // won't compile
```

`listGeneric` becomes the list of integers. If you try to add strings in it, the compiler will not allow it.

So, now if you retrieve an element from the list, it will give you an integer type. No type casting is required, which will save us from `ClassCastException` at runtime. Hence, it provides compile-time safety:

```
Integer intObject = listGeneric.get(0);
```

Creating your own generic type

In this section, we will create a class with generic type `T`. Classes will consist of the variable of type `T` and will also have a general purpose method that will return the variable of type `T`:

```
public class MyGeneric<T> {
  T input;
  public MyGeneric(T input) {
    this.input=input;
  }
  public T getInput()
  {
    return input;
  }
}
```

As described previously, `MyGeneric` is the class. It consists of the variable input of type `T`, a constructor to construct the object of the `MyGenric` class and initialize the variable input and a method that returns the value of `T`.

Now, let's implement it:

```
public class MyGenericsDemo {

  public static void main(String[] args) {
    MyGeneric<Integer> m1 =new MyGeneric<Integer>(1);
    System.out.println(m1.getInput());
    //It will print '1'
    MyGeneric<String> m2 =new MyGeneric<String>("hello");
    System.out.println(m2.getInput());
    //It will print 'hello'
  }
}
```

Here, we have created two objects of the `MyGeneric` class, one with an integer type and the other with a string type. When we invoke the `getInput` method on both objects, they will return the value of their respective type.

Interfaces

Interfaces are the reference types in Java. They are used in Java to define contracts among classes. Any class that implements that interface has to adhere to the contract that the interface defines.

For example, we have an interface `car` as follows that consists of three abstract methods:

```
public interface Car {
    void shape();
    void price();
    void color();
}
```

Any class that implements this interface has to implement all the abstract methods of this interface unless it is an abstract class. Interfaces can only be implemented or extended by other interfaces, they cannot be instantiated.

Prior to Java 8, interfaces consisted only of abstract methods and final variables. In Java 8, interfaces may contain default and static methods as well.

Static method in an interface

The static method in an interface is similar to the static method in a class. Users cannot override them. So even if a class implements an interface, it cannot override a static method of an interface.

Like a static method of a class, static method in an interface is called by using an interface name or class type reference, not using instance variables:

```
public interface MyInterface {
    static String hello()
    {
        return "Inside static method in interface";
    }
    void absmethod();
}
```

Here is an interface with an abstract method and a static method:

```
public class MyInterfaceImpl implements MyInterface{
    @Override
    public void absmethod() {
        System.out.println("Abstract method implementaion in class");
    }
}
```

Here is the class that implements the interface given previously, so to adhere to the contract it has to provide implementation of the abstract method as it is not an abstract class. However, it does not need to implement the static method.

Now, let's try to call the static method:

```
public class MyInterfaceDemo {
public static void main(String[] args) {
    System.out.println(MyInterface.hello()); // it works
    MyInterfaceImpl obj =new MyInterfaceImpl();
    obj.hello(); // wont-complie
}
}
```

So, calling the static method using the interface name reference works, but it does not work using the instance variable to a class that implements the interface.

Default method in interface

The default method is another extension in an interface provided in Java 8. An interface can consist of default methods. Classes that implement that interface may or may not implement the default method. Default methods are useful to extend an existing interface. Suppose you have an interface that is implemented by a lot of classes. Now, you want to extend functionality of the interface.

The first option you have is to add a new abstract method in the interface and force every class to implement it, which will break the existing implementation and require lots of new code. The second option is to add default methods in the interface, if some class wants to override them, it is free to do that. With this option, an existing implementation won't break as well. The `foreach` method in an iterable interface is the classic example of extending functionality using default methods.

Default methods can be created using default keywords. Let's change the static method in the preceding example to the default method:

```
public interface MyInterface {
    default String hello() {
        return "Inside static method in interface";
    }
    void absmethod();
}
```

The class implementing this interface does not need to provide the implementation of this method:

```
public class MyInterfaceImpl implements MyInterface {
    @Override
    public void absmethod() {
        System.out.println("Abstract method implementaion in class");
    }
}
```

Now, let's try to call the default method:

```
public class MyInterfaceDemo {
    public static void main(String[] args) {
        System.out.println(MyInterface.hello()); // won't compile
        MyInterfaceImpl obj =new MyInterfaceImpl();
        obj.hello(); // works
    }
}
```

Note that default methods are instance methods. They can be called using the instance of the class that implements the interface.

What if a class implements two interfaces which have default methods with same name and signature?

Interfaces in Java are used to provide multiple inheritances. Classes can implement more than one interface. As interface can consist of default methods in Java 8, which a class does not necessarily need to implement. We can have two interfaces that have default methods with the same name and signature.

Let's create two interfaces with the same default method:

```
public interface Interface1 {
   default void hello(){
      System.out.println("Hello from Interface1");
   }
}

public interface Interface2 {
   default void hello(){
      System.out.println("Hello from Interface1");
   }
}
```

So, we have two interfaces with the default method `hello` with the same signature:

```
public class InterfaceImpl implements Interface1,Interface2{
   @Override
   public void hello() {
      Interface1.super.hello();
   }
}
```

Now, once you create a class that implements both of these interfaces, the compiler will force you to override the `hello` method. You can call `hello` of any of the interfaces if you want using the syntax given previously or you can given a different implementation to it.

Anonymous inner classes

Anonymous inner classes are essentially inner classes in Java. They are called anonymous as they don't possess a name. They are declared and instantiated at the same time.

Anonymous inner classes are used whenever you need to provide the implementation of the interface or override the abstract method of a class. They are useful if the implementation of the interface or abstract class is needed only once.

Let's discuss it with the example of the `FilenameFilter` interface, which has been included in Java since JDK1.0.

Suppose you want to print all the files in a directory whose name ends with `java`.

The first approach is to create a class that implements the `FilenameFilter` interface as follows:

```
public class MyFileNameFilter implements FilenameFilter {
    @Override
    public boolean accept(File dir, String name) {
        return name.endsWith("java");
    }
}
```

Then, use the object of this class in your implementation as follows:

```
public class MyFilterImpl {
    public static void main(String[] args) {
        File dir = new File("src/main/java");
        dir.list(new MyFileNameFilter());
    }
}
```

However, you may require the implementation of this interface only once in your code, so instead of creating a separate class you can provide the implementation of this interface anonymously as follows:

```
public class MyFilterImpl {
    public static void main(String[] args) {
        File dir = new File("src/main/java");
        dir.list(new FilenameFilter() {
            @Override
            public boolean accept(File dir, String name) {
                return name.endsWith("java");
            }
        });
    }
}
```

This is an example of anonymous inner classes. The code might look weird at the time, but this is a very concise way of implementing an interface or abstract class if implementation is needed only once.

Lambda expressions

Lambda expressions are the brand new feature of Java. Lambda expressions are introduced in Java 8 and it is a step towards facilitating functional programming in Java.

Lambda expressions help you to define a method without declaring it. So, you do not need a name for the method, return-type, and so on. Lambda expressions, like anonymous inner classes, provide the way to pass behaviors to functions. Lambda, however, is a much more concise way of writing the code.

For example, the preceding example of an anonymous inner class can be converted to Lambda as follows:

```
public class MyFilterImpl {
    public static void main(String[] args) {
        File dir = new File("src/main/java");
        dir.list((dirname,name)->name.endsWith("java")); //Lambda Expression
        }
}
```

Note that the signature of the Lambda expression is exactly matching the signature of the `accept` method in the `FilenameFilter` interface.

 One of the huge differences between Lambda and anonymous inner classes lies in the way Lambdas are invoked. Lambdas are invoked dynamically using **Method Handle** (**MH**) calls, unlike anonymous inner classes where a separate inner class is created at compile time for reference.

Functional interface

In Java 8, all the **Single Abstract Method interfaces** (**SAM interfaces**), such as `java.util.Comparator`, `java.io.FilenameFilter`, `java.lang.Comparable`, `java.lang.Runnable`, and so on, are given a new name called the **Functional interface**.

Functional interfaces are the interfaces that consist of the Single Abstract Method. These interfaces are the target for Lambda expressions. So in other words, Lambda expressions can only implement the interfaces that have only one abstract method. This is the other difference between Lambda and anonymous inner classes.

A new annotation type `@FunctionalInterface` is added in Java 8. So if an interface is annotated with `@FunctionalInterface`, it is not allowed to have more than one abstract method.

The following declaration will work:

```
@FunctionalInterface
public interface Interface1 {
  void method1();
}
```

If you try to add one more abstract method to this interface, the compiler will throw an error stating - `Interface1 is not a Functional Interface`.

Syntax of Lambda expressions

A Lambda expression consists of two parts: 0 or more arguments and the function body:

```
argument -> function
(argument1,argument2,...argument) -> function
```

Let's discuss it with examples. Consider a list of integers as follows:

```
List<Integer> list = Arrays.asList(1,2,3,4,5);
```

Print each element of the list using Lambda:

```
list.forEach(n-> System.out.println(n));
```

Multiply each element of the list by 2:

```
list.stream().map(n -> n*2 );
```

 The stream method will convert the list to a stream of numbers. We will discuss more about it in another section. For now, just consider that the stream will convert all the elements of the list into the stream.

Here, we do not need to specify the type of n. The type of n is auto-inferred in Lambda. Also, we have not specified any return statement. The return statement is implicit in Lambda. If you want, you can specify the return statement explicitly as follows:

```
list.stream().map(n -> {
    return n*2;
  });
}
```

For specifying the return type explicitly, you need to enclose the function body in braces and provide a semicolon (;) at the end of the return statement.

Lexical scoping

Lexical scoping is also referred to as **Static scoping**. As per lexical scoping, a variable will be accessible in the scope in which it is defined. Here, the scope of the variable is determined at compile time.

Let us consider the following example:

```
public class LexicalScoping {
    int a = 1;
    // a has class level scope. So It will be available to be accessed
    // throughout the class

    public void sumAndPrint() {
        int b = 1;
        int c = a + b;
        // b and c are local variables of method. These will be accessible
        // inside the method only
    }
    // b and c are no longer accessible
}
```

Variable a will be available throughout the class (let's not consider the difference of static and non-static as of now). However, variables b and c will be available inside the sumAndPrint method only.

Similarly, a variable given inside lambda expressions are accessible only to that Lambda. For example:

```
list.stream().map(n -> n*2 );
```

Here n is lexically scoped to be used in the Lambda expression only, and n does not have any scope outside the Lambda expression.

Method reference

To improve code readability of Lambda expressions for functions having a name method reference is used. Method references have been identified in four different categories:

- **Static method reference**: For a static method isOdd, the method can be directly referenced as MethodReferenceExample::isOdd:

```
public static boolean isOdd(Integer n) { return n % 2 != 0; };
public static void main(String[] args) {
IntStream.range(1,
8).filter(MethodReferenceExample::isOdd).forEach(x->System.out.prin
tln(x));
}
```

- **Instance method reference**: For referencing an instance method, the instance of the method can be called separated by a double colon (::). Here System.out is an instance of PrintStream whose method println is being called:

```
//Instance Method Reference
IntStream.range(1, 8).filter(x->
x%2==0).forEach(System.out::println);
```

- **Constructor reference**: A constructor method reference can be called by adding the suffix new after :::

```
//Constructor Reference
TreeSet<String> hset=
streamSupplier.get().collect(Collectors.toCollection(TreeSet::new))
;
```

4. **Instance method reference of an arbitrary object of a particular type**: The following example is an instance method reference of an arbitrary object of a particular type:

```
System.out.println(" The sum of lengths are ::" +
streamSupplier.get().map(x->x.length()).reduce(Integer::sum));
```

Type	Lambda form	Method reference	Comments
Static method reference	`(a, b) -> Employee.data(a, b)`	`Employee::data`	Employee class has a static method, `data()`.
Instance method reference	`(a, b) -> sb.get(a, b)`	`sb::get`	The method `get()` is fetched using the instance object `sb`.
Constructor reference	`()->{ return new Integer ();}`	`Integer::new`	Constructor being called directly.
Instance method reference of an arbitrary object of a particular type	`x->System.out.println(x)`	`System.out::println`	A non-static method being called using a class name.

Understanding closures

As per the **Mozilla Developer Network** (**MDN**) -- "*A closure is a special kind of object that combines two things: a function, and the environment in which that function was created.*"

In other words, the closure remembers the variables in the environment in which it was created. In Java, closures can be implemented using Lambdas. Let us discuss this with an example. Suppose we have a class `ClosureExample` as follows:

```
public class ClosureExample {
    public static Function<Integer, Integer> closure() {
        int a=3;
        Function<Integer, Integer> function = t->{
            return t*a; // a is available to be accessed in this function
        };
        return function;
    }
}
```

This class consists of a function `closure()`, which returns a type of `java.util.function.Function`. In the previous example, variable `a` is in the scope of the function `closure`, so it is available to be accessed inside this function.

Then we have a nested function named `function` of type `java.util.function.Function`. This function takes an integer and multiplies it with `a` and returns the result. Then at last we are returning the nested function.

So according to the rules of scope, the value of a should vanish once a `closure()` call is finished. However, it is not the case. Let's call this function another class:

```
public class ClosureDemo {
    public static void main(String[] args) {
        List<Integer> list = Arrays.asList(1, 2, 3, 4, 5);
        Function<Integer, Integer> closure = ClosureExample.closure();
        list.stream().map(closure).forEach(n -> System.out.print(n+" "));
    }
}
```

If you run it, it multiplies every value by 3 and produces the following output:

```
3 6 9 12 15
```

So the nested function in the function `closure()` is an example where it has taken a snapshot of the environment it was created in and then it is able to access the variable `a` which was in scope when it was created.

However, one interesting thing to note with closures is the Java. Any variable, which it uses and is defined outside its definition, it assumes that variable to be final or effectively final. So, in other words, in the example given previously, if you try to change the value of a inside the nested function, `function` then the compiler will not allow it:

```
int a=3;
Function<Integer, Integer> function = t->{
            // a++  // will not compile
      return t*a; // a is available to be accessed in this function
   };
```

If you try to change the value compiler will throw an error saying: `Local variable a defined in an enclosing scope must be final or effectively final.`

Streams

A stream represents a collection of elements on which a chain of aggregate operations can be performed lazily. Streams have been optimized to cater to both sequential as well as parallel computation, keeping in mind the hardware capabilities of CPU cores. The Steams API was introduced in Java 8 to cater to functional programming needs of the developer. Streams are not Java based collections; however, they are capable enough to operate over collections by first converting them into streams. Some of the characteristics of streams that make them uniquely different from Java collection APIs are:

- Streams do not store elements. It only transfer values received from sources such as I/O channels, generating functions, data structures (Collections API), and perform a set of pipelined computation on them.
- Streams do not change the underlying data, they only process them and produce a new set of resultant data. When a `distinct()` or `sorted()` method is called on a stream, the source data does not change, but produces a result that is distinct or sorted.
- In general, streams are lazily evaluated; this leaves plenty of opportunity for code optimization. The thumb rule for lazy evaluation being that if an operation returns a stream then it is lazy or otherwise eager.
- Unlike collections streams, can be unbounded. This critically serves the purpose of processing streaming data in particular. Unbounded streams can be interrupted using the methods `limit()`, `findFirst()`, and so on.
- Streams are consumable, which means once a terminal operation gets fired on a stream it cannot be reused again. A similar parlance can be drawn from an iterator, which once iterated over needs to be regenerated again.

Generating streams

There are multiple ways in which stream objects can be created however, some of the most common ways in which stream objects can be generated are as follows:

1. **Using user/programmatically specified elements**: Streams can be generated using the method of `java.util.Stream interface`:

   ```
   //Creating Streams using user/programmatically specified elements
   Stream<String>Userstream = Stream.of("Creating", "Streams", "from",
   "Specific", "elements");
   //Creating Streams using array of objects
   Stream<String>ArrayStream = Stream.of( new
   String[]{"Stream","from","an","array","of","objects"} );
   ```

2. **From arrays**: The class `java.util.Arrays` has a method stream(array) that takes in arrays as an argument to create streams:

   ```
   //Creating Streams from an array
   String[] StringArray=new
   String[]{"We","can","convert","an","array","to","a","Stream","using
   ","Arrays","as","well"};
   Stream<String>StringStream=Arrays.stream(StringArray);
   ```

3. **From collections**: The Java class `java.util.Collection` also has the methods `stream()` and `parallelStream()` to construct serial and parallel streams, respectively:

   ```
   //Creating Streams from Collection
   List<Double>myCollection = new ArrayList<>();
   for(inti=0; i<10; i++){
       myCollection.add(Math.random());
   }
   //sequential stream
   Stream<Double>sequentialStream = myCollection.stream();
   //parallel stream
   Stream<Double>parallelStream = myCollection.parallelStream();
   ```

4. **From maps**: HashMaps have a slightly different way for creating streams as they contain keys and values. The streams are hence applied on `java.util.Map.entrySet().stream()` and `java.util.Map.values().stream()`:

   ```
   //Stream from Hashmap
   Map<String, Integer>mapData = new HashMap<>();
   mapData.put("This", 1900);
   ```

```
mapData.put("is", 2000);
mapData.put("HashMap", 2100);
mapData.entrySet()
        .stream()
        .forEach(p -> System.out.println(p));
mapData.keySet()
        .stream()
        .forEach(p-> System.out.println(p));
```

5. **Primitive streams:** The Stream API also supports three primitive streams `IntStream`, long stream, and double stream. From a performance point of view these stream APIs are more efficient, as the boxing and unboxing of elements do not take place and hence should be preferred wherever possible. The method `range()` generates a series where the starting number is inclusive while the last element is exclusive. On the other hand `rangeClosed()` generates a series where both the ends of the series are inclusive:

```
//primitive streams
IntStream.range(1, 4)
          .forEach(p -> System.out.println(p));
LongStream.rangeClosed(1, 4)
           .forEach(p -> System.out.println(p));
DoubleStream.of(1.0,2.0,3.0,4.0)
             .forEach(p -> System.out.println(p));
```

6. **Infinite streams** : Unlike collection, streams can be of infinite length. A stream interface provides methods `generate()` and `iterate()` to produce infinite streams. The `generate()` method is passed a function that always fetches the next element of the sequence:

```
//Infinite Streams using generate()
Stream <Double>sequentialDoubleStream = Stream.generate(Math ::
random);
Stream<Integer>sequentialIntegerStream = Stream.generate(new
AtomicInteger () :: getAndIncrement);
```

In the case of the `iterate()` method, an initial element seed is passed to the function, which generates the stream. The first element in such infinite streams is always the seed value that was passed in the iterate function:

```
//Infinite Streams using iterate()
Stream <Integer>sequentialIntegerStream1 = Stream.iterate
(Integer.MIN_VALUE, i ->i++);
Stream <BigInteger>sequentialBigIntegerStream =
Stream.iterate(BigInteger.ZERO, i ->i.add (BigInteger.TEN));
```

7. **Streams from files**: The Java `NIO` package also allows us to create streams from files using the method `lines()`. Each line in the file is treated as a stream element; the decoding charset can also be defined while parsing the file:

```
//Streams from File
Stream<String>streamOfStrings =
Files.lines(Paths.get("Apology_by_Plato.txt"));
Stream<String>streamWithCharset =
Files.lines(Paths.get("Apology_by_Plato.txt"),
Charset.forName("UTF-8"));
```

Streams are usually pipelined to perform a set of operations that comprises of a source (collectioxns, IO channel), zero or more **intermediate operations** and a **terminal operation**.

Intermediate operations

Intermediate operations always return another stream and get lazily evaluated only when terminal operations are called. The feature of lazy evaluation optimizes intermediate operations when multiple operations are chained together as evaluation only takes place after terminal operation. Another scenario where lazy evaluation tends to be useful is in use cases of infinite or large streams as iteration over an entire stream may not be required or even possible, such as `anyMatch`, `findFirst()`, and so on. In these scenarios, short circuiting (discussed in the next section) takes place and the terminal operation exits the flow just after meeting the criteria rather than iterating over entire elements.

Intermediate operations can further be sub-divided into stateful and stateless operations. Stateful operations preserve the last seen value, as in methods such as `sorted()`, `limit()`, `sequential()`, and so on since they need them while processing the current record. For example, the `limit()` method needs to keep a check on the maximum number of elements allowed in that stream and it can only be achieved if we possess the count of records previously stored in the stream. A stateless operation has no such obligation to manage the state of stream and hence operations such as `peek()`, `map()`, `filter()`, and so on do not possess any state as such:

Method	Intermediate Operation	Terminal Operation	Short Circuiting Operation	Stateful	Stateless
Filter	Y				Y
Map	Y				Y
flatMap	Y				Y
Distinct	Y			Y	
Sorted	Y			Y	
forEach		Y			Y
Peek	Y				Y
Limit	Y		Y	Y	
toArray		Y			Y
Reduce		Y			Y
Collect		Y			Y
Max		Y			
Min		Y			
anyMatch		Y	Y		
findFirst		Y	Y		
sequential	Y				
parallel	Y				

Working with intermediate operations

Following are some of the frequently used intermediate operations:

1. `filter()`: The method `filter()` method creates a new stream by first evaluating each element in the stream that passes a certain criteria that matches a given predicate:

```
//Filter Operation
IntStream.rangeClosed(1, 10)
        .filter(s -> s>4)
        .forEach(p -> System.out.println(p));
```

2. `map()`: A `map()` is an intermediate operation that produces an equal number of output values as there are input values. It is a unary operator that simply transforms the element so each time an element is passed to the map function it returns an object and hence there is a one-to-one mapping between the input values and the transformed output values. Map is usually required when we want to transform the elements of the stream, for example we want to create a stream of integers corresponding to the length of each string in the input stream. Such transformation can be achieved by using `map()`:

```
int sumOfLength=streamSupplier.get().map(x
->x.toString().length()).peek(x->System.out.println(Integer.parseIn
t(x.toString())))

.mapToInt(x->x.intValue()).sum();
```

As you may notice, we have also used special `map()` functions, such as `mapToInt()`, corresponding to primitive data types such as `int`, `long`, and `double`. The purpose of these special `map()` functions is to provide some added pipeline operations, such as `sum()`.

3. `flatmap()`: `flatMap()` is a combination of two operations, the `map()` and `flat()` operations. When the data is passed to `flatMap()` it may return more than one value to flatten the result. A simple corollary can be drawn from the following representation:

Input Data Stream	Operation	Result
`Stream<String[]>`	`flatMap()` Operation	`Stream<String>`
`Stream<Set<String>>`	`Stream<String>`	
`Stream<List<String>>`	`Stream<String>`	
`Stream<List<T>>`	`Stream<T>`	

Hence, `flatMap()` essentially takes an input element and transforms it in such a way that it may result in returning more than one value so that the resultant output is of the form `Stream<T>`:

```
//flatMap Example
Stream<List<String>>streamList = Stream.of(
Arrays.asList("FistList-FirstElement"),
Arrays.asList("SecondList-FirstElement", "SecondList-
```

```
SecondElement"),
Arrays.asList("ThirdList-FirstElement"));
//The streamList is of the form List<String>
Stream<String>flatStream = streamList
   .flatMap(strList ->strList.stream());
// But after applying flatMap operaton it translates into
Strem<String>
flatStream.forEach(System.out::println);
```

Similar to the `map()` operation, even the `flatMap()` operation has primitive variants of `flatMap()` functions to specially cater to int, long, and double data types.

4. **Sorted**: The elements of a stream can be sorted in their natural order by using the `sorted()` method. However, the element of the streams must be comparable or else `ClassCastException` is thrown:

```
//Natural Sorting
streamSupplier.get().sorted().forEach(System.out::println);
```

Apart from natural sorting, custom sorting of elements is also possible, where an overridden method of the `sorted()` method accepting a compartor can be used. If we want to change the natural sorting to reverse the order it can be achieved by:

```
//Comparing elements with reverse order
streamSupplier.get().sorted(Comparator.reverseOrder()).forEach(Syst
em.out::println);
```

Another way of sorting data is to use a Lambda function as an argument to the comparator:

```
//Sorting the element in reverse order based on their length
streamSupplier.get().sorted(Comparator.comparing(x
->x.toString().length()).reversed()).forEach(System.out::println);
```

Sorting on multiple fields is also possible as sorting algorithms can be chained to sort data in a specific sequence:

```
//Sorting on multiple fields
streamSupplier.get().sorted(Comparator.comparing(x
->x.toString().length()).thenComparing(x->x.toString())).forEach(Sy
stem.out::println);
```

5. **Distinct**: The `distinct()` method returns the unique values of the elements in the stream. The comparison property can be altered by using the overridden equals method:

```
//Distinct filters all the multiple records having same length
streamSupplier.get().mapToInt(x->x.toString().length()).distinct().
forEach(System.out::println);
```

6. **Limit**: In certain scenarios particularly in the case of infinite streams, the stream can be truncated using the `limit()` method with the appropriate value of `maxSize`:

```
//Limiting the size of the stream
streamSupplier.get().limit(2).forEach(System.out::println);
```

Terminal operations

Terminal operations act as the trigger point in a pipelined stream operation to trigger execution. Terminal operations either return a void or a non-stream type object and once the pipelined operations have been executed on the stream, the stream becomes redundant. A Terminal operation is always required for a pipelined stream operation to be executed.

Stream operations can further be classified as short-circuiting operations. An intermediate operation is said to be short circuited when an infinite input produces a finite stream such as in the case of the `limit()` method. Similarly, short circuiting operations in the case of terminal operations is when an infinite input may terminate in finite time, as is the case for the methods `anyMatch()`, `findAny()`, and so on.

Streams also support parallelism , but in the case of stateful operations, since each parallel operation can have its own state, a parallel stateful operation may have to undergo multiple passes to complete the operation. For example, the `distinct()` method will not produce the correct results if the results are processed parallel in one go. However, no such restriction of multiple passes exists for stateless operations. The entire set of operations remains the same for both serial and parallel execution, only differentiator being the stream itself. If the Stream is parallel the operation will happen in parallel, or else the operations take place serially. The streams API provides a helper method, `isParallel()`, to check if the stream is serial or parallel. The only pre-condition that is required for a parallel stream operation to match that of the serial stream is the values passed to the operation must be non-interfering , where non-interfering is defined as the data whose underlying value does not change for any given set of operations.

The order of data in a stream can be dependent upon the source, intermediate operation, or the terminal operation.

Working with terminal operations

A couple of terminal operations which require some attention in detail are as follows:

- `forEach()`: One of the most important paradigms where functional programming differs from imperative programming is the way it is focused on *what* to implement rather than *how* to implement. This cannot be explained any better than the new `foreach()` method of Java 8. Previous implementation of iteration, however unique each may be, focused on how the iteration will take place and each time it was different for the list, **HashMap**, array, set, and so on. This way of iterating over elements was also called external iteration, which inherently not only processed data serially, but also followed the storage and retrieval order of the collection. This in certain cases, had a performance impact and hence the **Stream API** introduced the `forEach()` method to overcome some of these limitations. The iteration using the `forEach()` method in the stream API is internal, which means that we do not define how to iterate, but rather what to do while iterating. This also provides the opportunity to both serialize as well as parallelize the iteration and is taken care of by the API itself:

```
Supplier<Stream<String>>streamSupplier =()->Stream.of( new
String[]{"Stream","from","an","array","of","objects"} ) ;

//Sequential For each
streamSupplier.get().sequential().forEach(P->System.out.println("Se
quential output :: "+P));
```

We can also iterate over the same elements in parallel as follows:

```
Supplier<Stream<String>>streamSupplier =()->Stream.of( new String[]
{"Stream","from","an","array","of","objects"} ) ;

//Parallel For each
streamSupplier.get().parallel().forEach(P->System.out.println("Para
llel
output :: "+P));
```

An important thing to notice however is that order of output has changed as parallel iteration does not guarantee the Collection order of operation.

- **Sum** : Sum is one of the simplest reduction terminal operators. What reduction operators essentially do is to iterate an entire stream and perform an operation that tends to reduce the size of result, which may be as small as one element. The sum function does exactly that, it iterates over the set of elements in the stream and sums the elements over the iteration:

```
System.out.println("Number of alphabets present in the stream
::"+streamSupplier.get().mapToInt(x ->x.length()).sum());
```

- **Reduce**: Reduce refers to an accumulation operation where each element of the stream is operated upon to produce a resultant element. Two basic tenets of a reduction operations is that it should have two operands:
    - A cumulative or derived collective value of the elements iterated so far which should be of the same type as the elements of the stream.
    - A subsequent non-iterated element of the stream.

  A fold operation is applied on both these operands to return the operated value as the first operand for the next non-iterated element. This operation continues until no unprocessed element is left behind in the stream. The reduce() method is a more generalized reduction operation that results in a single value.

  The signatures of the reduce() method in Java are:

```
Optional<T> reduce(BinaryOperator<T> reducer)
```

  This is the simplest of the available reduce methods; the argument reducer is an associative function, an accumulator, to combine two elements. Let's take an example of adding up the numbers using reduce() instead of sum as we did before:

```
Stream<Strings> streamSupplier = .......
Optional<Integer> simpleSum=
streamSupplier.map(x->x.length()).reduce((x,y)-> x+y);
```

Also note that if the input stream is empty then so is the result and hence the return type for such a signature is Optional. If we have just one element in the stream then the result is simply that value, in this case:

```
T r------educe(T identity, BinaryOperator<T> reducer)
```

This signature of the reduce method expects two arguments, identity, which acts as an initial value for the second argument, which is an associative function, an accumulator. The stream may be empty in this case, but the result is not empty and an `identity` value is taken as the default value. We can refactor the previous summing of the word length example as follows:

```
Stream<Strings> streamSupplier = .......
Integer defaulValSum=
streamSupplier.map(x->x.length()).reduce(0,(x,y)-> x+y);
```

Now we have seen that both the `reduce()` methods perform the same action, so which one to prefer and when? There is no straightforward answer to this, but to say that it is use case dependent. Let s take an example of a cricket match and applying a reduce `method()` to count the score. Here having an `identity` value of say 0 would mean that even those batsman yet to bat have a zero score just like the batsmen who have already had their chance. Now that can be misleading and we would want the reduce method to have no default values in this case. So the choice of the reduce method is subjective to the use case being developed:

```
<U> U reduce(U identity, BiFunction<U,? super T,U> reducer,
BinaryOperator<U> combiner)
```

The `reduce()` method also has a signature where it accepts three parameters. An identity element that also acts as the default value and hence the return type is the same as well. The second parameter `reducer` is an accumulator function that operates upon the next element of the stream and the previous accumulated partial result. The `reducer` accumulator is special in a sense that the input parameter can be of different types. The third parameter is a combiner that combines all partial results to form other partial results.

What makes this `reduce()` method special is that it is ideally designed to work in parallel or in use cases where an accumulator and combiner are required for performance reasons to say the least. In parallel execution, the stream is split into segments, which are processed in separate threads each having a copy of the `identity` elements and the accumulator function producing intermediate results. These intermediate results are then fed to the combiner to arrive at a result. Carrying forward the same summation example, but by using the three argument signature, the reducer function will look like this:

```
Stream<Strings> streamSupplier = .......
Integer valSum= streamSupplier.reduce(0,(x,y)->
x+y.length(),(acc1,acc2)->acc1+acc2);
```

Also it is important to note that if the reducer type is the same as that of the combiner then both reducer and combiner are essentially doing the same thing.

- **Collect**: Collect is a mutable reduction operation, and unlike the `reduce()` method which reduces the data into a single value or element, the `collect()` method returns mutable objects such as list, set, array, HashMap, and so on.

  The signature of the `collect()` method in Java is:

```
<R> R collect(Supplier<R> resultFactory, BiConsumer<R,? super T>
accumulator, BiConsumer<R,R> combiner)
```

  The `collect()` method accepts three parameters and similar to `reduce()` method, it also has an accumulator and combiner. Where it differs from the `reduce()` method is the `resultFactory`, which is an empty result container. The relationship among the parameters being passed to the `collect()` method therefore becomes that of creating result containers, accumulating partial results in containers, and finally combining the partial containers. String concatenation can be an example to show these functional relationships:

```
StringBuilder concat = streamSupplier.get().collect(() ->
new StringBuilder(),(sbuilder, str) ->sbuilder.append(str),
(sbuilder1, sbuiler2) ->sbuilder1.append(sbuiler2));
```

Now here in the example, the first parameter creates a result container in the form of an empty `StringBuilder` object, the second parameter accumulates the next stream elements to the `StringBuilder` object and finally, the combiner combines the partial `StringBuilder` object into one:

```
<R> R collect(Collector<? super T,R> collector)
```

The `collect()` method also has a simplified method signature in which the role of accumulator, combiner, and result container generation can be encapsulated into a single abstraction called the Collector interface. The Collectors class is an implementation of the Collector interface which has abundant factory methods to perform various reduction operations.

String collectors

The string concatenation example can be written using the collector as follows:

```
//String Concatenation using non parameterized joining
String concatedString = streamSupplier.collect(Collectors.joining());
```

The factory method `joining()` will concatenate all the string elements of the stream into a string. There are other overloaded `joining()` methods, one accepting a delimiter to separate each element of the concatenated string. This comes in handy while generating special delimited text files such as CSVs:

```
//String Concatenation using joining with delimiter parameter
String delimitedString = streamSupplier.collect(Collectors.joining(","));
```

The `joining()` function also has an overloaded function with three parameters, which are delimiter, prefix, and suffix. The overloaded method has been designed in such a way that the developer does not need to worry about the element being iterated in the stream. The method smartly appends a suffix in the end instead of the delimiter:

```
//String Concatenation using joining with delimiter parameter
String concatString =
streamSupplier.collect(Collectors.joining(",","[","]"));
```

The `joining()` method not only provides the simplest optimized way to concatenate the strings, but high performance as well. As you will notice the strings can be concatenated using the `reduce()` method as well, but strings are immutable and hence accumulators concatenating strings tend to copy the string each time. While one can also use the `forEach()` method along with a Lambda function to append the `StringBuffer` or `StringBuilder`, all these options do not perform as well as the `joining()` method of the collectors.

Collection collectors

The Collectors method also provides ways to reduce the stream into mutable data structures such as lists and sets:

```
//Collection Collectors
List<String>listCollected =
streamSupplier.get().collect(Collectors.toList());
System.out.println("The list collected value of Stream are :: " +
listCollected);
Set<String>setCollected=streamSupplier.get().collect(Collectors.toSet());
System.out.println("The set collected value of Stream are :: " +
setCollected);
```

By default, the `toSet()` method produces a **HashSet** and hence the results are unsorted. If we want the results to be sorted, we can use the `toCollection()` method to specify an ordered set, in our case let's use Tree Set:

```
Set<String>orderedSetCollected=streamSupplier.get().collect(Collectors.toCo
llection(TreeSet::new));
System.out.println("The ordered set collected value of Stream are ::
"+orderedSetCollected);
```

Map collectors

The streams can also be collected as a map; however, the key-value pairs need to be identified in order to create a map:

```
//Map Collectors
Map<String ,
Integer>mapCollected=orderedSetCollected.stream().collect(Collectors.toMap(
x->x.toString(),x->x.toString().length() ));
System.out.println("The generated Map values are :: "+mapCollected);
```

In the preceding implementation, it is assumed that the keys are unique; however, that may not be always the case and we might get an `IllegalStateException` exception saying that a duplicate key exists. To handle such scenarios, an overloaded method of `toMap()` can be used as follows:

```
//Map Collectors with duplicate key handling
Map<Object, List<Integer>>
mapWithDupVals=streamSupplier.get().collect(Collectors.toMap(x->x.toString(
),
//KeyMapper
x -> {List <Integer>tmp = new ArrayList <> ();
tmp.add(x.toString().length()); returntmp;},
//ValueMapper
(L1, L2) -> { L1.addAll(L2); returnL1;} //MergeFunction
));
System.out.println("The generated Map values with duplicate values::" +
mapWithDupVals);
```

Here the `toMap()` method accepts three arguments: `KeyMapper`, `ValueMapper`, and `MergeFunction`. The role of `KeyMapper` is to produce the key value of the map, while the role of `ValueMapper` is to map the value in this case in a list. Merge function has a special role of conflict avoidance as per the logic of the function, here the logic being to add both the elements in a list. There can be multiple ways to handle duplicate keys; the preceding case is only one of the many ways of doing so.

Groupings

The elements of streams can also be grouped using Collectors, returning a map, such that for a key of type `T`, the Collector generates a `Map<T,List<Y>>`:

```
//Grouping Collectors
Map<Integer,List<String>>groupExample=
streamSupplier.get().collect(Collectors.groupingBy(x->
x.toString().length()));
System.out.println("Grouping stream elements on the basis of its length ::
" + groupExample);
```

Partitioning

Partitioning is a special condition of grouping where the elements of the streams are partitioned based on the logic of the predicate function being passed to the Collectors. The predicate function based on a Boolean logic evaluates each element of the stream to either be true or false. The resultant output of the `partitioningBy()` method is a Map having two keys, true and false, and a list of values of streams associated with each Boolean value depending on the output of the predicate function:

```
//Partition Collectors
Map<Boolean,List<String>>partitionExample=streamSupplier.get().collect(Coll
ectors.partitioningBy( x->x.toString().length() > 5 ));
System.out.println("Patitioning of elements on the basis of its length ::
"+partitionExample);
```

Matching

Streams APIs provide multiple terminal methods to match a predicate against the elements of the stream:

- **All element match the predicate**: For validating if all the elements match the predicate, the `allMatch()` method is used. If all the elements match the predicate only then will the result be a Boolean true:

  ```
  boolean matchesAll
  =streamSupplier.get().allMatch(x->x.toString().length() > 1);
  System.out.println("All the elemetns have lenght greater than 1
  ::"+matchesAll);
  ```

- **No elements match the predicate**: If none of the elements match the predicate condition, the `noneMatch()` method returns the Boolean value true or else it is false:

  ```
  boolean noneMatches
  =streamSupplier.get().noneMatch(x->x.toString().length() > 1);
  System.out.println("None of the elemetns have lenght greater than 1
  ::"+noneMatches);
  ```

- **Any element matches the predicate**: This is a special matching function as it short circuits the result, that is, the moment an element matches the predicate, the anyMatch() method returns a true and exits the operation:

```
boolean anyMatches
=streamSupplier.get().peek(x->System.out.println("Element being
iterated is :: "+x)).anyMatch(x->x.toString().length() == 2);
System.out.println("The short circuit terminal operation finished
with return value :: "+anyMatches);
```

Finding elements

Finding elements in Java streams has the following variants:

- **Find any element of the stream**: The method findAny() is a short circuited terminal operation where the terminal operation returns the first encountered value of the stream before exiting the operation. In the case of an empty stream an empty optional is returned. It is also a non-deterministic function and hence the execution in parallel may return different values in each execution:

```
System.out.println("In a paralled stream from 5-100 finding any
element :: "+IntStream.range(5, 100).parallel().findAny());
```

- **Find first elements of the stream:** This is a deterministic function and it returns the first element of the stream or an empty optional in the case of an empty stream:

```
System.out.println("In a paralled stream from 8-100 finding the
first element :: "+IntStream.range(8, 100).parallel().findFirst());
```

- **Count**: This counts the number of elements present in a stream and then returns its value as a long:

```
Long elementCount=streamSupplier.get().count();
System.out.println("The number of elements in the stream are::
"+elementCount);
```

Summary

This chapter dealt with various concepts of Java and more particularly topics around generics and interfaces. We also discussed new features introduced in Java 8 such as Lambda expressions and streams. Introduction to the default method in Java 8 was also covered in detail.

In the next chapter, we will discuss the installation of Spark and Scala. We will also discuss Scala's REPL and the Spark UI along with exposure of Spark's REST API for working with Spark jobs, Sparks componentsm, and various configuration parameters.

3

Let Us Spark

This chapter serves the purpose of providing instructions so that the reader becomes familiar with the process of installing Apache Spark in standalone mode, along with its dependencies. Then we will start our first interaction with Apache Spark by doing a couple of hands on exercises using Spark CLI as known as REPL.

We will move on to discuss Spark components and common terminologies associated with spark, and then finally discuss the life cycle of a Spark Job in a clustered environment. We will also explore the execution of Spark jobs in a graphical sense, from creation of DAG to execution of the smallest unit of tasks by the utilities provided in Spark Web UI.

Finally, we will conclude the chapter by discussing different methods of Spark Job configuration and submission using Spark-Submit tool and Rest APIs.

Getting started with Spark

In this section, we will run Apache Spark in local mode or standalone mode. First we will set up Scala, which is the prerequisite for Apache Spark. After the Scala setup, we will set up and run Apache Spark. We will also perform some basic operations on it. So let's start.

Since Apache Spark is written in Scala, it needs Scala to be set up on the system. You can download Scala from `http://www.scala-lang.org/download/` (we will set up Scala 2.11.8 in the following examples).

Once Scala is downloaded, we can set it up on a Linux system as follows:

```
sparkuser@~$ ls
examples.desktop   scala-2.11.8.tgz
sparkuser@~$ sudo mv scala-2.11.8.tgz /usr/local
sparkuser@~$ cd /usr/local
sparkuser@/usr/local$ sudo tar -zxf scala-2.11.8.tgz
sparkuser@/usr/local$ ls
bin  etc  games  include  lib  man  sbin  scala-2.11.8  scala-2.11.8.tgz  share  src
sparkuser@/usr/local$ cd scala-2.11.8/
sparkuser@/usr/local/scala-2.11.8$ ls
bin  doc  lib  man
sparkuser@/usr/local/scala-2.11.8$ bin/scala
Welcome to Scala 2.11.8 (Java HotSpot(TM) 64-Bit Server VM, Java 1.8.0_101).
Type in expressions for evaluation. Or try :help.

scala>
```

Also, it is recommended to set the `SCALA_HOME` environment variable and add Scala binaries to the `PATH` variable. You can set it in the `.bashrc` file or `/etc/environment` file as follows:

```
export SCALA_HOME=/usr/local/scala-2.11.8
export PATH=$PATH:/usr/local/scala-2.11.8/bin
```

It is also shown in the following screenshot:

```
# Alias definitions.
# You may want to put all your additions into a separate file like
# ~/.bash_aliases, instead of adding them here directly.
# See /usr/share/doc/bash-doc/examples in the bash-doc package.

if [ -f ~/.bash_aliases ]; then
    . ~/.bash_aliases
fi

# enable programmable completion features (you don't need to enable
# this, if it's already enabled in /etc/bash.bashrc and /etc/profile
# sources /etc/bash.bashrc).
if ! shopt -oq posix; then
  if [ -f /usr/share/bash-completion/bash_completion ]; then
    . /usr/share/bash-completion/bash_completion
  elif [ -f /etc/bash_completion ]; then
    . /etc/bash_completion
  fi
fi

export SCALA_HOME=/usr/local/scala-2.11.8
export PATH=$PATH:/usr/local/scala-2.11.8/bin
```

Now, we have set up a Scala environment successfully. So, it is time to download Apache Spark. You can download it from `http://spark.apache.org/downloads.html`.

The Spark version can be different, as per requirements.

After Apache Spark is downloaded, run the following commands to set it up:

```
tar -zxf spark-2.0.0-bin-hadoop2.7.tgz
sudo mv spark-2.0.0-bin-hadoop2.7 /usr/local/spark
```

Directory location can be different as per user's requirement.

Also, you can set environment variable SPARK_HOME. It is not mandatory; however, it helps the user to find the installation directory of Spark. Also, you can add the path of Spark binaries in the $PATH variable for accessing them without specifying their path:

```
export SPARK_HOME=/usr/local/spark
export PATH=$PATH:/usr/local/scala-2.11.8/bin:$SPARK_HOME/bin
```

It is shown in the following screenshot:

```
# enable programmable completion features (you don't need to enable
# this, if it's already enabled in /etc/bash.bashrc and /etc/profile
# sources /etc/bash.bashrc).
if ! shopt -oq posix; then
  if [ -f /usr/share/bash-completion/bash_completion ]; then
    . /usr/share/bash-completion/bash_completion
  elif [ -f /etc/bash_completion ]; then
    . /etc/bash_completion
  fi
fi

export SCALA_HOME=/usr/local/scala-2.11.8
export SPARK_HOME=/usr/local/spark
export PATH=$PATH:/usr/local/scala-2.11.8/bin:$SPARK_HOME/bin
```

Now, we are ready to start Spark in standalone mode. Let's run the following command to start it:

```
$SPARK_HOME/bin/spark-shell
```

Also, we can simply execute the `spark-shell`command as Spark binaries are added to the environment variable `PATH`.

```
sparkuser@spark$
sparkuser@spark$
sparkuser@spark$
sparkuser@spark$
sparkuser@spark$spark-shell
Using Spark's default log4j profile: org/apache/spark/log4j-defaults.properties
Setting default log level to "WARN".
To adjust logging level use sc.setLogLevel(newLevel). For SparkR, use setLogLevel(newLevel).
17/05/22 06:49:41 WARN NativeCodeLoader: Unable to load native-hadoop library for your platform... using builtin-java classes where applicable
17/05/22 06:49:45 WARN ObjectStore: Failed to get database global_temp, returning NoSuchObjectException
Spark context Web UI available at http://10.204.136.223:4040
Spark context available as 'sc' (master = local[*], app id = local-1495435781982).
Spark session available as 'spark'.
Welcome to



      ____              __
     / __/__  ___ _____/ /__
    _\ \/ _ \/ _ `/ __/  '_/
   /___/ .__/\_,_/_/ /_/\_\   version 2.1.1
      /_/

Using Scala version 2.11.8 (Java HotSpot(TM) 64-Bit Server VM, Java 1.8.0_121)
Type in expressions to have them evaluated.
Type :help for more information.

scala>
```

Also, you can access Spark Driver's UI at `http://localhost:4040`:

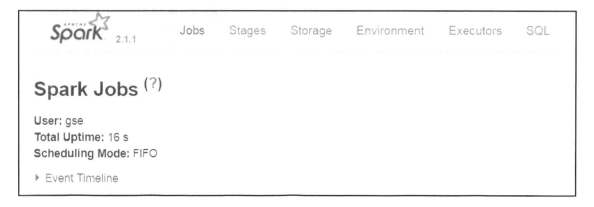

We will discuss more about Spark UI in the *Spark Driver Web UI* section of this chapter.

In this section, we have completed the Spark setup in standalone mode. In the next section, we will do some hands on Apache Spark, using `spark-shell` or `spark-cli`.

Spark REPL also known as CLI

In Chapter 1, *Introduction to Spark*, we learnt that one of the advantages of Apache Spark over the MapReduce framework is interactive processing. Apache Spark achieves the same using Spark REPL.

Spark REPL or Spark shell, also known as Spark CLI, is a very useful tool for exploring the Spark programming. REPL is an acronym for Read-Evaluate-Print Loop. It is an interactive shell used by programmers to interact with a framework. Apache Spark also comes with REPL that beginners can use to understand the Spark programming model.

To launch the Spark REPL, we will execute the command that we executed in the previous section:

```
$SPARK_HOME/bin/spark-shell

Using Spark's default log4j profile: org/apache/spark/log4j-
defaults.properties
Setting default log level to "WARN".
To adjust logging level use sc.setLogLevel(newLevel).
16/11/01 16:38:43 WARN NativeCodeLoader: Unable to load native-hadoop
library for your platform... using builtin-java classes where applicable
16/11/01 16:38:43 WARN Utils: Your hostname, dlla1424 resolves to a
loopback address: 127.0.0.1; using 192.168.0.15 instead (on interface
wlp1s0)
16/11/01 16:38:43 WARN Utils: Set SPARK_LOCAL_IP if you need to bind to
another address
16/11/01 16:38:45 WARN SparkContext: Use an existing SparkContext, some
configuration may not take effect.
Spark context Web UI available at http://192.168.0.15:4040
Spark context available as 'sc' (master = local[*], app id =
local-1477998525363).
Spark session available as 'spark'.
Welcome to
      ____              __
     / __/__  ___ _____/ /__
    _\ \/ _ \/ _ `/ __/  '_/
   /___/ .__/\_,_/_/ /_/\_\   version 2.1.1.
      /_/

Using Scala version 2.11.8 (Java HotSpot(TM) 64-Bit Server VM, Java
1.8.0_101)
Type in expressions to have them evaluated.
Type :help for more information.

scala>
```

Some basic exercises using Spark shell

Note that Spark shell is available only in the Scala language. However, we have kept examples easy to understand by Java developers.

Checking Spark version

Execute the following command to check the Spark version using `spark-shell`:

```
scala>sc.version
res0: String = 2.1.1
```

It is shown in the following screenshot:

Creating and filtering RDD

Let's start by creating an RDD of strings:

```
scala>val
stringRdd=sc.parallelize(Array("Java","Scala","Python","Ruby","JavaScript",
"Java"))
stringRdd: org.apache.spark.rdd.RDD[String] = ParallelCollectionRDD[0] at
parallelize at <console>:24
```

Now, we will filter this RDD to keep only those strings that start with the letter J:

```
scala>valfilteredRdd = stringRdd.filter(s =>s.startsWith("J"))
filteredRdd: org.apache.spark.rdd.RDD[String] = MapPartitionsRDD[2] at
filter at <console>:26
```

In the first chapter, we learnt that if an operation on RDD returns an RDD then it is a transformation, or else it is an action.

The output of the preceding command clearly shows that filter the operation returned an RDD so the filter is a transformation.

Now, we will run an action on `filteredRdd` to see it's elements. Let's run `collect` on the `filteredRdd`:

```scala
scala>val list = filteredRdd.collect
list: Array[String] = Array(Java, JavaScript, Java)
```

As per the output of the previous command, the `collect` operation returned an array of strings. So, it is an action.

Now, let's see the elements of the `list` variable:

```scala
scala> list
res5: Array[String] = Array(Java, JavaScript, Java)
```

We are left with only elements that start with J, which was our desired outcome:

```scala
scala> val stringRdd=sc.parallelize(Array("Java","Scala","Python","Ruby","JavaScript","Java"))
stringRdd: org.apache.spark.rdd.RDD[String] = ParallelCollectionRDD[7] at parallelize at <console>:24

scala> val filteredRdd = stringRdd.filter(s => s.startsWith("J"))
filteredRdd: org.apache.spark.rdd.RDD[String] = MapPartitionsRDD[8] at filter at <console>:26

scala> val list = filteredRdd.collect
list: Array[String] = Array(Java, JavaScript, Java)

scala> list
res3: Array[String] = Array(Java, JavaScript, Java)

scala>
```

Word count on RDD

Let's run a word count problem on `stringRDD`. Word count is the `HelloWorld` of the big data world. Word count means that we will count the occurrence of each word in the RDD:

So first we will create `pairRDD` as follows:

```scala
scala>valpairRDD=stringRdd.map( s => (s,1))
pairRDD: org.apache.spark.rdd.RDD[(String, Int)] = MapPartitionsRDD[6] at
map at <console>:26
```

The `pairRDD` consists of pairs of the word and one (integer) where word represents strings of `stringRDD`.

Now, we will run the `reduceByKey` operation on this RDD to count the occurrence of each word as follows:

```
scala>valwordCountRDD=pairRDD.reduceByKey((x,y) =>x+y)
wordcountRDD: org.apache.spark.rdd.RDD[(String, Int)] = ShuffledRDD[8] at
reduceByKey at <console>:28
```

Now, let's run `collect` on it to see the result:

```
scala>valwordCountList=wordCountRDD.collect
wordCountList: Array[(String, Int)] = Array((Python,1), (JavaScript,1),
(Java,2), (Scala,1), (Ruby,1))
scala>wordCountList
res3: Array[(String, Int)] = Array((Python,1), (JavaScript,1), (Java,2),
(Scala,1), (Ruby,1))
```

As per the output of `wordCountList`, every string in `stringRDD` appears once expect `Java`, which appeared twice.

It is shown in the following screenshot:

```
scala> val pairRDD=stringRdd.map( s => (s,1))
pairRDD: org.apache.spark.rdd.RDD[(String, Int)] = MapPartitionsRDD[9] at map at <console>:26

scala> val wordCountRDD=pairRDD.reduceByKey((x,y) => x+y)
wordCountRDD: org.apache.spark.rdd.RDD[(String, Int)] = ShuffledRDD[10] at reduceByKey at <console>:28

scala> val wordCountList=wordCountRDD.collect
wordCountList: Array[(String, Int)] = Array((Python,1), (JavaScript,1), (Java,2), (Scala,1), (Ruby,1))

scala> wordCountList
res4: Array[(String, Int)] = Array((Python,1), (JavaScript,1), (Java,2), (Scala,1), (Ruby,1))

scala>
```

Finding the sum of all even numbers in an RDD of integers

Let's first create an RDD of integers as follows:

```
scala>valintRDD = sc.parallelize(Array(1,4,5,6,7,10,15))
intRDD: org.apache.spark.rdd.RDD[Int] = ParallelCollectionRDD[0] at
parallelize at <console>:24
```

The next step is to filter all the even elements in this RDD. So, we will execute a `filter` operation on the RDD, as follows:

```
scala>valevenNumbersRDD=intRDD.filter(i => (i%2==0))
evenNumbersRDD: org.apache.spark.rdd.RDD[Int] = MapPartitionsRDD[3] at
filter at <console>:26
```

The preceding operation will fetch those elements for which 2 is a factor, that is, even elements .

Now, we will sum all the elements of this RDD as follows:

```
scala>val sum =evenNumbersRDD.sum
sum: Double = 20.0
scala> sum
res5: Double = 20.0
```

It is shown in the following screenshot:

```
scala> val intRDD = sc.parallelize(Array(1,4,5,6,7,10,15))
intRDD: org.apache.spark.rdd.RDD[Int] = ParallelCollectionRDD[0] at parallelize at <console>:24

scala> val evenNumbersRDD=intRDD.filter(i => (i%2==0))
evenNumbersRDD: org.apache.spark.rdd.RDD[Int] = MapPartitionsRDD[1] at filter at <console>:26

scala> val sum =evenNumbersRDD.sum
sum: Double = 20.0

scala> sum
res0: Double = 20.0

scala>
```

Counting the number of words in a file

Let's read the file `people.txt` placed in `$SPARK_HOME/examples/src/main/resources`:

```
sparkuser@~$ cd $SPARK_HOME/examples/src/main/resources
sparkuser@/usr/local/spark/examples/src/main/resources$ ls
full_user.avsc  kv1.txt  people.json  people.txt  user.avsc  users.avro  users.parquet
sparkuser@/usr/local/spark/examples/src/main/resources$ cat people.txt
Michael, 29
Andy, 30
Justin, 19
sparkuser@/usr/local/spark/examples/src/main/resources$ █
```

The `textFile()` method can be used to read the file as follows:

```
scala>val
file=sc.textFile("/usr/local/spark/examples/src/main/resources/people.txt")
file: org.apache.spark.rdd.RDD[String] =
/usr/local/spark/examples/src/main/resources/people.txt MapPartitionsRDD[1]
at textFile at <console>:24
```

The next step is to flatten the contents of the file, that is, we will create an RDD by splitting each line with , and flatten all the words in the list, as follows:

```
scala>valflattenFile = file.flatMap(s =>s.split(", "))
flattenFile: org.apache.spark.rdd.RDD[String] = MapPartitionsRDD[5] at
flatMap at <console>:26
```

The contents of `flattenFile` RDD looks as follows:

```
scala>flattenFile.collect
res5: Array[String] = Array(Michael, 29, Andy, 30, Justin, 19)
```

Now, we can count all the words in this RDD as follows:

```
scala>val count = flattenFile.count
count: Long = 6
scala> count
res2: Long = 6
```

It is shown in the following screenshot:

```
scala> val file=sc.textFile("/usr/local/spark/examples/src/main/resources/people.txt")
file: org.apache.spark.rdd.RDD[String] = /usr/local/spark/examples/src/main/resources/people.txt MapPartitionsRDD[4] at tex
tFile at <console>:24

scala> val flattenFile = file.flatMap(s => s.split(", "))
flattenFile: org.apache.spark.rdd.RDD[String] = MapPartitionsRDD[5] at flatMap at <console>:26

scala> flattenFile.collect
res1: Array[String] = Array(Michael, 29, Andy, 30, Justin, 19)

scala> val count = flattenFile.count
count: Long = 6

scala> count
res2: Long = 6

scala>
```

Whenever any action such as `count` gets called, the Spark creates a **directed acyclic graph** (**DAG**) to depict the lineage dependency of each RDD. Spark provides a debug method `toDebugString()` to show such lineage dependencies of the RDD:

```
scala>flattenFile.toDebugString
```

It is shown in the following screenshot:

```
scala> val file=sc.textFile("/usr/local/spark/examples/src/main/resources/people.txt")
file: org.apache.spark.rdd.RDD[String] = /usr/local/spark/examples/src/main/resources/people.txt MapPartitionsRDD[5] at textFile at <console>:24

scala>  val flattenFile = file.flatMap(s => s.split(", "))
flattenFile: org.apache.spark.rdd.RDD[String] = MapPartitionsRDD[6] at flatMap at <console>:26

scala> flattenFile.toDebugString
res2: String =
(2) MapPartitionsRDD[6] at flatMap at <console>:26 []
 |  /usr/local/spark/examples/src/main/resources/people.txt MapPartitionsRDD[5] at textFile at <console>:24 []
 |  /usr/local/spark/examples/src/main/resources/people.txt HadoopRDD[4] at textFile at <console>:24 []

scala>
```

The indentations represent the shuffle while the number in the parentheses indicates the parallelism level at each stage.

In this section, we became familiar with some Spark CLI concepts. In the next section, we will discuss various components of Spark job.

Spark components

Before moving any further let's first understand the common terminologies associated with Spark:

- **Driver**: This is the main program that oversees the end-to-end execution of a Spark job or program. It negotiates the resources with the resource manager of the cluster for delegate and orchestrate the program into smallest possible data local parallel programming unit.

- **Executors**: In any Spark job, there can be one or more executors, that is, processes that execute smaller tasks delegated by the driver. The executors process the data, preferably local to the node and store the result in memory, disk, or both.

- **Master**: Apache Spark has been implemented in master-slave architecture and hence master refers to the cluster node executing the driver program.

- **Slave**: In a distributed cluster mode, slave refers to the nodes on which executors are being run and hence there can be (and mostly is) more than one slave in the cluster.

- **Job**: This is a collection of operations performed on any set of data. A typical word count job deals with reading a text file from an arbitrary source and splitting and then aggregating the words.

- **DAG**: Any Spark job in a Spark engine is represented by a DAG of operations. The DAG represents the logical execution of Spark operations in a sequential order. Re-computation of RDD in case of a failure is possible lineage can be derived from the DAG.

- **Tasks**: A job can be split into smaller units to be operated upon in silos which are called **Tasks**. Each task is executed upon by an executor on a partition of data.

- **Stages**: Spark jobs can be divided logically into stages, where each stage represents a set of tasks having the same shuffle dependencies, that is, where data shuffling occurs. In shuffle map stage the tasks results are input for the next stage where as in result stage the tasks compute the action that started the evaluation of Spark job such as `take()`, `foreach()`, and `collect()`.

Following diagram shows logical representation of how different components of Spark application interacts:

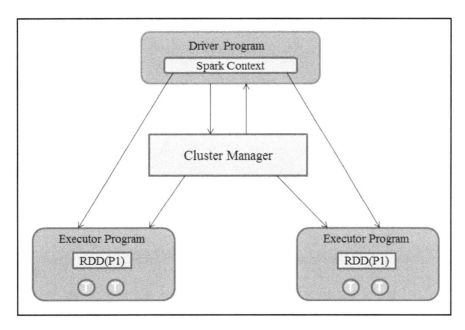

How a Spark job gets executed:

- A Spark Job can comprise of a series of operations that are performed upon a set of data. However big or small a Spark job may be, it requires a `SparkContext` to execute any such job. In the previous examples of working with REPL, one would notice the use of an environment variable called `sc`, which is how a `SparkContext` is accessible in an REPL environment.

- `SparkContext` creates an operator graph of different transformations of the job, but once an action gets called on such a transformation, the graph gets submitted to the `DAGScheduler`. Depending on the nature of the RDD or resultant being produced with narrow transformation or the wide transformation (those that require the shuffle operation), the `DAGScheduler` produces stages.

- The `DAGScheduler` splits the DAG in such a way that each stage comprises of the same shuffle dependency with common shuffle boundaries. Also, stages can either be a shuffle map stage in which case its tasks' results are input for another stage or a result stage in which case its tasks directly compute the action that initiated a job, for example, `count()`.

- Stages are then submitted to `TaskScheduler` as `TaskSets` by the `DAGScheduler`. The `TaskScheduler` schedules the `TaskSets` via cluster manager (YARN, Mesos, and Spark standalone) and monitors its execution. In case of the failure of the any task, it is rerun and finally the results are sent to the `DAGScheduler`. In case the result output files are lost, then `DAGScheduler` resubmits such stages to the `TaskScheduler` to be rerun again.

- Tasks are then scheduled on the designated executors (JVMs running on a slave node) meeting the resource and data locality constraints. Each executor can also have more than one task assigned.

Following diagram provides logical representation of different phases of Spark jJob execution:

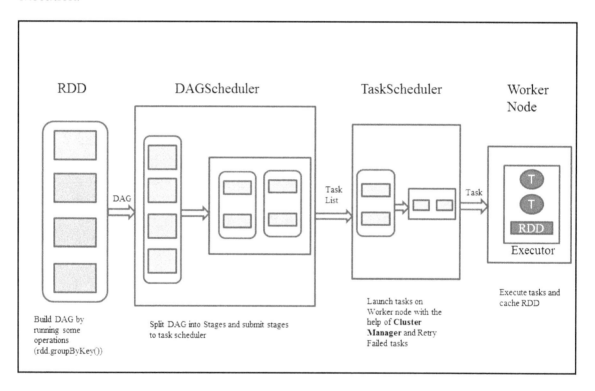

In this section, we became familiar with different components of a Spark job. In the next section, we will learn capabilities of Spark driver's UI.

Spark Driver Web UI

This section will provide some important aspects of the Spark driver's UI. We will see the statistics of the jobs we executed using Spark shell on Spark UI.

As described in the *Getting started with Apache Spark* section, Spark driver's UI runs at `http://localhost:4040/` (unless you make any changes to default settings).

When you start Spark shell, Spark driver's UI will look as follows:

`SparkContext` is an entry point to every Spark application. Every Spark job is launched with a `SparkContext` and can consist of only one `SparkContext`.

Spark shell, being a Spark application starts with `SparkContext` and every `SparkContext` launches its own web UI. The default port is `4040`. Spark UI can be enabled/disabled or can be launched on a separate port using the following properties:

Property	Default value
spark.ui.enabled	True
spark.ui.port	4040

For example, Spark shell application with Spark UI running on `5050` port can be launched as:

```
spark-shell --confspark.ui.port=5050
```

If multiple Spark applications are launched in parallel on one system without providing any of the preceding `conf` parameters, then Spark UI for those applications will be launched on successive ports starting from `4040` (that is, `4040`, `4041`, and so on).

Spark UI consists of the following tabs:

Jobs

Jobs is the default tab of Spark UI. It shows the status of all the applications executed within a `SparkContext`. It can be accessed at `http://localhost:4040/jobs/`.

It consists of three sections:

- **Active Jobs**: This section is for the jobs that are currently running
- **Completed Jobs**: This section is for the jobs that successfully completed
- **Failed Jobs**: This section is for the jobs that were failed

It is shown in the following screenshot:

 Sections of Spark UI are created lazily and can be visible if required. For example, the **Active Jobs** section will only be visible if there is a job that is currently running. Similarly, the **Failed Jobs** and **Completed Jobs** sections are visible only if there is a job that failed or successfully completed.

The **Jobs** tab section of Spark UI is rendered using the
`org.apache.spark.ui.jobs.JobsTab` class that uses
`org.apache.spark.ui.jobs.JobProgressListener` to get the statistics of the job.

After executing all the jobs mentioned in the *Spark REPL also known as CLI* section, Spark UI will look as follows:

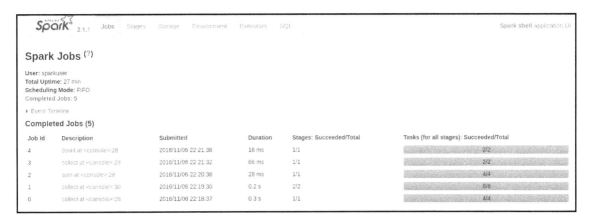

Also, if you expand the **Event Timeline** section, you can see the time at which `SparkContext` started (that is, driver was initiated) and the jobs were executed along with their status:

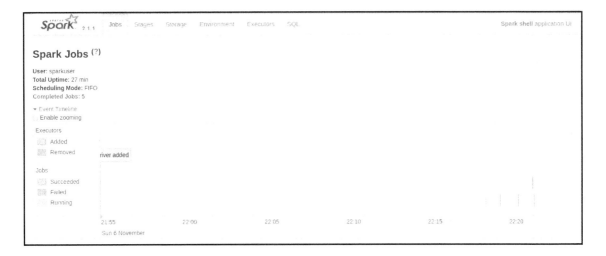

Also, by clicking on any of the jobs, you can see the details of the job, that is, the **Event Timeline** of the job and the DAG of the transformations and stages executed during the execution of the job, as follows:

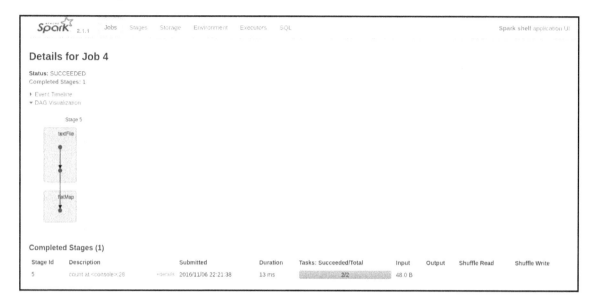

Stages

The **Stages** tab lists and provides, current state of all the stages of every job executed in the SparkContext. It can be accessed at http://localhost:4040/stages/. The **Stages** tab of Spark UI is rendered using the org.apache.spark.ui.jobs.StagesTab class.

Like the **Jobs** tab, the **Stages** tab also consists of three sections:

- **Active Stages**: This section is for the stages of an active that are currently running
- **Completed Stages**: This section is for the stages of active/failed/completed jobs that successfully completed
- **Failed Stages**: This section is for the stages of active/failed/completed jobs that were failed

After executing all the jobs mentioned in the *Spark REPL also known as CLI* section, the
Stages tab will look as follows:

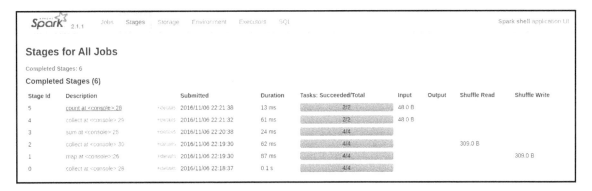

If you click on any of the stages you can see various details of the stage, that is, the DAG of
tasks executed, **Event Timeline**, and so on. Also, this page provides metrics of various
details of executors and tasks executed in the stage:

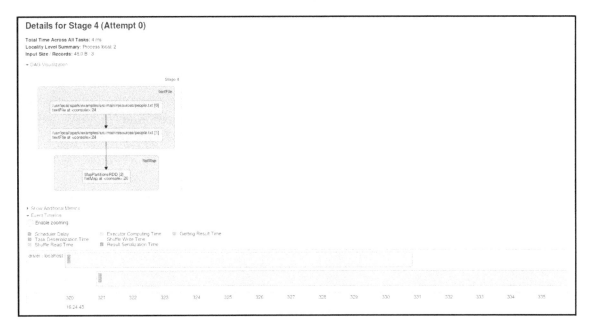

Storage

If during the execution of a job, the user persists/cache an RDD then information about that RDD can be retrieved on this tab. It can be accessed at `http://localhost:4040/storage/`.

Let's launch Spark shell again, read a file, and run an action on it. However, this time we will cache the file before running an action on it.

Initially, when you launch Spark shell, the **Storage** tab appears blank.

Let's read the file using `SparkContext`, as follows:

```
scala>val
file=sc.textFile("/usr/local/spark/examples/src/main/resources/people.txt")
file: org.apache.spark.rdd.RDD[String] =
/usr/local/spark/examples/src/main/resources/people.txt MapPartitionsRDD[1]
at textFile at <console>:24
```

This time we will cache this RDD. By default, it will be cached in memory:

```
scala>file.cache
res0: file.type = /usr/local/spark/examples/src/main/resources/people.txt
MapPartitionsRDD[1] at textFile at <console>:24
```

As explained earlier, the DAG of transformations will only be executed when an action is performed, so the cache step will also be executed when we run an action on the RDD. So let's run a collect on it:

```
scala>file.collect
res1: Array[String] = Array(Michael, 29, Andy, 30, Justin, 19)
```

Now, you can find information about an RDD being cached on the **Storage** tab.

If you click on the RDD name, it provides information about the partitions on the RDD along with the address of the host on which the RDD is stored.

Environment

The **Environment** tab provides information about various properties and environment variables used in Spark application (or `SparkContext`). It can be accessed at `http://localhost:4040/environment/`.

Users can get extremely useful information about various Spark properties on this tab without having to churn through the property files.

Executors

The **Executors** tab of Spark UI provides information about memory, cores, and other resources being used by executors. This information is available both at each executor level and an aggregated level. It is accessible at `http://localhost:4040/executors/`.

All the information on the **Executors** tab is retrieved using the `org.apache.spark.ui.exec.ExecutorsListener` class.

	RDD Blocks	Storage Memory	Disk Used	Cores	Active Tasks	Failed Tasks	Complete Tasks	Total Tasks	Task Time (GC Time)	Input	Shuffle Read	Shuffle Write
Active(1)	1	16.3 KB / 366.3 MB	0.0 B	4	0	0	20	20	1.2 s (0 ms)	96.0 B	0.0 B	309.0 B
Dead(0)	0	0.0 B / 0.0 B	0.0 B	0	0	0	0	0	0 ms (0 ms)	0.0 B	0.0 B	0.0 B
Total(1)	1	16.3 KB / 366.3 MB	0.0 B	4	0	0	20	20	1.2 s (0 ms)	96.0 B	0.0 B	309.0 B

Executors

Executor ID	Address	Status	RDD Blocks	Storage Memory	Disk Used	Cores	Active Tasks	Failed Tasks	Complete Tasks	Total Tasks	Task Time (GC Time)	Input	Shuffle Read	Shuffle Write	Thread Dump
driver	192.168.0.106:38543	Active	1	16.3 KB / 366.3 MB	0.0 B	4	0	0	20	20	1.2 s (0 ms)	96.0 B	0.0 B	309.0 B	Thread Dump

Also, this tab provides an option to make a **Thread Dump** of the executor process, which is very useful for debugging the issue. The user can turn off this option by setting `spark.ui.threadDumpsEnabled` to `false` (by default, this is set to `true`).

SQL

The **SQL** tab in Spark UI provides the really useful Spark SQL queries. We will learn about the working of Spark SQL framework in `Chapter 8`, *Working with Spark SQL*. For now, let us run the following commands on Spark shell. It is accessible at `http://localhost:4040/SQL`.

In the following example, we will read a JSON file in Spark using the `SparkSession` library and creating temporary views on JSON data and then we will run a Spark SQL query on the table:

```
scala> import org.apache.spark.sql.SparkSession
importorg.apache.spark.sql.SparkSession
scala> import spark.implicits._
importspark.implicits._

scala>val spark = SparkSession.builder().appName("Spark SQL basic
example").getOrCreate()
16/11/13 22:27:51 WARN SparkSession$Builder: Use an existing SparkSession,
some configuration may not take effect.
spark: org.apache.spark.sql.SparkSession =
org.apache.spark.sql.SparkSession@53fd59d4
```

```
scala>valdf =
spark.read.json("/usr/local/spark/examples/src/main/resources/people.json")
df: org.apache.spark.sql.DataFrame = [age: bigint, name: string]

scala>df.createOrReplaceTempView("people")

scala>valsqlDF = spark.sql("SELECT * FROM people")
sqlDF: org.apache.spark.sql.DataFrame = [age: bigint, name: string]

scala>sqlDF.show()
+----+-------+
| age| name|
+----+-------+
|null|Michael|
| 30| Andy|
| 19| Justin|
+----+-------+
```

After running the preceding example, details of the SQL query can be found in the **SQL** tab. It provides the DAG of the SQL query along with the query plan that shows how Spark optimized the executed SQL query.

The **SQL** tab retrieves all this information using `org.apache.spark.sql.execution.ui.SQLListener`:

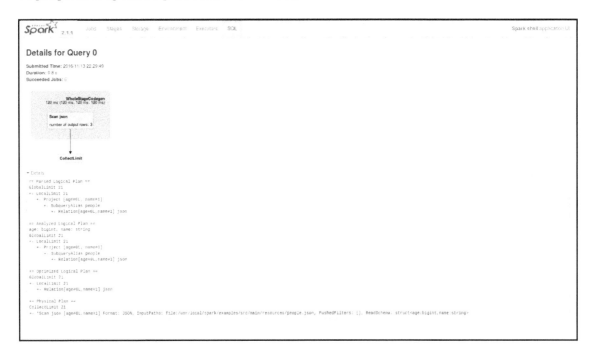

Streaming

As you may have guessed, the **Streaming** tab shows information about Spark Streaming jobs. This tab appears when you execute a streaming job in `SparkContext`.

We will learn about the working of Spark Streaming framework in `Chapter 9`, *Near Real-Time Processing with Spark Streaming*. For now, let us run the following job that will listen to port `10000` and run word count on the incoming messages.

First, open a connection on port `10000`:

```
sparkuser@~$ nc -lk 10000
```

Now, execute a `NetworkWordCount` example bundled in Spark Package:

```
sparkuser@~$ $SPARK_HOME/bin/run-example
streaming.NetworkWordCountlocalhost 10000
```

When you run it, the **Streaming** tab appears and it can be accessed at `http://localhost:4040/streaming/`:

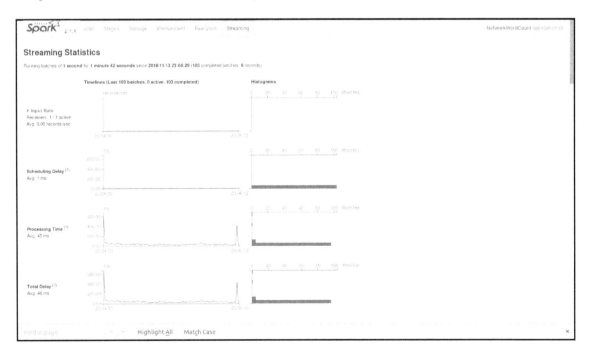

It provides a lot of information about the streaming job such as the input rate, the scheduling delay while processing streams, the processing time of the streams, and so on. This information becomes really useful for performance tuning of Spark Streaming jobs as stream processing needs to cope with the speed of incoming data to avoid delays.

Also, it provides information about batches processed, which is useful while debugging issues.

In this section, we will learn about various capabilities of Spark UI.

In the next section, we will learn about some of the REST APIs, which are useful for monitoring Spark jobs.

Spark job configuration and submission

When a Spark job is launched, it creates a `SparkConf` object and passes it to the constructor of `SparkContext`. The `SparkConf()` object contains a near exhaustive list of customizable parameters that can tune a Spark job as per cluster resources. The `SparkConf` object becomes immutable once it is passed to invoke a `SparkContext()` constructor, hence it becomes important to not only identify, but also modify all the `SparkConf` parameters before creating a `SparkContext` object.

There are different ways in which Spark job can be configured.

Spark's `conf` directory provides the default configurations to execute a Spark job. The `SPARK_CONF_DIR` parameter can be used to override the default location of the `conf` directory, which usually is `SPARK_HOME/conf` and some of the configuration files that are expected in this folder are `spark-defaults.conf`, `spark-env.sh`, and `log4j.properties`. Log4j is used by Spark for logging mechanism and can be configured by modifying the `log4j.properties.template`. Spark environment variables can be configured using the shell script file `spark-env.sh`, however, it is not available by default and can be copied from `spark-env.sh.template`.

The list of environment variables are as follows:

Environment variable	Meaning
JAVA_HOME	path of Java available on the machines.
PYSPARK_PYTHON	The Python binary executable to use for PySpark in both driver and workers (default is Python 2.7 if available, otherwise Python).
PYSPARK_DRIVER_PYTHON	The Python binary executable to use for PySpark in driver only (default is PYSPARK_PYTHON).
SPARKR_DRIVER_R	The R binary executable to use for SparkR shell (default is R).
SPARK_LOCAL_IP	The IP address of the machine to bind to.
SPARK_PUBLIC_DNS	The hostname your Spark program will advertise to other machines.

The default values passed on to a Spark job via the SparkConf object are available in the spark-defaults.conf file. Some of the frequently used configurations are:

Parameter name	Default value	Meaning
spark.app.name	none	The Spark job's name, which appears in Spark UI and logs.
spark.driver.cores	1	In cluster mode, the number of CPU cores that can be used by the driver.
spark.driver.memory	1g	The amount of memory that can be utilized by the driver.
spark.executor.cores	YARN: 1 OTHERS: Available cores	The number of cores utilized by an executor. Default value is 1 in YARN and all available cores on worker in standalone mode.
spark.executor.memory	1g	The memory that can be utilized by each executor.
spark.master	none	The URL of cluster manager.
spark.submit.deployMode	none	The deploying the Spark job locally (client) or remotely (cluster) on a cluster.

spark.local.dir	/tmp	The directory to use for scratch space in Spark. From Spark 1.0 onward, it is overridden by SPARK_LOCAL_DIRS (Standalone, Mesos) or LOCAL_DIRS (YARN) environment variables set by the cluster manager.

Since the SparkContext object is available across the worker nodes for any Spark job, it cannot be used to configure node specific configurations. Hence, to set local directories for merging and sorting intermediate output files, SPARK_LOCAL_DIRS or LOCAL_DIRS is provided in Mesos and YARN clusters, respectively.

Spark job's configuration and properties, set through the spark-defaults.conf, SparkConf object and Spark-Submit tool, can be viewed on Spark UI at http://<driver>:4040 under the **Environment** tab.

Spark configuration can also be set dynamically using the Spark-Submit tool. The most common parameters can be set directly using the Spark-Submit tool such as --master, --name (every parameter starts with a double hyphen), however, other parameters can be passed using the --conf parameter:

```
$ bin/spark-submit \
--class com.foo.Bar \
--master local[3] \
--name "AnotherFoobar App" \
--confspark.ui.port=37777\
fooBar.jar
```

Another convenient way to pass the parameter is by using a configuration file that has whitespace-delimited key/value pairs. The parameter --properties-file can be used to specify the configuration filename. The default location of the configuration file is assumed to be the SPARK_HOME/conf directory, unless otherwise mentioned:

```
$ bin/spark-submit \
--class com.foo.Bar \
--properties-file job-config.conf \
fooBar.jar
+++++ Contents of job-config.conf +++++
spark.master local[3]
spark.app.name "AnotherFoobar App"
spark.ui.port 37777
+++++ Contents of job-config.conf finish +++++
```

The `SparkConf` can also be explicitly set programmatically by first constructing a `SparkConf()` object with required parameters and then invoking `SparkContext` constructor with it:

```
// Construct a Spark conf
SparkConf conf = new SparkConf();
conf.set("spark.app.name", "AnotherFoobar App");
conf.set("spark.master", "local[3]");
conf.set("spark.ui.port", "37777");
// InstantiateSparkContext with the Spark conf
JavaSparkContextsc = JavaSparkContext(conf);
```

When executing the Spark job in client mode, care should be taken to not pass the driver related parameters programmatically as the driver JVM has already started and hence, will have no impact on driver's configurations. In such scenarios, one can choose to pass the driver's related configurations using the `spark-defaults.conf` file or using the `--driver-memory` argument in the `Spark-Submit` tool.

The different ways in which `SparkConf` can be set, create the need to define a precedence order in which each option may be applicable. The highest preference is given to the values being passed explicitly in the Spark job itself. After this, the parameters that have been passed using `Spark-Submit` tools takes precedence. The rest of the parameters are finally fetched from the `spark-defaults.conf` file of the `SPARK_HOME/conf` folder.

Spark REST APIs

Representational state transfer (**REST**) architecture is used very often while developing web services. These days, a lot of frameworks such as Hadoop, Apache Storm, and so on, provide RESTful web services that help users to interact with or monitor the framework. Apache Spark, being in the same league, also provides REST web services that can be used to monitor the Spark applications. In this section, we will learn about the REST APIs provided by Apache Spark.

The response type of Spark REST APIs is JSON, which can be used to design custom monitoring over Spark applications. The REST endpoints are mounted at `/api/v1`, which means that for a `SparkContext` with UI running `https://localhost:4040`, the REST endpoints will be mounted at `https://localhost:4040/api/v1`.

It is time to explore some of the REST APIs provided by Apache Spark. For that, launch Spark shell and run any of the jobs mentioned in *Spark REPL also known as CLI* section:

Execute the following command to list the applications executed/running in `SparkContext`:

```
curl http://localhost:4040/api/v1/applications
[ {
  "id" : "local-1479401168077",
  "name" : "Spark shell",
  "attempts" : [ {
    "startTime" : "2016-11-17T16:46:05.429GMT",
    "endTime" : "1969-12-31T23:59:59.999GMT",
    "lastUpdated" : "2016-11-17T16:46:05.429GMT",
    "duration" : 0,
    "sparkUser" : "",
    "completed" : false,
    "startTimeEpoch" : 1479401165429,
    "endTimeEpoch" : -1,
    "lastUpdatedEpoch" : 1479401165429
  } ]
} ]
```

The REST API provided previously also accepts some request parameters, for example `status=running`, which provides the list of applications that have requested status:

```
curl http://localhost:4040/api/v1/applications?status=running
[ {
  "id" : "local-1479401168077",
  "name" : "Spark shell",
  "attempts" : [ {
    "startTime" : "2016-11-17T16:46:05.429GMT",
    "endTime" : "1969-12-31T23:59:59.999GMT",
    "lastUpdated" : "2016-11-17T16:46:05.429GMT",
    "duration" : 0,
    "sparkUser" : "",
    "completed" : false,
    "startTimeEpoch" : 1479401165429,
    "endTimeEpoch" : -1,
    "lastUpdatedEpoch" : 1479401165429
  } ]
} ]
```

Execute the following command to list the jobs executed by the application (REST URL: `http://localhost:4040/api/v1/applications/[app-id]/jobs`):

```
curl http://localhost:4040/api/v1/applications/local-1479401168077/jobs
[ {
  "jobId" : 1,
  "name" : "count at <console>:28",
  "submissionTime" : "2016-11-17T16:47:33.799GMT",
  "completionTime" : "2016-11-17T16:47:33.827GMT",
  "stageIds" : [ 1 ],
  "status" : "SUCCEEDED",
  "numTasks" : 2,
  "numActiveTasks" : 0,
  "numCompletedTasks" : 2,
  "numSkippedTasks" : 0,
  "numFailedTasks" : 0,
  "numActiveStages" : 0,
  "numCompletedStages" : 1,
  "numSkippedStages" : 0,
  "numFailedStages" : 0
}, {
  "jobId" : 0,
  "name" : "collect at <console>:29",
  "submissionTime" : "2016-11-17T16:47:26.329GMT",
  "completionTime" : "2016-11-17T16:47:26.754GMT",
  "stageIds" : [ 0 ],
  "status" : "SUCCEEDED",
  "numTasks" : 2,
  "numActiveTasks" : 0,
  "numCompletedTasks" : 2,
  "numSkippedTasks" : 0,
  "numFailedTasks" : 0,
  "numActiveStages" : 0,
  "numCompletedStages" : 1,
  "numSkippedStages" : 0,
  "numFailedStages" : 0
} ]
```

The following is the complete list of RESTful APIs provided by Apache Spark along with their usage:

REST endpoint	Usage	Allowed request parameters
`/applications`	To list all applications executed/running in a `SparkContext`.	The `?status=[completed|running]` is to list the applications that requested status. The `?minDate=[date]` is used to list all the applications started after provided date. Examples, `?minDate=2016-11-16`, `?minDate=2015-11-16T100:00:00.000GMT`. The `?maxDate=[date]` is used to list all the applications started before provided date. Examples, `?maxDate=2016-11-16`, `?maxDate=2015-11-16T100:00:00.000GMT`.
`/applications/[app-id]/jobs`	To list all jobs executed within a Spark application.	The `?status=[complete|succeeded|failed]` is used to list the jobs that requested status.
`/applications/[app-id]/jobs/[job-id]`	To fetch details of a specific job executed within a Spark application.	
`/applications/[app-id]/stages`	To list all stages executed within a Spark application.	
`/applications/[app-id]/stages/[stage-id]`	To fetch details of a specific stage executed within a Spark application.	The `?status=[active|complete|pending|failed]` is used to list the stages which requested status.
`/applications/[app-id]/stages/[stage-id]/[stage-attempt-id]`	To fetch details of a specific attempt of a particular stage.	
`/applications/[app-id]/stages/[stage-id]/[stage-attempt-id]/taskSummary`	To fetch the summary metrics of all tasks executed in a specific attempt of a particular stage.	The `?quantiles` is used to summarize the metrics with the given quantiles. Example: `?quantiles=0.01,0.5,0.99`.
`/applications/[app-id]/stages/[stage-id]/[stage-attempt-id]/taskList`	To list all the tasks of a specific attempt of a particular stage.	The `?offset=[offset]&length=[len]` is used to list tasks in the given offset range. The `?sortBy=[runtime|-runtime]` is used to sort the tasks by given value.
`/applications/[app-id]/executors`	To list all executors of a Spark application.	
`/applications/[app-id]/storage/rdd`	To list all the stored RDDs of a Spark application.	
`/applications/[app-id]/storage/rdd/[rdd-id]`	To fetch the details about the status of a particular stored RDD.	

`/applications/[base-app-id]/logs`	To download the event logs for all the attempts of a particular application. It will be in the form of a ZIP file.	
`/applications/[base-app-id]/[attempt-id]/logs`	To download the event logs for a particular attempt of an application. It will be in the form of a ZIP file.	

In the next section, we will learn about various configurations that can help in the performance tuning of Spark applications.

Summary

In this chapter, we learned how to set up an Apache Spark standalone cluster and interact with it using Spark CLI. We then focused on becoming familiar with various Spark components and how a Spark job gets executed in a clustered environment. Different Spark job configurations and Spark web UI were also discussed, along with REST API usage for job submission and status monitoring.

In the next chapter, we will discuss more on RDD and its operations.

4
Understanding the Spark Programming Model

This chapter will progress by explaining the word count problem in Apache Spark using Java and simultaneously setting up an IDE. Then we will progress towards explaining common RDD actions and transformations. We will also touch upon the inbuilt capability of Spark caching and the persistence of RDD for improving Spark job performance.

Hello Spark

In this section, we will create an `Hello World` program for Spark and will then get some understanding of the internals of Spark. The `Hello World` program in the big data world is also known as a `Word Count` program. Given the text data as input, we will calculate the frequency of each word or number of occurrences of each word in the text data, that is, how many times each word has appeared in the text. Consider that we have the following text data:

Where there is a will there is a way

The number of occurrences of each word in this data is:

Word	Frequency
Where	1
There	2
Is	2
A	2
Will	1
Way	1

Now we will solve this problem with Spark. So let's develop a Spark `WordCount` application.

Prerequisites

The following are the prerequisites for preparing the Spark application:

- **IDE for Java applications**: We will be using the **Eclipse** IDE to develop the Spark application. Users can use any IDE as per their choice. Also, the IDE should have the Maven plugin installed (the latest version of Eclipse such as **Mars** and **Neon** consists of inbuilt Maven plugins).
- Java 7 or above, but preferably Java 8.
- The Maven package.

The following are the steps to get started with the Maven project in Java IDE:

1. The first step is to create a Maven project. In Eclipse, it can be created as **File|New|Project**.

2. Then search for Maven, as shown in the following screenshot:

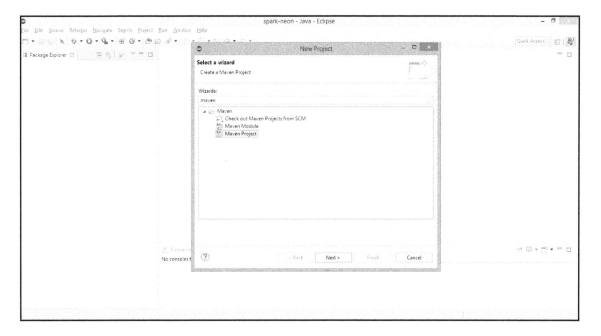

3. Select **Maven Project** and click **Next**. On the next, screen select the checkbox next to **Create a simple project** (skip the archetype selection) and click **Next**. On the next screen, add the **Group Id** and **Artifact Id** values as follows and then click **Finish**:

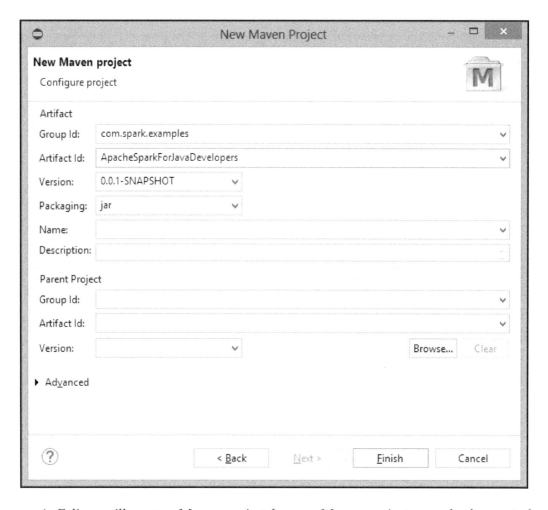

4. Eclipse will create a Maven project for you. Maven projects can also be created using the mvn command line tool as follows:

```
mvn archetype:generate -DgroupId=com.spark.examples -
DartifactId=ApacheSparkForJavaDevelopers
```

Once the project is created using the `mvn` command line tool, it needs to be imported to the IDE.

5. After creating a Maven project, expand the Maven project and edit `pom.xml` by adding the following dependency:

```
<dependency>
    <groupId>org.apache.spark</groupId>
    <artifactId>spark-core_2.11</artifactId>
    <version>2.0.0</version>
</dependency>
```

6. The following are the contents of the `pom.xml` file:

```
 1  <project xmlns="http://maven.apache.org/POM/4.0.0" xmlns:xsi="http://www.w3.org/2001/XMLSchema-instance"
 2      xsi:schemaLocation="http://maven.apache.org/POM/4.0.0 http://maven.apache.org/xsd/maven-4.0.0.xsd">
 3      <modelVersion>4.0.0</modelVersion>
 4      <groupId>com.spark.examples</groupId>
 5      <artifactId>ApacheSparkForJavaDevelopers</artifactId>
 6      <version>0.0.1-SNAPSHOT</version>
 7      <properties>
 8      <java-version>1.8</java-version>
 9      </properties>
10      <dependencies>
11          <dependency>
12              <groupId>org.apache.spark</groupId>
13              <artifactId>spark-core_2.11</artifactId>
14              <version>2.0.0</version>
15          </dependency>
16      </dependencies>
17  
18      <build>
19          <plugins>
20              <plugin>
21                  <groupId>org.apache.maven.plugins</groupId>
22                  <artifactId>maven-compiler-plugin</artifactId>
23                  <version>2.0.2</version>
24                  <configuration>
25                      <source>${java-version}</source>
26                      <target>${java-version}</target>
27                  </configuration>
28              </plugin>
29          </plugins>
30      </build>
31  </project>
```

The following are some useful tips about compilation of the Maven project:

- The Maven compiler plugin is added, which helps to set the Java version for compiling the project. It is currently set to 1.8 so Java 8 features can be used. The Java version can be changed as per the requirement.
- Hadoop is not a prerequisite to be installed in your system to run Spark jobs. However, for certain scenarios one might get an error such as `Failed to locate the winutils binary in the hadoop binary path` as it searches for a binary file called `winutils` in the bin folder of `HADOOP_HOME`.

The following steps may be required to fix such an error:

1. Download the `winutils` executable from any repository.
2. Create a dummy directory where you place the downloaded executable `winutils.exe`. For example, : `E:\SparkForJavaDev\Hadoop\bin`.
3. Add the environment variable `HADOOP_HOME` that points to `E:\SparkForJavaDev\Hadoop` using either of the options given here:
    - **Eclipse**|Your class which can be run as a Java application (containing the static main method)|Right click on Run as Run Configurations|Environment Tab:

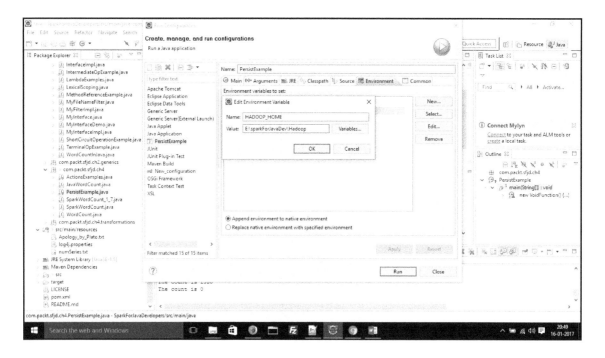

4. Add the following line of code in the Java main class itself:

```
System.setProperty("hadoop.home.dir", "PATH_OF_ HADOOP_HOME");
```

The next step is to create our Java class for the Spark application. The following is the
`SparkWordCount` application using Java 7:

```
public class SparkWordCount {
  public static void main(String[] args) {
    SparkConf conf =new
    SparkConf().setMaster("local").setAppName("WordCount");
    JavaSparkContext javaSparkContext = new JavaSparkContext(conf);
    JavaRDD<String> inputData =
    javaSparkContext.textFile("path_of_input_file");
    JavaPairRDD<String, Integer> flattenPairs =
    inputData.flatMapToPair(new PairFlatMapFunction<String,
    String, Integer>() {
      @Override
      public Iterator<Tuple2<String, Integer>> call(String text) throws
      Exception {
        List<Tuple2<String,Integer>> tupleList =new ArrayList<>();
        String[] textArray = text.split(" ");
        for (String word:textArray) {
          tupleList.add(new Tuple2<String, Integer>(word, 1));
        }
        return tupleList.iterator();
      }
    });
    JavaPairRDD<String, Integer> wordCountRDD = flattenPairs.reduceByKey(new
    Function2<Integer, Integer, Integer>() {
      @Override
      public Integer call(Integer v1, Integer v2) throws Exception {
        return v1+v2;
      }
    });
    wordCountRDD.saveAsTextFile("path_of_output_file");
  }
}
```

The following is the `SparkWordCount` application using Java 8:

```
public class SparkWordCount {
  public static void main(String[] args) {

    SparkConf conf =new
    SparkConf().setMaster("local").setAppName("WordCount");
    JavaSparkContext javaSparkContext = new JavaSparkContext(conf);
    JavaRDD<String> inputData =
```

```
    javaSparkContext.textFile("path_of_input_file");
    JavaPairRDD<String, Integer> flattenPairs =
    inputData.flatMapToPair(text -> Arrays.asList(text.split("
    ")).stream().map(word ->new
Tuple2<String,Integer>(word,1)).iterator());

    JavaPairRDD<String, Integer> wordCountRDD =
flattenPairs.reduceByKey((v1,
    v2) -> v1+v2);
    wordCountRDD.saveAsTextFile("path_of_output_file");
    }
}
```

In the preceding example of the `WordCount` application, we have performed the following steps:

1. **Initialize SparkContext**: We started with creating a `SparkConf` object:

   ```
   new SparkConf().setMaster("local").setAppName("WordCount");
   ```

   Here, `setMaster("local")` defines that the application will run inside a single JVM; that is, we can execute it in the IDE itself. This is very useful for debugging Spark applications and to create test units as well. For running Spark applications on a Spark cluster `setMaster()` should point to the Spark Master URL. (Note: we will learn more about it in detail in `Chapter 6`, *Spark On Cluster*.)

   `setAppName("WordCount")` helps to provide a name to our Spark application. In this case, we have named the application as `WordCount`. However, the user can provide any name to the application as per the requirement.

   All other configuration parameters can be set using the `SparkConf` object. Then with the help of the `SparkConf` object we initialized the `JavaSparkContext`:

   ```
   new JavaSparkContext(conf);
   ```

   `JavaSparkContext` is specifically for Java Spark applications. As described in previous chapters, `SparkContext` is the mandatory component of a Spark application. Also, one Spark application can contain only one `SparkContext`. Now, with the help of `SparkContext`, we can create RDDs and can create a DAG of RDD transformations.

2. **Load the input data**: Using the `javaSparkContext`, we loaded the data from a text file:

```
javaSparkContext.textFile("path_of_input_file");
```

There are other ways of loading the data as well. However, in this case we used text file as input. It is always advisable to provide an absolute path as a relative path depends upon the location from which the program is executed.

Also, we can create an RDD by executing the `parallelize()` function on `SparkContext` as follows:

```
JavaRDD<String> data
=javaSparkContext.parallelize(Arrays.asList("where there is
  a will there is a way"));
```

3. **Flatten the input data and create tuples**: Once the data was loaded, we flattened it and converted it into tuples such as `<key,value>` pairs using the transformation `flatMapToPair`:

```
inputData.flatMapToPair(text -> Arrays.asList(text.split("
")).stream().map(word
  ->new Tuple2<String,Integer>(word,1)).iterator())
```

Consider the content of the text file: `Where there is a will there is a way`.

So the `flatMapToPair` transformation will first break the text data into words (in our example, we have assumed the words are separated by space (" ")) and create the tuples as follows:

```
(where,1)
(there,1)
(is,1)
(a,1)
(will,1)
(there,1)
(is,1)
(a,1)
(way,1)
```

4. **Aggregate (sum) the values for every key**: Once data is transformed in the form of tuples as described previously, another transformation, `reduceByKey` is executed on the data to sum the values for every key which helps us to find the occurrence or frequency of every word in the data:

```
flattenPairs.reduceByKey((v1, v2) -> v1+v2);
```

So the preceding data will be reduced as follows:

```
(where, (1)) -> (where,1)
(there,(1+1) -> (there,2)
(is,(1+1)) -> (is,2)
(a,(1+1)) -> (a,2)
(will, (1)) -> (will,1)
(way, (1)) -> (way,1)
```

So this gives us the required result. If running in a cluster, the RDD is partitioned and then identical keys get shuffled to same executor, so this transformation allows network traffic as well (we will learn about partitioning concepts in `Chapter 7`, *Spark Programming Model-Advanced*).

5. **Run the final action**: As described in previous chapters, transformations are lazy operations. The DAG of transformations will only execute once an action is executed. So the final step is to execute the action. In this example, we have executed `saveToTextFile`, which saves the output in a text file:

```
wordCountRDD.saveAsTextFile("path_of_output_file");
```

In this section, we discussed the classical word count problem and learned to solve it using Spark and Java. In this process of solving the word count problem we also set up the Eclipse IDE for executing the Spark job.

In the next section, we will discuss some common RDD transformations and briefly touch upon narrow and wide dependencies of RDD operations.

Common RDD transformations

As described in `Chapter 1`, *Introduction of Spark*, if an operation on an RDD outputs an RDD then it is a transformation. In other words, transformation on an RDD executes a function on the elements of the RDD and creates a new RDD, which represents the transformed elements. The number of elements in the target RDD can be different than the source RDD.

Transformations in Spark are lazy operations that get triggered with an action; that is, a chain of transformations will only execute when an action is performed.

One important aspect of transformation also deals with the dependency on partition of the parent RDD. If each partition of the generated RDD depends on a fixed partition of the parent RDD then it's called a **narrow dependency**. Similarly, a wide dependency pertains to operations where the generated RDD depends on multiple partitions of the parent RDD. Typically, map, filter, and similar operations (which will be discussed in the coming section) have a narrow dependency, while `groupByKey`, `sortByKey`, and so on have a wide dependency.

Since narrow dependency relies on a specific partition to be operated upon, the sequential operations on these partitions become independent of each other. This not only increases parallelism, but also reduces compute time. Wide dependency, on the other hand depends on the efficacy of the shuffle operation that transfers data across different partitions. Even during node failures, the narrow dependency operation only recomputes the missing partition of the parent node, while in the case of wide dependency, all the dependent partitions of the parent RDD are recomputed.

Let's take a look at some useful Spark transformations:

Map

In a map transformation there is one-to-one mapping between elements of the source RDD and the target RDD. A function is executed on every element of source RDD and target RDD is created, which represents results of the executed function.

The following is an example of a map transformation, which increments every element of the RDD of integers by 1:

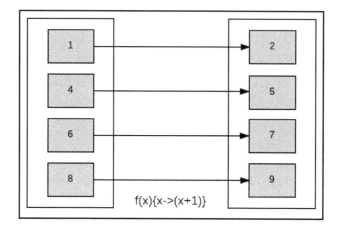

We will start with creating `JavaSparkContext` as follows:

```
SparkConf conf = new SparkConf().setMaster( "local" ).setAppName(
  "ApacheSparkForJavaDevelopers" );
JavaSparkContext javaSparkContext = new JavaSparkContext( conf );
```

Note that `setMaster` should point to a master URL for distributed clusters. However, setting to local specifies that the Spark job will run in single JVM. It is useful to run jobs inside the IDE, (for example, Eclipse) for debugging purposes.

Now, we will create an RDD of integers:

```
List<Integer> intList = Arrays.asList(1, 2, 3, 4, 5, 6, 7, 8, 9, 10);
JavaRDD<Integer> intRDD = javaSparkContext .parallelize( intList , 2);
```

Once created, a map transformation on the RDD to increment every element by one can be executed as follows:

```
Java 7:
intRDD .map( new Function<Integer, Integer>() {
@Override
public Integer call(Integer x ) throws Exception {
return x + 1;
}
});
Java 8:
intRDD.map(x -> x + 1);
```

Filter

With a filter transformation, the function is executed on all the elements of the source RDD and only those elements, for which the function returns true, are selected to form the target RDD. In this transformation, the number of elements in target RDD can be less than or equal to the number of elements in the source RDD.

The following is an example of a filter transformation that runs on the RDD of integers and selects only even elements, that is, elements that are divisible by 2:

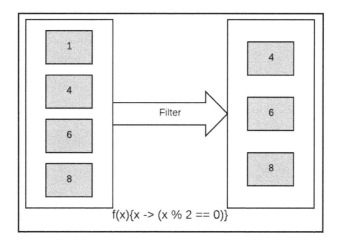

A filter transformation can be executed using Java 7 on intRDD created in the previous examples as follows:

```
intRDD .filter(new Function<Integer, Boolean>() {
  @Override
  public Boolean call(Integer x ) throws Exception {
    return ( x % 2 == 0);
  }
});
```

Example of intRDD using Java 8:

```
intRDD.filter(x -> (x % 2 == 0));
```

flatMap

In `flatMap()` transformation, an element of source RDD can be mapped to one or more elements of target RDD.A function is executed on every element of source RDD that produces one or more outputs. The return type of the `flatMap()` function is `java.util.iterator`, that is, it returns a sequence of elements.

The following example of `flatMap()` transformation will execute a function on an RDD of strings that will split every string element into words and produce an RDD with those words as its individual elements:

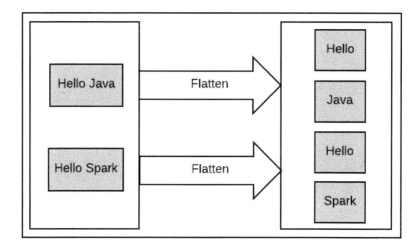

We will start with creating an RDD of strings using the `javaSparkContext`:

```
JavaRDD<String> stringRDD
=javaSparkContext.parallelize(Arrays.asList("Hello
  Spark", "Hello Java"));
```

Java 7:

```
stringRDD.flatMap(new FlatMapFunction<String, String>() {
@Override
public Iterator<String> call(String t) throws Exception {
return Arrays.asList(t.split(" ")).iterator();
}
});
```

Java 7:

```
stringRDD.flatMap(t -> Arrays.asList(t.split(" ")).iterator());
```

So in this case, the number of elements of target RDD is more than or equal to the number of elements of source RDD.

mapToPair

It is similar to `map` transformation; however, this transformation produces `PairRDD`, that is, an RDD consisting of key and value pairs. This transformation is specific to Java RDDs. With other RDDs, `map` transformation can perform both (`map` and `mapToPair()`) of the tasks.

Being similar to map transformation, it also creates one-to-one mapping between elements of source RDD and target RDD. So the number of elements of target RDD is equal to the number of elements of source RDD.

The following example of this transformation will convert intRDD created in *Map transformation* section to `JavaPairRDD` of `<String, Integer>` type, that is, the key of target RDD will be of string type and value will be of integer type with key specifying whether the element is even or odd:

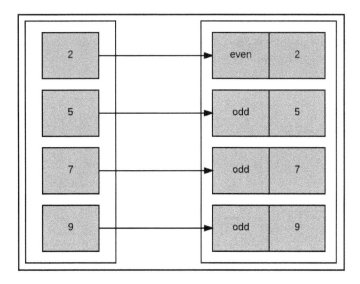

Java 7:

```
JavaPairRDD<String, Integer> pairRDD= intRDD.mapToPair(new
PairFunction<Integer,
  String, Integer>() {
    @Override
    public Tuple2<String, Integer> call(Integer i) throws Exception {
      return (i % 2 == 0) ? new Tuple2<String, Integer>("even", i) : new
      Tuple2<String,
      Integer>("odd", i);
    }
  });
```

Java 8:

```
JavaPairRDD<String, Integer> mapToPair = intRDD.mapToPair(i -> (i % 2 == 0)
? new
  Tuple2<String, Integer>("even", i) : new Tuple2<String, Integer>("odd",
i));
```

flatMapToPair

It is similar to `flatMap()`, however, the target RDD is a type of `PairRDD`, that is, an RDD consisting of key and value Pairs. Like `mapToPair()`, this operation is also specific to JavaRDDs.

Let's extend the example of `FlatMap()` transformation to create an RDD that consists of a word as the key and length of the word as its value:

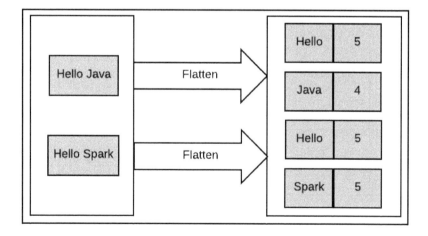

Java 7:

```
stringRDD.flatMapToPair(new PairFlatMapFunction<String, String, Integer>(){
@Override
  public Iterator<Tuple2<String, Integer>> call(String s) throws Exception
{
    List<Tuple2<String,Integer>> list =new ArrayList<>();
    for (String token : s.split(" ")) {
      list.add(new Tuple2<String, Integer>(token, token.length()));
    }
    return list.iterator();
  }
});
```

Java 8:

```
stringRDD.flatMapToPair(s -> Arrays.asList(s.split(" ")).stream().map(token
-> new Tuple2<String,Integer>(token,
token.length())).collect(Collectors.toList()).iterator());
```

union

As the name suggests, this transformation unites two RDDs into one. The target consists of all the elements of source RDDs. The following example of union transformation combines two Integer RDDs:

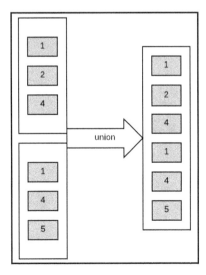

We will create an integer RDD using Java `SparkContext` and then create union of this RDD with the integer RDD created in the m*ap() transformation* section:

```
JavaRDD<Integer> intRDD2 =
javaSparkContext.parallelize(Arrays.asList(1,2,3));
intRDD.union(intRDD2);
```

Intersection

It produces an intersection of the elements of source RDDs, that is, the target RDD consists of the elements that are identical in source RDDs.

The following example will produce an intersection of two RDDs of integers:

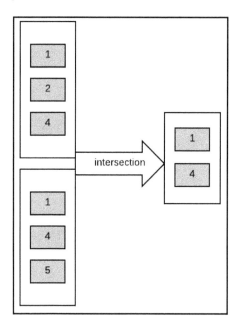

Intersection transformation can be executed as follows:

```
intRDD.intersection(intRDD2);
```

Distinct

As you would have already guessed, the distinct operation will return an RDD by fetching all the distinct elements of a source RDD. Distinct uses the `hashCode` and equals method of the objects to find distincts:

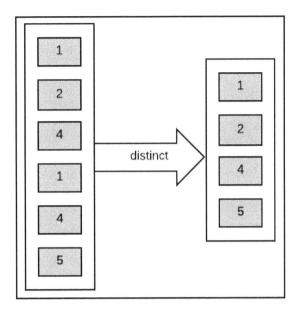

Let's create an RDD of integers that contains duplicates:

```
JavaRDD<Integer> rddwithdupElements =
javaSparkContext.parallelize(Arrays.asList(1,1,2,4,5,6,8,8,9,10,11,11));
```

The distinct operation on the RDD can be executed as follows:

```
rddwithdupElements.distinct();
```

Cartesian

Cartesian transformation generates a cartesian product of two RDDs. Each element of our first RDD is paired with each element of the second RDD. Therefore, if the cartesian operation is executed on an RDD of types X and an RDD of type Y it will return an RDD that will consist of <X,Y> pairs. The resultant RDD will consist of all the possible pairs of <X,Y>.

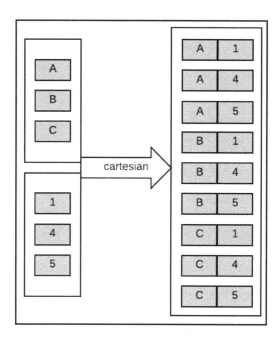

Cartesian transformation of RDD of Strings and RDD of integers can be executed as follows:

```java
JavaRDD<String> rddStrings =
javaSparkContext.parallelize(Arrays.asList("A","B","C"));
JavaRDD<Integer> rddIntegers =
javaSparkContext.parallelize(Arrays.asList(1,4,5));
rddStrings.cartesian(rddIntegers);
```

The next set of transformation works on PairRDDs:

groupByKey

groupbyKey transformation work with PairRDD (that is, RDD consists of (key, value) pairs). It is used to group all the values that are related to keys. It helps to transform a PairRDD consists of <key, value> pairs to PairRDD of <key, Iterable<value>>) pairs.

In the following example, we will execute the groupByKey operation on pairRDD generated in the mapToPair() transformation section.

The groupByKey operation can be executed as follows:

```
pairRDD.groupByKey()
```

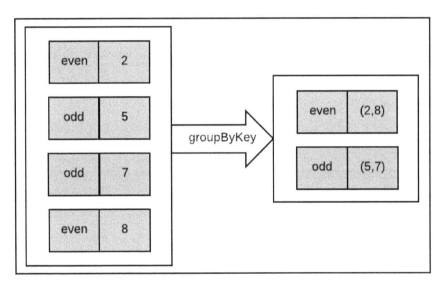

There is an overload available for this transformation function that lets the user provide Partitioner:

```
groupByKey(Partitioner partitioner)
```

As RDD is partitioned across multiple nodes. A key can be present in multiple partitions. In an operation such as `groupByKey` data will shuffled across multiple partitions. So key after shuffling will land on which of the executor running is decided by `Partitioner`. By default, Spark uses Hash Partitoner that uses `hashCode` of key to decide which executor it should be shuffled to. User can also provide custom partitioners based on the requirement.

> RDD Partitioning concepts will be explained in detail in `Chapter 7`, *Spark Programming Model-Advance*.

`groupByKey()` is a very costly operation as it requires a lot of shuffling. Data corresponding to one key is shuffled across the network, which can cause serious issues in case of large datasets.

reduceByKey

It is another transformation for Pair RDDs that helps to aggregate data corresponding to a key with the help of an associative reduce function. A function is passed as an argument to this transformation, which helps to aggregate the values corresponding to a key.

Given the same `PairRDD` that we used in `groupByKey`, for example, the `reduceByKey` operation can be performed on it as follows:

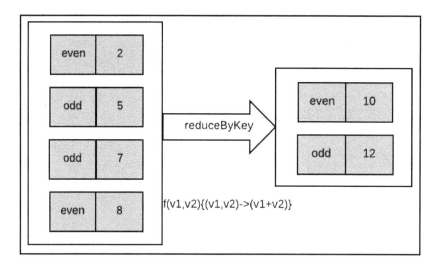

Java 7:

```
pairRDD.reduceByKey(new Function2<Integer, Integer, Integer>() {
@Override
  public Integer call(Integer v1, Integer v2) throws Exception {
    return v1 + v2;
  }
});
```

Java 8:

```
pairRDD.reduceByKey((v1, v2) -> v1 + v2);
```

In the previous example, the `reduceByKey` transformation will sum all the values corresponding to a key. The function accepts two parameters. The type of both parameters and return type of the function is the same as the value type of PairRDD. The first parameter is the cumulative value and the second value is the value of the pair that is next to be merged.

Similar to group by key, the `reduceByKey` function also provides an overload that accepts a partitioner as an argument:

```
reduceByKey(Partitioner partitioner,new Function2<T, T, T>() func)
```

For an RDD with multiple partitions, the `reduceByKey` transformation aggregates the values at partition level before shuffling, which helps in reducing the data travel of network. It is similar to the concept of combiner in Hadoop MapReduce. For a large dataset it is huge saving in the data being transferred over network. Therefore, `reduceByKey` is recommended over `groupByKey`.

sortByKey

`sortByKey()` belongs to `OrderedRDDFunctions`. It is used sort to a pair RDD by its key in ascending or descending order.

To execute `sortByKey()` on a `PairRDD`, Key should be of ordered type. In the Java world, key type should have implemented comparable, or else it throws an exception. So for a custom key type, the user should implement comparable interface.

The following is an example of the `sortByKey()` transformation:

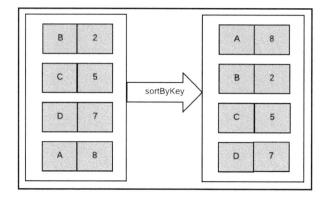

Let's first create a pair RDD of `<String,Integer>` type using `JAVaSparkContext`:

```
JavaPairRDD<String, Integer> unsortedPairRDD =
javaSparkContext.parallelizePairs (
Arrays.asList(new Tuple2<String, Integer>("B", 2), new Tuple2<String,
Integer>("C", 5), new Tuple2<String, Integer>("D", 7), new Tuple2<String,
Integer>("A", 8)));
```

Now, let's execute the `sortByKey` transformation on it to sort it in descending order:

```
unsortedPairRDD.sortByKey()
```

There is an overload available for the `sortByKey()` function that takes a Boolean argument:

```
sortByKey(boolean ascending)
```

This function can be used to sort an RDD in descending order by keys as follows:

```
unsortedPairRDD.sortByKey(false);
```

There are other overloads available for this function that allows users to provide a `Comparator` for the key type. So if the key has not implemented Comparable this function can be used:

```
sortByKey(Comparator<T> comp, boolean ascending)
```

This transformation also required shuffling of data between partitions. With the introduction of dataframes and datasets, Spark SQL operations can also be utilized to sort the data (these operations will discussed in detail in `Chapter 8`, *Working with Spark SQL*).

Join

It is used to join pair RDDs. This transformation is very similar to Join operations in a database. Consider, we have two pair RDDs of <X, Y> and <X, Z> types . When the Join transformation is executed on these RDDs, it will return an RDD of <X, (Y, Z) > type.

The following is an example of the join operation:

Let's start with creating two `PairRDD`:

```
JavaPairRDD<String, String> pairRDD1 =
javaSparkContext.parallelizePairs(Arrays.asList(new Tuple2<String,
String>("B", "A"), new Tuple2<String, String>("C", "D"), new Tuple2<String,
String>("D", "E"), new Tuple2<String, String>("A", "B"))
JavaPairRDD<String, Integer> pairRDD2 = javaSparkContext.parallelizePairs(
Arrays.asList(new Tuple2<String, Integer>("B", 2), new Tuple2<String,
Integer>("C", 5), new Tuple2<String, Integer>("D", 7), new Tuple2<String,
Integer>("A", 8)));
```

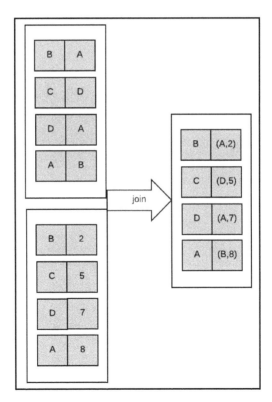

Now, `pairRDD1` will be joined with `pairRDD2` as follows:

```
JavaPairRDD<String, Tuple2<String, Integer>> joinedRDD =
pairRDD1.join(pairRDD2);
```

`LeftOuterJoin`, `RightOuterJoin` and `FullOuterJoin` are also supported which can be executed as :

```
pairRDD1.leftOuterJoin(pairRDD2);
pairRDD1.rightOuterJoin(pairRDD2);
pairRDD1.fullOuterJoin(pairRDD2);
```

In case of an RDD partitioned across multiple nodes, same keys will be shuffled to one of the executor nodes for the join operation. Therefore, overload is available for all of the join operations and it will let the user provide a partitioner as well:

```
join(JavaPairRDD<K,V> other,Partitioner partitioner)
leftOuterJoin(JavaPairRDD<K,V> other,Partitioner partitioner);
rightOuterJoin(JavaPairRDD<K,V> other,Partitioner partitioner);
fullOuterJoin(JavaPairRDD<K,V> other,Partitioner partitioner);
```

CoGroup

This operation also groups two `PairRDD`. Consider, we have two `PairRDD` of `<X, Y>` and `<X, Z>` types . When `CoGroup` transformation is executed on these RDDs, it will return an RDD of `<X, (Iterable<Y>, Iterable<Z>)>` type. This operation is also called `groupwith`.

The following is an example of `CoGroup` transformation. Let's start with creating two pair RDDs:

```
JavaPairRDD<String, String> pairRDD1 =
javaSparkContext.parallelizePairs(Arrays.asList(new Tuple2<String,
String>("B", "A"), new Tuple2<String, String>("B", "D"), new Tuple2<String,
String>("A", "E"), new Tuple2<String, String>("A", "B")));

JavaPairRDD<String, Integer> pairRDD2 =
javaSparkContext.parallelizePairs(Arrays.asList(new Tuple2<String,
Integer>("B", 2), new Tuple2<String, Integer>("B", 5), new Tuple2<String,
Integer>("A", 7), new Tuple2<String, Integer>("A", 8)));
```

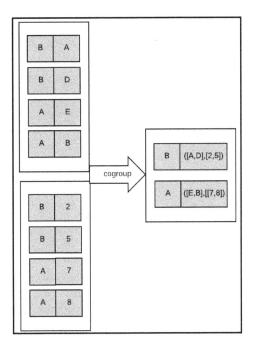

CoGroup transformation on these RDDs can be executed as follows:

```
JavaPairRDD<String, Tuple2<Iterable<String>, Iterable<Integer>>>
cogroupedRDD = pairRDD1.cogroup(pairRDD2);
```

or

```
JavaPairRDD<String, Tuple2<Iterable<String>, Iterable<Integer>>>
groupWithRDD = pairRDD1.groupWith(pairRDD2);
```

As this operation also requires shuffling of the same keys to one executor on a partitioned RDD, an overloaded function is available to provide partitioner:

```
cogroup(JavaPairRDD<K,V> other,Partitioner partitioner)
```

This section described various useful transformations, their usage, and their implementation in Java. In the next section, we will learn about various actions available in Spark that can be executed on RDDs.

Common RDD actions

In the previous section, we explored various RDD transformations that resulted in another RDD, however, an RDD operation that triggers Job computation and returns a non RDD value(s) is called an action. All the various transformations discussed previously do not get evaluated until an action gets called. Different transformations only help in materializing the lazily evaluated DAGs. It is the only action that triggers the data to be loaded in RDDs, transformation to be computed, and the final result to be either sent to the Driver program or written to a filesystem.

Some of the common actions widely used in Spark are discussed as follows:

isEmpty

`isEmpty` returns a Boolean value as *True*, if the RDD contains no element at all. It is important to note that RDD can be empty even when it is one or more partition. In the following example, we create the RDD with three integers and then filter an element that does not exist in the parent RDD hence the resultant creates an empty RDD:

Java 7:

```
// isEmpty
JavaRDD<Integer> intRDD = sparkContext.parallelize(Arrays.asList(1,2,3));
boolean isRDDEmpty = intRDD.filter(new Function<Integer, Boolean>() {
@Override
  public Boolean call(Integer v1) throws Exception {
    return v1.equals(5);
  }
}).isEmpty();
System.out.println("The RDD is empty ::"+isRDDEmpty);
```

Java 8:

```
JavaRDD<Integer> intRDD = sparkContext.parallelize(Arrays.asList(1,2,3));
boolean isRDDEmpty= intRDD.filter(a-> a.equals(5)).isEmpty();
System.out.println("The RDD is empty ::"+isRDDEmpty);
```

collect

Collect retrieves the data from different partitions of RDD into an array at the driver program. Care should be taken to call the collect action only on RDDs having considerably small data as otherwise it can crash the driver program.

Usually, after applying a set of transformations when the data size condenses, a collect action is called. The simplest example to call `collect()` can be filtering a specific value as follows:

```
//Collect
List<Integer> collectedList= intRDD.collect();
for(Integer elements: collectedList){
  System.out.println( "The collected elements are ::"+elements);
}
```

collectAsMap

The `collectAsMap` action is called on PairRDD to collect the dataset in key/value format at the driver program. Since all the partition data of RDD is dumped at the driver all the effort should be made to minimize the size:

```
// collectAsMap
List<Tuple2<String,Integer>> list= new ArrayList<Tuple2<String,Integer>>();
list.add(new Tuple2<String,Integer>("a", 1));
list.add(new Tuple2<String,Integer>("b", 2));
list.add(new Tuple2<String,Integer>("c", 3));
list.add(new Tuple2<String,Integer>("a", 4));
JavaPairRDD<String,Integer> pairRDD = sparkContext.parallelizePairs(list);
Map<String, Integer> collectMap=pairRDD.collectAsMap();
for(Entry<String, Integer> entrySet :collectMap.entrySet()) {
  System.out.println("The key of Map is : "+entrySet.getKey()+" and the
  value is : "+entrySet.getValue());
}
```

In the example, one can notice that the RDD has two tuples having the same key and it works fine as long as it is not collected as Map, as in such a scenario one of the values of key gets overridden by another.

count

The `count` method returns the number of element that exist in an RDD across partitions:

```
//count()
long countVal=intRDD.count();
System.out.println("The number of elements in the the RDD are :"+countVal);
```

countByKey

countByKey is an extension to what the action count() does, it works on pair RDD to calculate the number of occurrences of keys in a pair RDD. The CountByKey() method returns a Map having RDD elements's key as the Key of the Map and its value being the count of such Key:

```
//CountByKey
List<Tuple2<String,Integer>> list= new ArrayList<Tuple2<String,Integer>>();
list.add(new Tuple2<String,Integer>("a", 1));
list.add(new Tuple2<String,Integer>("b", 2));
list.add(new Tuple2<String,Integer>("c", 3));
list.add(new Tuple2<String,Integer>("a", 4));
JavaPairRDD<String,Integer> pairRDD = sparkContext.parallelizePairs(list);
Map<String, Long> countByKeyMap= pairRDD.countByKey();
for( Entry<String, Long> entrySet :countByKeyMap.entrySet() ){
  System.out.println("The key of Map is : "+entrySet.getKey()+" and the
  value is : "+entrySet.getValue());
}
```

countByValue

The countByValue() method can be applied on both RDD as well as pair RDD, however, the returned object has different signatures in both cases. For example, when countByValue() is applied on RDD , it counts the occurrence of elements having the specific value in that RDD and returns a Map having RDD elements as key and count of occurrence as value:

```
//countByValue
List<Tuple2<String,Integer>> list= new ArrayList<Tuple2<String,Integer>>();
list.add(new Tuple2<String,Integer>("a", 1));
list.add(new Tuple2<String,Integer>("b", 2));
list.add(new Tuple2<String,Integer>("c", 3));
list.add(new Tuple2<String,Integer>("a", 4));
JavaPairRDD<String,Integer> pairRDD = sparkContext.parallelizePairs(list);
Map<Tuple2<String, Integer>, Long> countByValueMap= pairRDD.countByValue();
for(Entry<Tuple2<String, Integer>, Long> entrySet
:countByValueMap.entrySet()) {
  System.out.println("The key of Map is a tuple having value :
  "+entrySet.getKey()._1()+" and "+entrySet.getKey()._2()+" and
  the value of count is : "+entrySet.getValue());
}
```

When `countByValue()` is applied on Pair RDD it returns the count of each unique value in the RDD as a map of (value, count) pairs where `value` is the Tuple for RDD. In the code snippet we can see that there are two tuples having the same key, that is, `a`, but the values are different. Hence when the `countByValue()` action is applied on them it treats both the keys having `a` as differently. The final combine step happens locally on the master, equivalent to running a single reduce task.

Max

The action `max` returns the largest value in the RDD where the comparison between the elements is decided by the comparator passed as an argument:

Java 7:

```
// max()
JavaRDD<Integer> intRDD = sparkContext.parallelize(Arrays.asList(1,2,3));
Integer maxVal=intRDD.max(new integerComparator());
System.out.println("The max value of RDD is "+maxVal);
//Also create a Comparator class as below
static class integer Comparator implements Comparator<Integer>,
Serializable
{
  private static finallongserialVersionUID = 1L;
  @Override
  public int compare(Integer a, Integer b) {
    return a.compareTo(b);
  }
}
```

Java 8:

```
JavaRDD<Integer> intRDD = sparkContext.parallelize(Arrays.asList(1,2,3));
Integer maxVal=intRDD.max(Comparator.naturalOrder());
System.out.println("The max value of RDD is "+maxVal);
```

Min

The method `min()` computes the smallest value in the RDD. A comparator is passed as an argument to the method `min()` to decide upon the comparison of elements in the RDD:

Java 7:

```
//min()
JavaRDD<Integer> intRDD = sparkContext.parallelize(Arrays.asList(1,2,3));
Integer minVal=intRDD.min(new integerComparator());
System.out.println("The min value of RDD is "+minVal);
//Also create a Comparator class as below
static class integerComparator implements Comparator<Integer>,Serializable{
private static finallongserialVersionUID = 1L;
@Override
  public int compare(Integer a, Integer b) {
    return a.compareTo(b);
  }
}
```

Java 8:

```
JavaRDD<Integer> intRDD = sparkContext.parallelize(Arrays.asList(1,2,3));
Integer minVal=intRDD.min(Comparator.naturalOrder());
System.out.println("The min value of RDD is "+minVal);
```

First

The `first` method returns the first element of the RDD:

```
//first()
JavaRDD<Integer> intRDD = sparkContext.parallelize(Arrays.asList(1,2,3));
Integer first=intRDD.first();
System.out.println("The first value of RDD is "+first);
```

Take

The action `take` returns a list on n elements where n is the argument to be passed to the method `take()`:

```
//take()
JavaRDD<Integer> intRDD = sparkContext.parallelize(Arrays.asList(1,2,3));
List<Integer> takeTwo=intRDD.take(2);
for(Integer intVal:takeTwo){
  System.out.println("The take elements are :: "+intVal);
}
```

As it can be observed now that the method `take()` with an argument as 1 will return the same value as the method `first()`. In other words, output of `take(1)` is same as running `first` action.

takeOrdered

Elements of the RDD can be returned based on natural or custom ordering of the dataset using the method `takeOrdered()`. An example for fetching the elements based on natural ordering of the elements is as follows:

```
//TakeOrdered()
JavaRDD<Integer> intRDD = sparkContext.parallelize(Arrays.asList(1,4,3));
List<Integer> takeOrderedTwo= intRDD.takeOrdered(2);
for(Integer intVal:takeOrderedTwo){
  System.out.println("The take ordered elements are :: "+intVal);
}
```

Similarly, if we are to fetch elements of the RDD based on custom ordering then we will have to implement and pass a custom comparator as an argument to the `takeOrdered()` method:

Java 7:

```
//TakeOrdered
JavaRDD<Integer> intRDD = sparkContext.parallelize(Arrays.asList(1,4,3));
List<Integer> takeCustomOrderedTwo= intRDD.takeOrdered(2, new
integerReverseComparator());
for(Integer intVal:takeCustomOrderedTwo){
  System.out.println("The take custom ordered elements are :: "+intVal);
}

//Also create a Comparator class as below
static class integerReverseComparator implements
Comparator<Integer>,Serializable {
private static finallongserialVersionUID = 1L;
@Override
  public int compare(Integer a, Integer b) {
    return b.compareTo(a);
  }
}
```

Java 8:

```
JavaRDD<Integer> intRDD = sparkContext.parallelize(Arrays.asList(1,4,3));
List<Integer> takeCustomOrderedTwo= intRDD.takeOrdered(2,
Comparator.reverseOrder());
for(Integer intVal:takeCustomOrderedTwo) {
  System.out.println("The take custom ordered elements are :: "+intVal);
}
```

takeSample

The `takeSample` method allows us to fetch a random list of elements from an RDD to the Driver program. One of the variants of the `takeSample()` method allows two parameters to be passed where the first parameter `withReplacement` is a Boolean value representing the possibility of each element of the RDD getting picked and being the same when set to `True`, or else any element of the RDD gets picked only once. The second parameter in the method is the size of the list of the sampled:

```
//takeSample()
JavaRDD<Integer> intRDD = sparkContext.parallelize(Arrays.asList(1,4,3));
List<Integer> takeSamepTrueList= intRDD.takeSample(true, 4);
for(Integer intVal:takeSamepTrueList) {
  System.out.println("The take sample vals for true are : "+intVal);
}
```

The output of the result will have four elements despite the RDD having only three elements, it is happening because we have set the `withReplacement` parameter as True and hence for fetching each sample element entire RDD datasets are considered. Now let's try the same example by passing the `withReplacement` parameter as False:

```
//TakeSample()
JavaRDD<Integer> intRDD = sparkContext.parallelize(Arrays.asList(1,4,3));
List<Integer> takeSamepFalseList=intRDD.takeSample(false, 4);
for(Integer intVal:takeSamepFalseList){
  System.out.println("The take sample vals for false are : "+intVal);
}
```

In this scenario, there will be only three element in the list despite setting the sample size to be four. It should be apparent now that if we set the `withReplacement` parameter as False then in such cases the elements for sample size does not get repeated, however, the sample size can be less than that may be required.

Another variant of the `takeSample()` method adds another parameter called seed, which when kept the same returns the same list of values any number to times the RDD with same dataset is sampled. i.e multiple executions with same seed value with return same result. It is very useful in replicating testing scenarios by keeping the sampled data the same:

```
//takeSample()
JavaRDD<Integer> intRDD = sparkContext.parallelize(Arrays.asList(1,4,3));
List<Integer> takeSamepTrueSeededList=intRDD.takeSample(true, 4,9);
for(Integer intVal:takeSamepTrueSeededList) {
  System.out.println("The take sample vals with seed are : "+intVal);
}
```

top

The RDD action `top` returns a list of n elements based on natural or custom ordering of the elements in the RDD:

```
//top()
JavaRDD<Integer> intRDD = sparkContext.parallelize(Arrays.asList(1,4,3));
List<Integer> topTwo=intRDD.top(2);
for(Integer intVal:topTwo) {
  System.out.println("The top two values of the RDD are : "+intVal);
}
```

For custom ordering of the elements a comparator is passed as an argument to the `top()` method:

Java 7:

```
//top()
JavaRDD<Integer> intRDD = sparkContext.parallelize(Arrays.asList(1,4,3));
List<Integer> topTwo=intRDD.top(2,new integerReverseComparator());
for(Integer intVal:topTwo) {
  System.out.println("The top two values of the RDD are : "+intVal);
}

//Also create a Comparator class as below
static class integerReverseComparator implements
Comparator<Integer>, Serializable {
private static finallongserialVersionUID = 1L;
@Override
  public int compare(Integer a, Integer b) {
    return b.compareTo(a);
  }
}
```

Java 8:

```
//top()
JavaRDD<Integer> intRDD = sparkContext.parallelize(Arrays.asList(1,4,3));
List<Integer> topTwo=intRDD.top(2,Comparator.reverseOrder());
for(Integer intVal:topTwo) {
  System.out.println("The top two values of the RDD are : "+intVal);
}
```

reduce

The reduce method passes the elements of the RDD to a function to be operated upon and then returns the computed output having the same data type as that of the input function. The simplest implementation of the reduce() function is of adding, multiplying, or counting all the elements of the RDD:

Java 7:

```
//reduce()
JavaRDD<Integer> intRDD = sparkContext.parallelize(Arrays.asList(1,4,3));
Integer sumInt=intRDD.reduce(new Function2<Integer, Integer, Integer>() {
  private static finallongserialVersionUID = 1L;
  @Override
    public Integer call(Integer v1, Integer v2) throws Exception {
      return v1+v2;
    }
  });
System.out.println("The sum of all the elements of RDD using reduce is
"+sumInt);
```

Java 8:

```
JavaRDD<Integer> intRDD =
sparkContext.parallelize(Arrays.asList(1,4,3));Integer
sumInt=intRDD.reduce((a,b)->a+b);
System.out.println("The sum of all the elements of RDD using reduce is
"+sumInt);
```

Fold

Just like a `reduce()` function, the `fold()` function too aggregates the value of RDD elements by passing each element to the aggregate function and computing a resultant value of the same data type. However, the `fold()` function also requires a *zero value* that is utilized while initializing the call to the partitions for the RDD. Depending on the type of aggregate function the zero value should ideally change , such as while adding the values of RDD elements zero value can be 0, similarly while multiplying it can be 1 and while concatenating a string it could be a blank space. Mathematically, the zero value should be the identity element of the aggregate function being computed:

Java 7:

```
//fold()
JavaRDD<Integer> intRDD = sparkContext.parallelize(Arrays.asList(1,4,3));
Integer foldInt=intRDD.fold(0, newFunction2<Integer, Integer, Integer>() {
  @Override
  public Integer call(Integer v1, Integer v2) throws Exception {
    return v1+v2;
  }
});
System.out.println("The sum of all the elements of RDD using fold is "+foldInt);
```

Java 8:

```
JavaRDD<Integer> intRDD = sparkContext.parallelize(Arrays.asList(1,4,3));
Integer foldInt=intRDD.fold(0, (a,b)-> a+b);
System.out.println("The sum of all the elements of RDD using fold is "+foldInt);
```

aggregate

Apart from `reduce` and `fold` functions Spark provides another method for aggregation of the RDD element called the `aggregate` function. The distinctive features of the aggregate function is that the return type of the function need not be of the same type as are the elements of RDD being operated upon.

An aggregate function has three input parameters, the first parameter being the zero value, which acts as an identity element of the data type in which the resultant aggregate of the RDD will be returned as an output. The second parameter is an accumulator function that defines the aggregation logic within each partition of the RDD and the third parameter is the function combining the output of each accumulator that worked on each partition of the RDD:

Java 7:

```
JavaRDD<Integer> rdd = sc.parallelize(Arrays.asList(1, 2, 3,4,5),3);
System.out.println("The no of partitions are ::"+rdd.getNumPartitions());
Function2<String,Integer,String> agg=newFunction2<String, Integer,
String>()
{
   @Override
   public String call(String v1, Integer v2) throws Exception {
     return v1+v2;
   }
};
Function2<String,String,String> combineAgg=newFunction2<String, String,
String>() {
   @Override
   public String call(String v1, String v2) throws Exception {
     return v1+v2;
   }
};
String result= rdd.aggregate("X", agg, combineAgg);
System.out.println("The aggerate value is ::"+result);
```

Java 8:

```
JavaRDD<Integer> rdd = sc.parallelize(Arrays.asList(1, 2, 3,4,5),3);
System.out.println("The no of partitions are ::"+rdd.getNumPartitions());
String result= rdd.aggregate("X", (x,y)->x+y, (x,z)->x+z);
System.out.println("The aggerate value is ::"+result);
```

It is to be noted that the zero value gets utilized once for each partition while accumulating the data from them and then once while combining all these accumulated output results. The output of the example has four x where three x represents the three partitions of the RDD while the fourth one represents the aggregation of partial outputs of various partitions. One can also notice that while the RDD elements were of Integer type the output of the aggregate function is a String.

forEach

In order to iterate over all the elements of the RDD to perform some repetitive tasks without fetching the entire set of data to the Driver program can be achieved by using the `foreach()` function:

Java 7:

```
//forEach()
JavaRDD<Integer> rdd = sc.parallelize(Arrays.asList(1, 2, 3,4,5),3);
intRDD.foreach(newVoidFunction<Integer>() {
  @Override
  public void call(Integer t) throws Exception {
    System.out.println("The element values of the RDD are ::"+t);
  }
});
```

Java 8:

```
JavaRDD<Integer> rdd = sc.parallelize(Arrays.asList(1, 2, 3,4,5),3);
intRDD.foreach(x->System.out.println("The element values of the RDD are
::"+x));
```

saveAsTextFile

The data of RDD can be saved to some local filesystem, HDFS, or any other Hadoop-supported filesystem using the action `saveAsTextFile()`. Each element of the RDD is first converted to a line of string by calling the `toString()` function on them before saving it on a filesystem:

Example for `saveAsTextFile()` using Java 7:

```
//saveAsTextFile()
JavaRDD<Integer> rdd = sc.parallelize(Arrays.asList(1, 2, 3,4,5),3);
intRDD.saveAsTextFile("TextFileDir");
JavaRDD<String> textRDD= sparkContext.textFile("TextFileDir");
textRDD.foreach(newVoidFunction<String>() {
@Override
public void call(String x) throws Exception {
System.out.println("The elements read from TextFileDir are :"+x); }
});
```

Java 8:

```
JavaRDD<Integer> rdd = sc.parallelize(Arrays.asList(1, 2, 3, 4, 5),3);
intRDD.saveAsTextFile("TextFileDir");
JavaRDD<String> textRDD= sparkContext.textFile("TextFileDir");
textRDD.foreach(x->System.out.println("The elements read from TextFileDir
are :"+x));
```

The text files on the filesystem can be read using the `testFile()` method of `SparkContext` as shown in the example.

saveAsObjectFile

RDD elements are converted string objects while reading and writing files using the `saveAsTextFile()` method and hence we lose important metadata information about the datatype of the object being written or read from a file. In order to store and retrieve the data and metadata information about its data type `saveAsObjectFile()` can be used. It uses Java Serialization to store the data on filesystems and similarly the data can be read using the `objectFile()` method of `SaprkContext`:

Java 7:

```
//saveAsObjectFile()
JavaRDD<Integer> rdd = sc.parallelize(Arrays.asList(1, 2, 3,4,5),3);
intRDD.saveAsObjectFile("ObjectFileDir");
JavaRDD<Integer> objectRDD= sparkContext.objectFile("ObjectFileDir");
objectRDD.foreach(newVoidFunction<Integer>() {
@Override
  public void call(Integer x) throws Exception
  {
    System.out.println("The elements read from ObjectFileDir are :"+x);
  }
});
```

Java 8:

```
JavaRDD<Integer> rdd = sc.parallelize(Arrays.asList(1, 2, 3,4,5),3);
intRDD.saveAsObjectFile("ObjectFileDir");
JavaRDD<Integer> objectRDD= sparkContext.objectFile("ObjectFileDir");
objectRDD.foreach(x->System.out.println("The elements read from
ObjectFileDir are :"+x));
```

This section covered the RDD operation action and its significance in Spark job evaluation. We also discussed commonly used actions and their usage and implication. The next section covers RDD caching and how RDD caching can improve the performance of Spark Job.

RDD persistence and cache

Spark jobs usually contains multiple intermediate RDDs on which multiple actions can be called to compute different problems. However, each time an action is called the complete DAG for that action gets called, this not only increases the computing time, but is also wasteful as per CPU and other resources are concerned. To overcome the limitation of re-computing the entire iterative job, Spark provides two different options for persisting the intermediate RDD, that is, `cache()` and `persist()`. The `cache()` method persists the data unserialized in the memory by default .This possibly is the fastest way to retrieve the persisted data, However, use of `cache()` comes with some trade off. Each node computing a partition of the RDD persist the resultant on that node itself and hence in case of node failure the data of the RDD partition gets lost. It is then recomputed again, but certain computation time gets lost in the process. Similarly, the persisted data is also unserialized and hence consumes more memory.

These limitations can be overcome by using the `persist()` method with optimal replication and serializing the data . The `persist()` method also gives the flexibility of choosing different storage level, that is, Memory, Disk, and Off heap. The numeral value (`_2`) in storage level defines the replication factor of the persisted data.

Storage Level	Memory Footprint	Computation Time	Replication	Serialized Objects	Memory Usage	Disk Usage
`MEMORY_ONLY`	HIGH	LOW	NO	NO	YES	NO
`MEMORY_ONLY_2`	HIGH	LOW	YES	NO	YES	NO
`MEMORY_ONLY_SER`	LOW	HIGH	NO	YES	YES	NO
`MEMORY_ONLY_SER_2`	LOW	HIGH	YES	YES	YES	NO
`DISK_ONLY`	LOW	HIGH	NO	YES	NO	YES
`DISK_ONLY_2`	LOW	HIGH	YES	YES	NO	YES
`MEMORY_AND_DISK`	HIGH	MEDIUM	NO	PARTIAL	PARTIAL	PARTIAL
`MEMORY_AND_DISK_2`	HIGH	MEDIUM	YES	PARTIAL	PARTIAL	PARTIAL
`MEMORY_AND_DISK_SER`	LOW	HIGH	NO	YES	PARTIAL	PARTIAL
`MEMORY_AND_DISK_SER_2`	LOW	HIGH	YES	YES	PARTIAL	PARTIAL
`OFF_HEAP`	LOW	HIGH	NO	YES	OFF-HEAP MEMORY	NO

List of Storage Level in Persist()

Data is always serialized when it is written to `DISK_ONLY` or `OFF_HEAP` and hence there is no storage level with `_SER` in its name when choosing only disk or off heap. With storage level `MEMORY_ONLY` a situation can arise when the amount of data to be persisted is more than that available in the memory, in such scenarios Spark uses the **Least Recently Used** (**LRU**) algorithm to drop partitions. However, if such dropped partitions are ever required then it is recomputed again. To overcome such memory constraint limitation one can choose between `MEMORY_ONLY_SER`, which reduces the memory footprint of the data slightly or otherwise can choose from `MEMORY_AND_DIST` storage level variants:

```
//cache() and persist()
JavaRDD<Integer> rdd = sparkContext.parallelize(Arrays.asList(1, 2,
3, 4, 5),3).cache();
JavaRDD<Integer> evenRDD=
rdd.filter(neworg.apache.spark.api.java.function.Function<Integer,
Boolean>() {
@Override
  public Boolean call(Integer v1) throws Exception {
    return ((v1%2)==0)?true:false;
  }
});
evenRDD.persist(StorageLevel.MEMORY_AND_DISK());
evenRDD.foreach(newVoidFunction<Integer>() {
  @Override
    publicvoid call(Integer t) throws Exception {
      System.out.println("The value of RDD are :"+t);
    }
  });
//unpersisting the RDD
evenRDD.unpersist();
rdd.unpersist();
```

It is important to note that the `cache()` method is just a syntactic sugar for using the `persist()` method with storage level as `MEMORY_ONLY`. Choosing a storage level for RDD persistence is of paramount importance as far as performance of Spark jobs are concerned, but there are no rules that govern the choice to be made. Some of the factors, however, can act as guiding principles to choose a better storage level for any Spark job:

- Prefer `MEMORY_ONLY` storage as long as complete RDD can be persisted in memory.
- Try `MEMORY_ONLY_SER` if memory required for RDD persistence is slightly more than available, however, this option increases the operation time as some computation gets consumed in serializing and de-serializing the data.

- Spilling the RDD data on disk may sometimes be a far more expensive operation than re-computing the partition itself.
- Data replication should be chosen for use cases where extremely high throughput is required such that the time lost in recomputation of lost partitions be avoided at all cost.

`cache()` usage is monitored in Spark using **Least Recently Used (LRU)** algorithms where unused old partitions are dropped automatically , however, one can manually evict an RDD from cache using the `unpersist()` method.

Summary

In this chapter, we started with a `Hello World` program and setting up an IDE (Eclipse) for executing Spark Jobs. Then we discussed various RDD Transformation and various common transformations such as `map`, `flatMap`, `mapToPair`, and so on. We also explored commonly used RDD actions and some of the use cases associated with it. We also gained some understanding in improving Spark Job performance by using Apache Spark's inbuilt cache and persist mechanism.

The next chapter will focus on the interactional aspect of Apache Spark as far as the Data and Storage layer is concerned. We will learn about Spark integration with external storage systems such as HDFS, S3 etc and its ability to process various data formats such as xml, json etc.

5
Working with Data and Storage

In the previous chapter, we discussed the various transformations and actions that we can execute on data in Spark. To load data in Spark for processing, it needs to interact with external storage systems. In this chapter, we will learn how to read/store data in Spark from/to different storage systems. Also, we will discuss the libraries that help to process different varieties of structured/unstructured data in Spark.

Interaction with external storage systems

As we know, Spark is a processing engine that can help to process a humongous amount of data; however, to process the data it should be read from external systems. In this section, we will learn how to store/read data in Spark from/to different storage systems.

We will start with the local filesystem and then will implement Spark with some popular storage systems used in the big data world.

Interaction with local filesystem

It is very straightforward and easy to read data from a local filesystem in Spark. Let's discuss this with examples, as follows:

Let's put first things first. First, create (or reuse) the Maven project described in the previous chapter and create a Java class (with main method) for our application. We will start by creating a `JavaSparkContext`:

```
SparkConf conf =new SparkConf().setMaster("local").setAppName("Local File
system Example");
JavaSparkContext jsc=new JavaSparkContext(conf);
```

To read a text file in Spark, the `textFile` method is provided by `SparkContext`. The following is the signature of the method:

```
textFile(String path)
```

This method can be used to read the file from local filesystems, as follows:

```
JavaRDD<String> localFile =
jsc.textFile("absolutepathOfTheFileOnLocalFileSystem");
```

As shown previously, the file will be read as RDD of strings. Now we can run transformation and/or actions on the data of the file. For example, wordcount on this data can be executed as follows:

```
JavaPairRDD<String, Integer> wordCountLocalFile =localFile.flatMap(x ->
Arrays.asList(x.split(" ")).iterator())
            .mapToPair(x -> new Tuple2<String, Integer>((String) x, 1))
            .reduceByKey((x, y) -> x + y);
wordCountLocalFile.collect();
```

 As we already know, DAG of Spark operations starts to execute only when an action is performed. Here, reading the file from the local filesystem is also a part of DAG. Therefore, file reading operations will also be performed only when an action is executed, that is, the `collect()` operation in the preceding case.

The `textfile` method can be used to read multiple files as follows:

- To read more than one file:

    ```
    jsc.textFile("absolutepathOfTheFile1,absolutepathOfTheFile2");
    ```

- To read all the files in a directory:

    ```
    jsc.textFile("absolutepathOfTheDir/*");
    ```

- To read all the files in multiple directories:

    ```
    jsc.textFile("absolutepathOfTheDir1/*,absolutepathOfTheDir2/*");
    ```

The `textfile` method also provides an overload that allows users to provide the minimum number of partitions:

```
textFile(String path,int minPartitions)
```

The `minPartitons` parameters help to calculate the number of splits the file is distributed into.

The Spark `textFile` method internally uses `FileInputFormat` [1] of Hadoop to calculate the input splits. The following is the formula used to calculate input splits:

```
Math.max(minSize, Math.min(goalSize, blockSize));
```

Where `minSize = mapred.min.split.size` or `mapreduce.input.fileinputformat.split.minsize`:

```
goalSize = totalSize / (numSplits == 0 ? 1 : numSplits); (total size is
total size of input data)
```

`blockSize` is the block size of the file, which is considered to be 32 MB (`hadoop fs.local.block.size`) in the case of local filesystems and 64 MB/128 MB (`dfs.blocksize`) in the case of HDFS.

The `numSplits` value, which is used to calculate goal Size is the `minPartitons` parameter value.

We will study more about RDD partitioning in `Chapter 7`, *Spark Programming Model – Advanced*.

`SparkContext` provide another method to read the files:

```
wholeTextFiles(String path)
wholeTextFiles(String path,int minPartitions)
```

This method returns a pair RDD with key as the filename and value as the content of the file:

```
JavaPairRDD<String, String> localFile =
jsc.wholeTextFiles("absolutepathOfTheFile");
```

Similar to the `textFile`method, multiple files can be read using the `wholeTextFiles` method as follows:

- To read more than one file

```
jsc.wholeTextFiles
("absolutepathOfTheFile1,absolutepathOfTheFile2");
```

- To read all the files in a directory

```
jsc.wholeTextFiles ("absolutepathOfTheDir/*");
```

- To read all the files in multiple directories

```
jsc.wholeTextFiles
("absolutepathOfTheDir1/*,absolutepathOfTheDir2/*");
```

To save the output back to the local file, the `system,saveAsTextFile()` method can be used as follows:

```
wordCountLocalFile.saveAsTextFile("absolutePathOfTheOutputDir");
```

> Output Path should not be an existing path, or else it will throw the following exception:
> ```
> Exception in thread "main"
> org.apache.hadoop.mapred.FileAlreadyExistsException
> ```

Interaction with Amazon S3

Simple Storage Service, also known as S3, is an auto scalable storage platform provided by **Amazon Web Services** (**AWS**). It is a widely used service for storing data. Once connected to the internet, users can store and retrieve any amount of data at any time from S3. Being one of the cheapest storage services available on the internet, it is used extensively to store huge amounts of data. As it is an AWS service, users do not have to worry about its availability and management.

> If you have not used S3, it is suggested that you refer to the AWS S3 documentation (`http://docs.aws.amazon.com/AmazonS3/latest/dev/Welcome.html`) for more information.

The following filesystem schemes can be used to access S3 data in Spark:

- **S3 (URL: s3://)**: This scheme is bound the to Hadoop File System. In other words, this scheme is the Hadoop implementation of the HDFS, backed up by S3. So, files will be actually stored in blocks using this scheme and as those are stored in blocks, tools other than Hadoop are unable to read them as regular files. This scheme is deprecated now.

> As this scheme is deprecated, we have not considered it for our code examples.

- **S3N (URI : s3n://)**: S3N, aka **S3 Native**, is the scheme used to read/write files as regular S3 objects. Using this scheme, files written by Hadoop are accessible by other tools and vice versa. It requires the `jets3t` library to work.

  With this scheme, there is an upper limit of 5GB, that is, files larger than 5GB can't be read using this scheme. Although this scheme is widely used, it is not considered for new enhancements anymore.

- **S3A (URI : s3a://)**: This is the latest filesystem scheme. This scheme has removed the upper limit constraint of S3N and provides various performance improvements. This scheme leverages Amazon's libraries to access S3 objects. S3A is also backward compatible with S3N.

  As per Amazon documentation, this scheme is recommended for any newer developments.

To read the data from S3, the following AWS credentials are required:

- AWS Access key ID
- AWS Secret access key

Users can configure AWS credentials using any of the following ways:

- The credentials can be set inline in the Spark program, as follows:
    - **Using S3N**

      ```
      jsc.hadoopConfiguration().set("fs.s3n.awsAccessKeyId",
      "accessKeyIDValue");
      jsc.hadoopConfiguration().set("fs.s3n.awsSecretAccessKey",
      "securityAccesKeyValue");
      ```

    - **Using S3A**

      ```
      jsc.hadoopConfiguration().set("fs.s3a.awsAccessKeyId",
      "accessKeyIDValue");
      jsc.hadoopConfiguration().set("fs.s3a.awsSecretAccessKey",
      "securityAccesKeyValue");
      ```

      It can be read using a property file to avoid security issues. These credentials can be set using environment variables, as follows:

      ```
      export AWS_ACCESS_KEY_ID=accessKeyIDValue
      export AWS_SECRET_ACCESS_KEY=securityAccesKeyValue
      ```

Also, to use the S3A filesystem, the `hadoop-aws` library is required to be added in the classpath. The following is the Maven dependency template for the same:

```
<dependency>
    <groupId>org.apache.hadoop</groupId>
    <artifactId>hadoop-aws</artifactId>
    <version>2.7.1</version>
</dependency>
```

S3 scheme, to read the data from S3, can be provided in Spark as follows:

- **Using S3N:**

```
JavaRDD<String> s3File = jsc.textFile("s3n://"+"bucket-name"+"/"+"file-path");
```

- **Using S3A:**

```
JavaRDD<String> s3File = jsc.textFile("s3a://"+"bucket-name"+"/"+"file-path");
```

Once RDD is created, further operations (transformation/actions) can be performed on the data to get the required results. For example, the following transformations can be executed on it to generate word count:

```
JavaPairRDD<String, Integer> s3WordCount=s3File .flatMap(x
-> Arrays.asList(x.split(" ")).iterator())
                .mapToPair(x -> new Tuple2<String,
Integer>((String) x, 1))
                .reduceByKey((x, y) -> x + y);
```

The `textfile` method can be used to read multiple files from HDFS as follows:

- To read more than one file:
  - **Using S3N**

```
jsc.textFile("s3n://"+"bucket-name"+"/"+"path-of-
file1"+","+"s3n://"+"bucket-name"+"/"+"path-of-file2");
```

  - **Using S3A**

```
jsc.textFile("s3a://"+"bucket-name"+"/"+"path-of-
file1"+","+"s3a://"+"bucket-name"+"/"+"path-of-file2");
```

- To read all the files in a directory:
    - **Using S3N**

      ```
      jsc.textFile("s3n://"+"bucket-name"+"/"+"path-of-dir/*");
      ```

    - **Using S3A**

      ```
      jsc.textFile("s3a://"+"bucket-name"+"/"+"path-of-dir/*");
      ```

- To read all the files in multiple directories
    - **Using S3N**

      ```
      jsc.textFile("s3n://"+"bucket-name"+"/"+"path-of-
      dir1/*"+","+"s3n://"+"bucket-name"+"/"+"path-of-dir2/*");
      ```

    - **Using S3A**

      ```
      jsc.textFile("s3a://"+"bucket-name"+"/"+"path-of-
      dir1/*"+","+"s3a://"+"bucket-name"+"/"+"path-of-dir2/*");
      ```

- To save the output back to the S3 schemes can be used as follows:
    - **Using S3N**

      ```
      s3WordCount.saveAsTextFile("s3n://"+"buxket-
      name"+"/"+"outputDirPath");
      ```

    - **Using S3A**

      ```
      s3WordCount.saveAsTextFile("s3a://"+"buxket-
      name"+"/"+"outputDirPath")
      ```

Interaction with HDFS

Hadoop Distributed File System (HDFS), is widely used for storing huge amounts of data. It is the most popular storage system in the big data world. Its scalability, high availability, and fault tolerance make it an ideal filesystem for storing large chunks of data.

We have already explained some basics of HDFS in Chapter 1, *Introduction to Spark*. Please refer to it for further clarification of its workings.

For reading or writing data on HDFS, the client has to connect to NameNode, which holds all the metadata of HDFS. Then, NameNode redirects the client to the DataNode(s) where the actual data resides if the client has requested to read, or to the DataNode(s) where resources (that is, storage space) are available to write the data in the case of write requests.

So, to read from HDFS, the client requires the NameNode address and path of the file(s) that needs to be read. Users can read a file in Spark from HDFS as follows:

```
JavaRDD<String> hadoopFile= jsc.textFile("hdfs://"+"namenode-
host:port/"+"absolute-file-path-on-hdfs");
```

For example:

```
JavaRDD<String> hadoopFile=
jsc.textFile("hdfs://localhost:8020/user/spark/data.csv")
```

As the `textFile` method always returns an RDD of Strings, further operations can be done similarly:

```
JavaPairRDD<String, Integer> hadoopWordCount=hadoopFile.flatMap(x ->
Arrays.asList(x.split(", ")).iterator())
                .mapToPair(x -> new Tuple2<String, Integer>((String) x, 1))
                .reduceByKey((x, y) -> x + y);
```

The `textfile` method can be used to read multiple files from HDFS as follows:

- To read more than one file:

  ```
  jsc.textFile("hdfs://"+"namenode-host:port/"+"absolute-file-path-
  of-file1"+", "+"hdfs://"+"namenode-host:port/"+"absolute-file-path-
  of-file2");
  ```

- To read all the files in a directory:

  ```
  jsc.textFile("hdfs://"+"namenode-host:port/"+"absolute-file-path-
  of-dir/*");
  ```

- To read all the files in multiple directories:

  ```
  jsc.textFile("hdfs://"+"namenode-host:port/"+"absolute-file-path-
  of-dir1/*"+", "+"hdfs://"+"namenode-host:port/"+"absolute-file-path-
  of-dir2/*");
  ```

To write the output back to HDFS, users can provide the HDFS URL as follows:

```
hadoopWordCount.saveAsTextFile("hdfs://"+"namenode-host:port/"+"absolute-
file-path-of-output-dir");
```

Interaction with Cassandra

Apache Cassandra is an open source NoSQL database. It falls in the **Column family** based database category. It is developed at Facebook and built on the concepts on Amazon's Dynamo. It is designed to store large amounts of data in a distributed fashion.

Cassandra is highly scalable with no single point of failure. It satisfies availability and partition tolerance categories of the CAP theorem with tunable consistency, that is, Cassandra is by default eventually consistent, however, consistency in Cassandra can be increased at the cost of availability. Cassandra is made to support very high-speed writes and due to its excellent features, it is one of the most widely used databases in the NoSQl World.

To read more about Cassandra, you can refer to `https://academy.datastax.com/planet-cassandra`.

To interact with Cassandra from Spark, `spark-cassandra-connector` is required. The following is the Maven template for `spark-cassandra-connector`:

```
<dependency>
            <groupId>com.datastax.spark</groupId>
            <artifactId>spark-cassandra-connector_2.11</artifactId>
            <version>2.0.0-M1</version>
</dependency>
```

 The preceding specified version works with Spark 2.x.x versions. Users can change the version as per their requirement.

Consider, we have a table in Cassandra with the following definition in keyspace named `my_keyspace`:

```
CREATE TABLE my_keyspace.emp (
    empid int PRIMARY KEY,
    emp_dept text,
    emp_name text
)
```

To read the data, an `Employee` POJO object is needed, as follows:

```
public class Employee implements Serializable{
    private Integer empid;
    private String emp_name;
    private String emp_dept;
    public String toString() {
        return "Employee [empid=" + empid + ", emp_name=" + emp_name + ",
        emp_dept=" + emp_dept + "]";
    }
      public Integer getEmpid() {
        return empid;
    }
    public void setEmpid(Integer empid) {
        this.empid = empid;
    }
    public String getEmp_name() {
        return emp_name;
    }
    public void setEmp_name(String emp_name) {
        this.emp_name = emp_name;
    }
    public String getEmp_dept() {
        return emp_dept;
    }
    public void setEmp_dept(String emp_dept) {
        this.emp_dept = emp_dept;
    }
  }
```

 The name of the columns of the Cassandra table should exactly match the name of the fields on the class, or else it throws exceptions. Also, the object must be serializable.

To connect Spark to Cassandra, Cassandra configurations need to provide to Spark as follows:

```
SparkConf conf =new SparkConf().setMaster("local").setAppName("Cassandra
Example");
conf.set("spark.cassandra.connection.host", "127.0.0.1");

JavaSparkContext jsc=new JavaSparkContext(conf);
```

Now, the rows of the Cassandra table can be mapped to the preceding POJO class using the `CassandraJavaUtil` library provided by `spark-cassandra-connector` as follows:

```
JavaRDD<Employee> cassandraRDD =
CassandraJavaUtil.javaFunctions(jsc).cassandraTable("my_keyspace",
"emp",CassandraJavaUtil.mapRowTo(Employee.class));
```

As shown in the preceding snippet, Cassandra rows have mapped to `Employee` objects and this returns an RDD of `employee` objects. An example of the `collect()` action can be executed on this RDD as follows:

```
cassandraRDD.collect().forEach(System.out::println);
```

To load only one column from the table, the `CassandraJavaUtil` library can be used as follows:

```
JavaRDD<String> selectEmpDept
=CassandraJavaUtil.javaFunctions(jsc).cassandraTable("my_keyspace",
"emp",CassandraJavaUtil.mapColumnTo(String.class)).select("emp_dept");
```

Here we have a used datatype of column `emp_dept` as an argument of the `mapColumnTo` method. To find out the other operations that can be executed on Cassandra data using the `CassandraJavaUtil` library, please refer to the following URL: `https://github.com/datastax/spark-cassandra-connector`.

To write the results back to Cassandra, the same library can be used, as follows:

```
CassandraJavaUtil.javaFunctions(cassandraTable)
        .writerBuilder("my_keyspace", "emp",
CassandraJavaUtil.mapToRow(Employee.class)).saveToCassandra();
```

Similar to the read operation, the POJO object is mapped to the column of the Cassandra table before persisting the results.

 `saveToCassandra()` is an action.

This is a bit of a tedious way. Let's look into another way to load the Cassandra table as a dataset. A dataset is an RDD with schema. Using the dataset API, an RDD can be viewed as a tabular structure, as it loads schema as well as data.

To load a Cassandra table as a datasets, we need to create a `SparkSession` object. As explained in `Chapter 1`, *Introduction to Spark*, `SparkSession` is the single entry point for a Spark program. Prior to Spark 2.x, `SparkContext`, `SQLContext`, and so on needed to be created separately. However, in Spark 2.x, `SparkSession` performs all these roles.

> We will discuss more about dataset and `SparkSession` while discussing **Spark SQL** in `Chapter 8`, *Working with Spark SQL*.

Let's start by creating a `SparkSession` object:

```
SparkSession sparkSession =
SparkSession.builder().master("local").appName("My App")
                    .config("spark.cassandra.connection.host",
"localhost").getOrCreate();
```

The next step is to load the data from Cassandra using the `SparkSession` object:

```
Map<String, String> map = new HashMap<>();
    map.put("table", "table_name");
    map.put("keyspace", "keyspace_name");

Dataset<Row> cassDataset =
sparkSession.read().format("org.apache.spark.sql.cassandra").options(map).l
oad();
```

As per the preceding code, it accepts a `map` object where users can specify table properties.

Now, similar to the `collect()` function of RDD, the `show()` function can be executed on the dataset to read the data:

```
cassDataset.show();
```

> The `show()` function is an action.

This will return the data along with column names. So, it is easier to interpret the data, as a schema is also provided. Also, temporary view can be created on the dataset, using which, users can run SQL on the data:

```
cassDataset.createOrReplaceTempView("cass_data_view");
  sparkSession.sql("Select * from cass_data_view");
```

Similar to Cassandra, Spark Connectors are available for other databases, for example, MongoDB, HBase, and so on, which can be leveraged to connect Spark to these databases.

In this section, we learnt about connecting Spark to various data sources and reading the data. In the next section, we will learn how to handle different types of structured data in Spark.

Working with different data formats

Apache Spark extensively supports various file formats either natively or with the support of libraries written in Java or other programming languages. Compressed file formats, as well as Hadoop's file format, are very well integrated with Spark. Some of the common file formats widely used in Spark are as follows:

Plain and specially formatted text

Plain text can be read in Spark by calling the `textFile()` function on `SparkContext`. However, for specially formatted text, such as files separated by white space, tab, tilde (~), and so on, users need to iterate over each line of the text using the `map()` function and then split them on specific characters, such as tilde (~) in the case of tilde-separated files.

Consider, we have tilde-separated files that consist of data of people in the following format:

```
name~age~occupation
```

Let's load this file as an RDD of `Person` objects, as follows:

Person POJO:

```
public class Person implements Serializable {
  private String Name;
  private Integer Age;
  private String occupation;
  public String getOccupation() {
    return occupation ;
  }
  public void setOccupation(String occupation ) {
    this.occupation = occupation;
  }
  public String getName() {
    return Name;
```

```
    }
    public void setName(String name) {
      Name = name;
    }
    public Integer getAge() {
      return Age ;
    }
    public void setAge(Integer age ) {
      Age = age ;
    }
  }
```

Example for plain and specially formatted text using Java 7:

```
JavaRDD<String> textFile = jsc.textFile("Path of the file");

JavaRDD<Person> people = textFile.map( new Function<String, Person>() {
  public Person call(String line ) throws Exception {
    String[] parts = line .split("~");
    Person person = new Person();
    person.setName(parts [0]);
    person.setAge(Integer.parseInt(parts [1].trim()));
    person.setOccupation(parts[2]);
    return person ;
  }
});

people.foreach(new VoidFunction<Person>() {
  @Override
  public void call(Person p) throws Exception {
    System.out.println(p);
  }
});
```

Example for plain and specially formatted text using Java 7:

```
JavaRDD<String> textFile = jsc.textFile( "Path of the file" );

JavaRDD<Person> people = textFile.map(line -> {
  String[] parts = line.split("~");
  Person person = new Person();
  person.setName(parts [0]);
  person.setAge(Integer.parseInt( parts [1].trim()));
  person.setOccupation(parts [2]);
  return person ;
});
people.foreach(p -> System.out.println(p));
```

POJO objects should be serializable, as RDD is a distributed data structure and while shuffling operations during transformations/actions, data gets transferred over the network.

This arrangement of reading a text file, creating an RDD of string, and then applying a map() function to map text fields to Java objects works perfectly fine as long as creating Java objects in the map() function for each row is not an expensive process. However, there is some performance gain if we choose mapPartitions() over map() in general, as it gives an iterator of the elements on the RDD for each partition. Later, in other sections, wherever we have the option to work on map() we must also consider the suitability of mapPartitions() in such scenarios as a thumb rule. Any pre-build stage, such as creating a database connection, opening a socket port, or maybe creating a web session has some overhead associated with it, and also the same object can be reused. Hence, in all such scenarios, mapPartitions() will work much better than map().

Java 7:

```
JavaRDD <Person> peoplePart = textFile.mapPartitions( new
FlatMapFunction<Iterator<String>, Person>() {
  @Override
  public Iterator<Person> call(Iterator<String> p) throws Exception {
    ArrayList<Person> personList = new ArrayList<Person>();
    while ( p .hasNext()){
      String[] parts = p.next().split("~");
      Person person = new Person();
      person.setName(parts [0]);
      person.setAge(Integer.parseInt(parts[1].trim()));
      person.setOccupation(parts[2]);
      personList.add( person );
    }
    return personList .iterator();
  }
});
peoplePart .foreach( new VoidFunction<Person>() {
  @Override
  public void call(Person p) throws Exception {
    System.out.println(p);
  }
});
```

Java 8:

```
JavaRDD<Person> peoplePart = textFile.mapPartitions( p -> {
  ArrayList<Person> personList = new ArrayList<Person>();
  while (p .hasNext()) {
    String[] parts = p.next().split("~");
    Person person = new Person();
    person.setName(parts [0]);
    person.setAge(Integer.parseInt(parts [1].trim()));
    person.setOccupation(parts [2]);
    personList add(person);
  }
  return personList.iterator();
});
peoplePart.foreach(p -> System.out.println(p));
```

Similarly, saving a text file in some specific format can also be done in a similar manner by calling the `saveAsTextFile()` method on RDD. It will write the data in a text file, where the `.toString()` method is called on each RDD element and one element is written per line:

```
people.saveAsTextFile( "Path of output file" );
```

The number of output files are equal to the number of partitions in the RDD, hence it can be controlled by calling the `repartition()` method on the RDD with the appropriate number before saving the text file:

```
people.repartition(1).saveAsTextFile("Path of output file");
```

Although the `repartition()` method achieves the task of managing the output file while saving, it may be an expensive process because of data shuffle. Coalesce is another option that can be used in place of `repartition()`, which will try to avoid the shuffling of data, hence may be better suited for these kinds of operations:

```
people.coalesce(1).saveAsTextFile( "Path of output file" );
```

 Refer to the *Advance Spark Transformations* section in Chapter 7, *Spark Programming Model – Advanced* for a detailed explanation about the working of repartitioning and coalesce transformations .

Working with CSV data

CSV files can be treated as plain text files, having a comma as a delimiter and will generally work as expected. Consider, we have data of movies in the following format:

```
movieId, title, genre
```

Let's load this file as an RDD of the `Movie` object, as follows:

Movie POJO:

```java
public class Movie implements Serializable {
private Integer movieId;
private String title;
private String genre;
public Movie()
{};
public Movie(Integer movieId, String title, String genere ) {
  super();
  this.movieId = movieId;
  this.title = title;
  this.genre = genere;
}
public Integer getMovieId() {
  return movieId;
}
public void setMovieId(Integer movieId ) {
  this.movieId = movieId ;
}
public String getTitle() {
  return title;
}
public void setTitle(String title ) {
  this.title = title;
}
public String getGenere() {
  return genre;
}
public void setGenere(String genere ) {
  this.genre = genere;
}
public static Movie parseRating(String str ) {
  String[] fields = str.split(",");
  if ( fields . length != 3) {
    System.out.println("The elements are ::");
    Stream.of( fields ).forEach(System. out ::println);
    throw new IllegalArgumentException("Each line must contain 3 fields
    while the current line has ::" + fields.length );
```

```
  }
  Integer movieId = Integer.parseInt( fields [0]);
  String title = fields [1].trim();
  String genere = fields [2].trim();
  return new Movie(movieId, title, genere);
  }
}
```

Spark Code:

Example for working on CSV data using Java 7:

```
JavaRDD<Movie> moviesRDD = sparkSession.read().textFile("movies.csv")
                                .javaRDD().filter( str -> !(null ==
str))
                                .filter( str -> !(str.length()==0))
                                .filter( str ->
!str.contains("movieId"))
                                .map(new Function<String, Movie>()
{
  private static final long serialVersionUID = 1L;
  public Moviee call(String str ) {
    return Movie.parseRating( str );
  }
});

moviesRDD .foreach( new VoidFunction<Movie>() {
  @Override
  public void call(Movie m) throws Exception {
    System. out .println( m );
  }
});
```

Example for working on CSV data using Java 8:

```
JavaRDD<Movie> moviesRDD = sparkSession.read().textFile("movies.csv")
                                .javaRDD().filter(str -> !(null ==
str))
                                .filter(str -> !(str.length()==0))
                                .filter(str ->
!str.contains("movieId"))
                                .map(str -> Movie.parseRating(str));
moviesRDD.foreach(m -> System.out.println(m));
```

However, in certain cases such as fields having a comma within the field, fails if we do not handle such cases explicitly, or in certain cases, one would like to infer the schema of CSV, or maybe even get the header information. For all such scenarios, one can use the Spark CSV library by **Databricks** for CSV datatypes:

```
Dataset<Row> csv_read =
sparkSession.read().format("com.databricks.spark.csv")
                                    .option("header", "true")
                                    .option("inferSchema", "true")
                                    .load("movies.csv");
csv_read.printSchema();
csv_read.show();
```

The default inferred schema can be overridden by specifying the schema of StructType having StructField as elements representing the CSV fields:

```
StructType customSchema = new StructType(new StructField[] {
   new StructField( "movieId", DataTypes.LongType, true, Metadata.empty()),
   new StructField("title", DataTypes.StringType, true, Metadata.empty()),
   new StructField("genres", DataTypes.StringType, true, Metadata.empty())
});

Dataset<Row> csv_custom_read =
sparkSession.read().format("com.databricks.spark.csv")
                .option("header", "true")
                .schema(customSchema)
                .load("movies.csv");
csv_custom_read.printSchema();
csv_custom_read.show();
```

Some of the features that can be used in the options() method while reading a CSV file are:

- **Header**: When set to true, the first line of files will be used to name columns and will not be included in the data. All types will be assumed string. The default value is false.
- **Delimiter**: By default, columns are delimited using , , but the delimiter can be set to any character.
- **Quote**: By default, the quote character is ", but it can be set to any character. Delimiters inside quotes are ignored.
- **Escape**: By default, the escape character is \, but it can be set to any character. Escaped quote characters are ignored.

- **Mode**: Determines the parsing mode. By default it is Permissive. Possible values are:
  - **PERMISSIVE**: Tries to parse all lines: nulls are inserted for missing tokens and extra tokens are ignored.

  - **DROPMALFORMED**: Drops lines that have fewer or more tokens than expected or tokens that do not match the schema.

  - **FAILFAST**: Aborts with a `RuntimeException` if it encounters any malformed lines.

- **Charset**: Defaults to UTF-8, but can be set to other valid charset names.
- **InferSchema**: Automatically infers column types. It requires one extra pass over the data and is false by default.

The data from RDD can be saved to disk by using the `write()` method over RDD, and along with its format and compression codec if any, as follows:

```
csv_custom_read.write()
                .format("com.databricks.spark.csv")
                .option("header", "true")
                .option("codec", "org.apache.hadoop.io.compress.GzipCodec")
                .save("newMovies.csv");
```

Some of the common features that can be used in the `options()` method while writing a CSV file are:

- **Header**: When set to true, the header (from the schema in the dataframe) will be written at the first line.
- **Delimiter**: By default columns are delimited using `,`, but delimiter can be set to any character.
- **Quote**: By default the quote character is `"`, but it can be set to any character. This is written according to `quoteMode`.
- **Escape**: By default the escape character is `\`, but it can be set to any character. Escaped quote characters are written.
- **Codec**: Compression codec to use when saving to file. Should be the fully qualified name of a class implementing `org.apache.hadoop.io.compress.CompressionCodec` or one of the case-insensitive shortened names (`bzip2`, `gzip`, `lz4`, and `snappy`). Defaults to no compression when a codec is not specified.

Instead of comma (,), the library can be used to read any character-separated file by specifying such a character with delimiter options.

Working with JSON data

JSON is a schemaless human-readable file format. The rise in web and mobile applications has made JSON a very popular web interchange format for API services and data storage. There are different approaches in which we can read Json files, such as reading the file as text and then processing it on a record basis, or by using SparkSession/Spark SQL, which support JSON natively.

Let's first understand how we can process JSON using records using external JSON libraries/parser with an assumption that each record in the file is of type JSON. Consider the JSON file that consists of data of people. The following is an example JSON record:

```
{ "year": "2013", "firstName": "DAVID", "county": "KINGS", "sex": "M",
"cid": 272,"dateOfBirth":"2016-01-07T00:01:17Z" }
```

Let's load this data as an RDD of `PersonDetails` object as follows:

PersonDetails POJO:

```
public class PersonDetails implements Serializable {
private Integer cid;
private String county;
private String firstName;
private String sex;
private String year;
private Timestamp dateOfBirth;
public Integer getCid() {
  return cid;
}
public void setCid(Integer cid ) {
  this.cid = cid;
}
public String getCounty() {
  return county;
}
public void setCounty(String county ) {
  this.county = county;
}
public String getFirstName() {
  return firstName;
```

```
  }
  public void setFirstName(String firstName ) {
    this.firstName = firstName;
  }
  public String getSex() {
    return sex;
  }
  public void setSex(String sex ) {
    this.sex = sex;
  }
  public String getYear() {
    return year;
  }
  public void setYear(String year ) {
    this.year = year;
  }
  public Timestamp getDateOfBirth() {
    return dateOfBirth ;
  }
  public void setDateOfBirth(Timestamp dateOfBirth ) {
    this.dateOfBirth = dateOfBirth ;
  }
}
```

Example for working with JSON data using Java 7:

```
RDD<String>textFile=sparkSession.sparkContext().textFile("pep_json.json",
2);

JavaRDD<PersonDetails>mapParser=textFile.toJavaRDD().map(new
Function<String, PersonDetails>() {
  @Override
  public PersonDetails call(String v1) throws Exception {
    return new ObjectMapper().readValue(v1, PersonDetails.class );
  }
});
mapParser .foreach( new VoidFunction<PersonDetails>() {
  private static final long serialVersionUID = 1L;
  @Override
  public void call(PersonDetails t) throws Exception {
    System.out.println(t);
  }
});
```

Example for working with JSON data using Java 8:

```
JavaRDD<PersonDetails>mapParser=textFile.toJavaRDD().map( v1 -> new
ObjectMapper().readValue(v1, PersonDetails.class));

mapParser.foreach(t -> System.out.println(t));
```

The code flow for parsing a JSON file is as follows:

- Read the file having JSON records, where each line must contain a separate, self-contained valid JSON object

- Once we have an RDD of String, we can use the map function to parse each line of the self-contained JSON object into an RDD of JSON class

This approach to handling a JSON object has certain benefits, such as we can filter out the data that we do not need and also the datatypes and validations on them can be done at the parsing stage itself. We also have the privilege of modifying the content, as well as erroring out data in types and formats the way we need. However, using the map function on RDD is not an optimal solution as in this case, the JSON parser object will be created for each record or line, hence one optimization can use mapPartitions() instead of the map() function, which will give access to all the records in a partition instead of one record, as in the case of the map() function.

Another approach to handling JSON is to use Spark SQL, which has the capability of handling JSON natively. Spark SQL provides automatic inference of JSON schemas for both reading and writing data. It also handles the nested fields in JSON data and provides direct access to these fields without any transformation using dataframes:

 We will discuss Spark SQL in detail in Chapter 8, *Working with Spark SQL*.

```
Dataset<Row>json_rec=sparkSession.read().json( "pep_json.json" );
json_rec.printSchema();

json_rec.show();
```

Considering the fact that schema definition is not mentioned in the JSON data, Spark SQL will automatically infer the schema of the JSON dataset. If the JSON fields are array then Spark creates a `STRUCT` of array to represent the type fields. DataFames provides a `printSchema()` method that helps in visualizing the inferred schema.

If one needs to change the inferred schema then Spark provides the option to create custom schema, which can then be imposed on the JSON file that one would like to read. In the preceding dataset, timestamp is being treated as string by default, but if we want to change this default behavior, we can create a custom schema to override the defaults. One can apply the schema definition while loading the JSON file as follows:

```
StructType schema = new StructType( new StructField[] {
DataTypes.createStructField("cid", DataTypes.IntegerType, true),
DataTypes.createStructField("county", DataTypes.StringType, true),
DataTypes.createStructField("firstName", DataTypes.StringType, true),
DataTypes.createStructField("sex", DataTypes.StringType, true),
DataTypes.createStructField("year", DataTypes.StringType, true),
DataTypes.createStructField("dateOfBirth", DataTypes.TimestampType, true)
});

Dataset <Row> person_mod =
sparkSession.read().schema(schema).json(textFile);
person_mod .printSchema();
person_mod .show();
```

In the previous example, the JSON field `cid` is long, while `dateOfBirth` is string if we consider the output of inferred schema. However, one can make modifications to the inferred schema by creating an explicit schema of `StructType` having an array of `StructField` with respective datatypes. An advantage of explicitly mentioning the schema of JSON is that the elements of DataFrame are not iterated twice, which will always create an overhead while parsing the JSON object. It also constrains the data with a restricted schema having specific datatypes.

RDD can be saved in JSON format as follows:

```
person_mod.write().format("json").mode("overwrite").save("pep_out.json");
```

Working with XML Data

XML is another important file format that has extensive usage and coverage in Spark. One way to deal with XML would be to read each XML as a string of RDD and then map over each XML, parsing them using Java libraries such as DOM parser or JAXB. Though there is nothing wrong with this approach, Spark also supports a library provided by Databricks that can process a format-free XML file in a distributed way. This feature is in contrast with JSON support by Spark, where each JSON object is expected to be in-line JSON format:

```
HashMap<String, String> params = new HashMap<String, String>();
params.put("rowTag", "food");
params.put("failFast", "true");
Dataset<Row>docDF=sparkSession.read()
                .format("com.databricks.spark.xml")
                .options(params)
                .load("breakfast_menu.xml");
docDF.printSchema();
docDF.show();
```

You will notice, the similarity in the approach to handling the XML file with that of the CSV file; both libraries follow a similar structure. Some of the common features that can be used in the options() method while reading the XML files are :

- rowTag: The row tag of your XML files to treat as a row.
- samplingRatio: Sampling ratio for inferring schema (0.0 ~ 1). The default is 1.
- mode: The mode for dealing with corrupt records during parsing. The default is PERMISSIVE.
    - **PERMISSIVE**: Sets other fields to null when it meets a corrupted record, and puts the malformed string into a new field configured by columnNameOfCorruptRecord. When a schema is set by a user, it sets null for extra fields.
    - **DROPMALFORMED**: Ignores all corrupted records.
    - **FAILFAST**: Throws an exception when it meets corrupted records.
- columnNameOfCorruptRecord: The name of new fields where malformed strings are stored. The default is _corrupt_record.
- valueTag: The tag used for the value when there are attributes in the element having no child. The default is _VALUE.
- charset: Defaults to UTF-8, but can be set to other valid charset names.

The inferred schema can be overridden by specifying custom schema of `StructType` having `StructField` as row elements. RDDs can be saved in XML format using the method `write()` over RDD, along with options as follows:

- `path`: Location to write files.
- `rowTag`: The row tag of your XML files to treat as a row.
- `rootTag`: The root tag of your XML files to treat as the root.
- `valueTag`: The tag used for the value when there are attributes in the element having no child. Default is `_VALUE`.
- `compression`: Compression codec to use when saving to file. Should be the fully qualified name of a class implementing `org.apache.hadoop.io.compress.CompressionCodec` or one of case-insensitive shortened names (`bzip2`, `gzip`, `lz4`, and `snappy`). Defaults to no compression when a codec is not specified:

```
docDF.write().format("com.databricks.spark.xml")
             .option("rootTag", "food")
             .option("rowTag", "food")
             .save("newMenu.xml");
```

The `POM` file entry to use XML library is:

```
<dependency>
        <groupId>com.databricks</groupId>
        <artifactId>spark-xml_${scala.binary.version}</artifactId>
        <version>0.3.3</version>
</dependency>
```

References

- https://github.com/apache/hadoop/blob/branch-2.4/hadoop-mapreduce-project/hadoop-mapreduce-client/hadoop-mapreduce-client-core/src/main/java/org/apache/hadoop/mapred/FileInputFormat.java#L299-373
- https://github.com/databricks/spark-csv
- https://github.com/databricks/spark-xml

Summary

In the first part of this chapter, we talked about how to load data in Spark from various data sources. We have seen code examples of connecting to some popular data sources such as HDFS, S3, and so on. In later parts, we discussed processing data in some widely used structured formats, along with the code examples.

In the next chapter, we will discuss Spark clusters in detail. We will discuss the cluster setup process and some popular cluster managers available with Spark in detail. Also, we will look at how to debug Spark applications in cluster mode.

6
Spark on Cluster

In the previous chapters, we have seen Spark examples using Spark shell in local mode or executing Spark programs using local master mode. As Spark is a distributed processing engine, it is designed to run on a cluster for high performance, scalability, and fault-tolerant behavior.

In this chapter, we will discuss Spark application architecture in distributed-mode. This chapter will also explain how various components of Spark in distributed mode interact. Along with that, this chapter will focus on various cluster managers that can be used to run Spark jobs in clusters. Also, we will discuss some effective performance parameters for running jobs in cluster mode. After this chapter, the reader will be able to execute Spark jobs effectively in distributed mode.

Spark application in distributed-mode

A Spark application is made of up of **Driver** and **Executor(s)** processes. Each application in Spark contains one driver process and one or more executor processes. The driver is the central coordinator of the application that drives the application. Spark Driver communicates and divides work among one or more executors. In distributed mode, Spark driver and each executor runs in separate JVM.

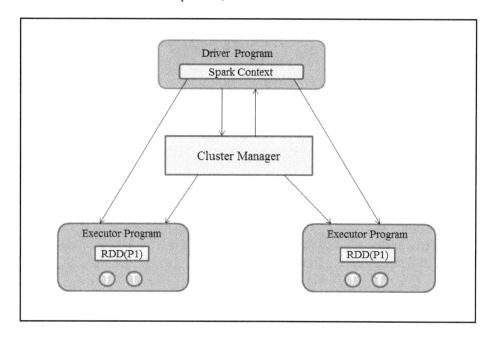

Logical Representation of a Spark Application in Distributed Mode

Driver program

`SparkContext` is initialized in the Driver JVM. Spark driver can be considered as the master of Spark applications. The following are the responsibilities of Spark Driver program:

- It creates the physical plan of execution of tasks based on the DAG of operations.
- It schedules the tasks on the executors. It passes the task bundle to executors based. Data locality principle is used while passing the tasks to executors.
- Spark driver tracks RDD partitions to executor mapping for executing future tasks.

Spark Driver is the single point of failure for a Spark application. If a driver dies, the application is finished. So, the application needs to be restarted again if the Driver terminates.

Executor program

Executors can be considered as slave JVMs for Driver processes. These are the JVM processes where actual application logic executes. An application in Spark consists of a number of a tasks where a task is the smallest unit of work to be executed, for example, reading all blocks of a file from HDFS, running map operation of RDD partitions, and so on.

In the traditional MapReduce of Hadoop, multiple mappers and reducers are executed for a chain of MR jobs and every mapper and reducer runs as a separate JVM. So, there is a lot of overhead of initiating JVMs of each mapper and reducer tasks. However, in the case of Spark, executors are initiated once at the beginning of the application execution and they run until the application finishes. All the application logic runs inside executors, being individual tasks, as separate threads. The following are the main responsibilities of executors:

1. Execute the tasks as directed by the Driver.
2. Cache RDD partitions in memory on which the tasks execute.
3. Report the tasks result to the driver.

Executors are not a single point of failure. If an executor dies, it is the responsibility of the cluster manager to restart it. We will discuss cluster manager operations in the next section.

So far in this book, we were running Spark applications in local mode.

 In local mode, Spark Driver and Executor both run inside the single JVM process.

Cluster managers

Cluster managers are used to deploy Spark applications in cluster mode. Spark can be configured to run various cluster managers. Spark distribution provides an inbuilt cluster manager known as *Spark standalone*. Apart from that Spark can run on top of other popular cluster managers in the big data world such as YARN and Mesos. In this section, we will discuss how to deploy Spark applications with Spark standalone and YARN.

Spark standalone

Spark standalone manager is available in the Spark distribution. It helps to deploy Spark applications in cluster mode in a very efficient and convenient way.

Spark standalone manager follows the master-slave architecture. It consists of a Spark master and multiple worker nodes where worker nodes are the slave nodes for Spark master node. Similar to other master-slave frameworks, Spark master works a scheduler for the submitted Spark applications. It schedules the applications on worker nodes and the processes that executed the application will run on the worker nodes.

Installation of Spark standalone cluster

In this section, we will learn how to install Spark Standalone cluster. Spark distribution provides the `init` scripts to install Spark standalone clusters. We first have to download Scala and Spark. Please refer to the *Getting Started with Spark* section in `Chapter 3`, *Lets Start* for detailed explanation about downloading and setting up Scala and Spark. Let's quickly recap the steps about setting up Spark.

Users can download the Spark distribution from the following URL:
`https://spark.apache.org/downloads.html`.

In this book, we are working with Spark 2.1.1, which is the latest at the time of publishing this book. Once downloaded, run the following commands:

```
tar -zxf spark-2.1.1-bin-hadoop2.7.tgz
sudo mv spark-2.1.1-bin-hadoop2.7  /usr/local/spark
```

 Directory location can be different as per user's requirement.

Also, it is suggested to set the following environment variables as well (not mandatory):

```
export SPARK_HOME=/usr/local/spark
export PATH=$PATH$SPARK_HOME/bin
```

As we are going to start the Spark cluster, please repeat the preceding steps on all nodes. Once the steps are performed, Spark standalone cluster can be started as follows:

Start master

Let's first start Spark master as follows:

```
$cd $SPARK_HOME
sbin/start-master.sh
```

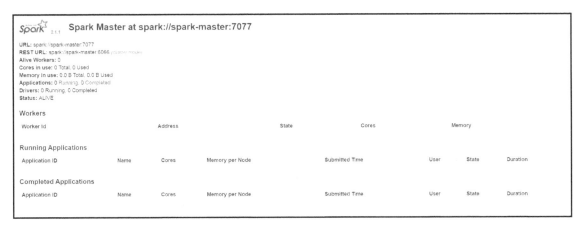

Initializing Spark Master

Users can access Spark Master UI on port 8080. After Spark master gets started, the web UI will look as follows:

Spark Master UI

Here, spark-master is the Hostname of the node on which Spark master is running.

The URL shown in the previous screenshot is used while starting slave nodes.

Start slave

After starting Spark master, Spark slave can be started using the Spark master URL, as follows:

```
cd $SPARK_HOME
sbin/start-slave.sh spark://spark-master:7077
```

```
[sparkuser@spark-slave1 ~]$
[sparkuser@spark-slave1 ~]$
[sparkuser@spark-slave1 ~]$ cd $SPARK_HOME
[sparkuser@spark-slave1 spark]$ sbin/start-slave.sh spark://spark-master:7077
starting org.apache.spark.deploy.worker.Worker, logging to /opt/spark/logs/spark-sparkuser-org.apache.spark.deploy.worker.Worker-1-spark-slave1.out
[sparkuser@spark-slave1 spark]$
```

Initializing Spark Slave

The following is the Spark master web UI showing two active workers:

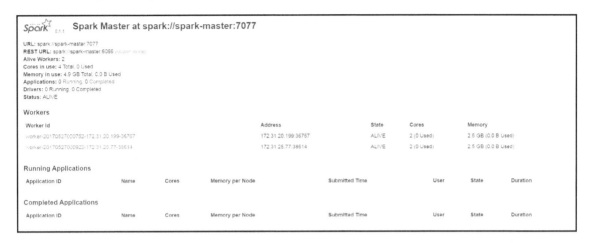

Spark Master UI with Two Slave Nodes

All slave/worker nodes can be started together. Hostnames of the nodes should be added in the $SPARK_HOME/conf/slaves file on the master node, as follows:

```
[sparkuser@master spark]$cd $SPARK_HOME
[sparkuser@master spark]$cat conf/slaves
spark-slave1
spark-slave2
[sparkuser@master spark]$
```

Spark slaves file

Then, execute the following command to start all slave nodes together:

```
cd $SPARK_HOME
sbin/start-slaves.sh
```

- start-slaves.sh script helps to login to all slave nodes using SSH protocol. Hence, it is suggested to set up password less SSH between master and slave nodes. Otherwise, passwords need to be entered manually for every login.
- If a username on Spark master is different than Spark slave node then entry is Hostname should be added as follows: username@slave-host.

Stop master and slaves

Spark master and slaves can be stopped using the following scripts:

`$SPARK_HOME/sbin/stop-master.sh`: This script is used to stop Spark Master nodes.

- `$SPARK_HOME/sbin/stop-slave.sh`: This script is used to stop individual slave nodes. This should be executed to the individual nodes
- **`$SPARK_HOME/sbin/stop-slaves.sh`**: This script is used to stop all slave nodes together. This should be executed on the Spark master node. All Hostnames of slave nodes should be added in the `$SPARK_HOME/conf/slaves` file.

Apart from the preceding scripts, the following scripts are available to start/stop Spark master and Spark slaves together:

`sbin/start-all.sh`- This script is used to start both Spark master and Spark slave nodes. This should be executed on Spark master node. All hostnames of slave nodes should be added in the `$SPARK_HOME/conf/slaves` file.

`sbin/stop-all.sh`- This script is used to stop both Spark master and Spark slave nodes. This should be executed on Spark master node. All hostnames of slave nodes should be added in the `$SPARK_HOME/conf/slaves` file.

Deploying applications on Spark standalone cluster

In the previous section, we learned how to start and stop Spark standalone cluster. Once the Spark standalone cluster is running, Spark applications can be deployed on the cluster. Before deploying the application on the cluster, let's first discuss how applications components run in Spark Standalone mode:

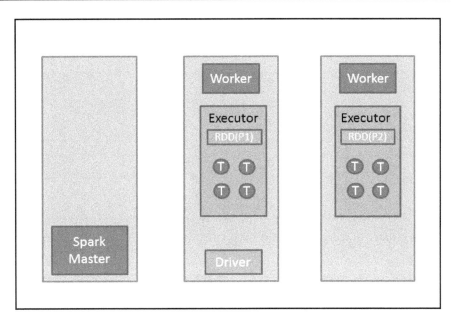

Logical Representation of Spark Application on Standalone Cluster

The preceding figure shows a Spark standalone cluster of three nodes. Spark master is running on one node and workers on two other nodes. A Spark application is deployed on the cluster. Driver JVMs is running on one of the worker nodes. The application consists of two Executor JVMs running on each worker node. Executors JVMs show an RDD with two partitions cached in the memory and in each Executor four tasks are running, which execute the actual business logic of the application.

In Spark standalone mode, a maximum of one executor per application can be executed per worker node.

When the client submits Spark Application requests to Spark Master, Spark driver starts in the client program or a separate JVM of the worker nodes (depends upon the deploy mode of the application). After the Driver of the application is started, it contacts spark master with the required cores for the application. Then, Spark master will start executors for the applications that register with the driver. After which, the Driver submits the physical plan of execution to executors to process. Spark master generally starts one executor each on every worker node to load balance the application processing.

Spark distribution provides a Binary `spark-submit`, which is used to deploy Spark applications on every cluster manager.

Spark application on standalone cluster can be deployed in the following two modes:

Client mode

In client mode, the driver executes in the client process that submits the application. Therefore, the client program remains alive until Spark application's execution completes. In this example, we will run a Spark PI application on a spark standalone cluster in client mode.

To run a spark application in client mode on the spark standalone cluster, log in to any of the nodes in the cluster and run the following commands:

```
cd $SPARK_HOME
./bin/spark-submit --master spark://spark-master:7077--deploy-mode client -
-class org.apache.spark.examples.SparkPi examples/jars/spark-
examples_2.11-2.1.1.jar
```

In the preceding code:

- `--master`: Defines the spark master URL to which an application is submitted.
- `--deploy-mode`: Defines mode of application execution. If this parameter is not provided then by default the application starts in *client* mode.
- `--class`: Defines main class of Spark Application.

Finally, application bundle (JAR file) is provided that contains the main class. Also, spark-shell can be executed in client mode as follows:

```
bin/spark-shell --master spark:// spark-master:7077
```

Cluster mode

In cluster mode, a client submits the request to the Spark master and exits. Spark master will schedule the driver on one of the nodes and then the process continues as described in the previous section. In this example, we will run a Spark PI application on a Spark standalone cluster in cluster mode.

To run a Spark application in cluster mode in client mode on the Spark standalone cluster, log in to any of the nodes in the cluster and run the following commands:

```
cd $SPARK_HOME
./bin/spark-submit --master spark://spark-master:7077--deploy-mode cluster
--class org.apache.spark.examples.SparkPi examples/jars/spark-
examples_2.11-2.1.1.jar
```

 Spark Shell is not supported in Cluster mode.

Useful job configurations

In this section, we will discuss some useful job configurations that can be configured while submitting the job:

- `--dirs`: This parameter is used to provide external jar files that the Spark application is referring. If the user has not created uber jar of the application, external libraries can be provided to the job using this parameter:

  ```
  ./bin/spark-submit --master spark://spark-master:7077 -jars
  /path/of/external/lib --deploy-mode cluster --class
  com.Spark.ApplicationMain  /path/to/application/jar
  ```

- `--driver-memory`: This parameter is used to specify the memory required for spark driver:

  ```
  ./bin/spark-submit --master spark://spark-master:7077 -driver-
  memory 1G --deploy-mode cluster --class com.Spark.ApplicationMain
  /path/to/application/jar
  ```

- `--executor-memory`: This parameter is used to specify the memory required for each executor:

  ```
  ./bin/spark-submit --master spark://spark-master:7077 -executor-
  memory 1G --deploy-mode cluster --class com.Spark.ApplicationMain
  /path/to/application/jar
  ```

- `--total-executor-cores`: This parameter is used to specify the total number of cores needed for an application:

In Spark standalone, there is no option to specify the total number of executors for an application. Spark master generally runs each executor per worker node to balance load of processing for an application.

```
./bin/spark-submit --master spark://spark-master:7077 --total-
executor-cores 10 --deploy-mode cluster --class
com.Spark.ApplicationMain  /path/to/application/jar
```

- `--supervise`: When supervise configuration is provided, Spark master will supervise Spark Driver and if the Driver dies, it restarts the driver:

If Spark driver is restarted, then all of the Spark executors also need to be restarted. In other words, all Spark applications are restarted.

```
./bin/spark-submit --master spark://spark-master:7077 -- supervise
--deploy-mode cluster --class com.Spark.ApplicationMain
/path/to/application/jar
```

`--executor-cores`: This parameter is used to specify the total number of cores per executor. In standalone mode, default value is all available cores on the worker.

Useful cluster level configurations (Spark standalone)

In this section, we will discuss some useful cluster level configurations in Spark standalone. These configurations can be set in *spark-env.sh* in $Spark_HOME/confdir. Any change in these configurations requires a restart of the worker JVM or the cluster. Here are some useful configurations:

- `SPARK_LOCAL_DIRS`: This parameter specifies the comma separated list of local directories on a node of each node of the cluster that will be used for Spark shuffle operations and RDD persistence on disk
- `SPARK_MASTER_HOST`: This parameter is used to bind Spark master to an IP or Hostname

- `SPARK_MASTER_PORT`: This parameter is used to Spark master to a port on the system. The default value for this parameter is 7077
- `SPARK_WORKER_CORES`: This parameter is used to specify total number of cores that a worker can provide to executors process running on that node
- `SPARK_WORKER_MEMORY`: This parameter is used to specify total amount of memory that a worker can provide to executors process running on that node

Yet Another Resource Negotiator (YARN)

Hadoop YARN is one of the most popular resource managers in the big data world. Apache Spark provides seamless integration with YARN. Apache Spark applications can be deployed to YARN using the same `spark-submit` command.

Apache Spark requires `HADOOP_CONF_DIR` or `YARN_CONF_DIR` environment variables to be set and pointing to the Hadoop configuration directory, which contains `core-site.xml`, `yarn-site.xml`, and so on. These configurations are required to connect to the YARN cluster.

To run Spark applications on YARN, the YARN cluster should be started first. Refer to the following official Hadoop documentation that describes how to start the YARN cluster: `https://hadoop.apache.org/docs`

YARN in general consists of a **resource manager** (**RM**) and multiple **node managers** (**NM**) where resource manager is the master node and node managers are slave nodes. NMs send detailed report to RM at every defined interval that tell RM how many resources (such as CPU slots and RAM) are available on NMs.

To deploy an application, a client connects to RM and submits the application. Based on application configuration, RM finds an available slot on one of the NM and runs the **application master** (**AM**) for the submitted application on that slot. As soon as the AM initializes, it connects to RM and negotiates resources (asks for containers) to run the application. Then based on cluster resource availability, RM gives addresses of NMs to the AM along with credentials (security tokens) to run containers on NMs. The AM connects to NMs with security credentials and NM schedules containers for that application. When containers are launched, they connect to the AM and run the application.

 In YARN, if the AM crashes then RM restarts it (on the same node or different node), however, in that case all application containers need to be restarted.

Similar to the standalone cluster, Spark applications in Yarn also run the following modes:

YARN client

In YARN client mode, Spark Driver runs in client nodes. The client submits requests to RM, RM launches applications for the application on the cluster, which negotiates resources with RM. Then the AM connects to the NM as per the info given by RM, which launches the container for the application. Executor processes run inside containers and run the applications. Executor processes connect to the driver application on the client node.

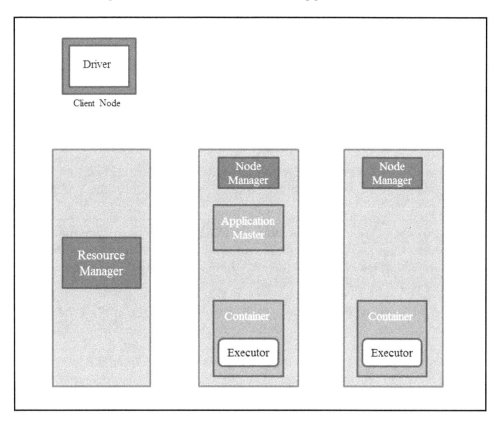

Logical Representation of Spark Applications in YARN Client Mode

In YARN, the AM and containers are scheduled by RM, however, tasks that run the application are scheduled by Spark Driver itself.

To run spark shell in YARN client mode, execute the following commands:

```
cd $SPARK_HOME
./bin/spark-shell –master yarn –deploy-mode client
```

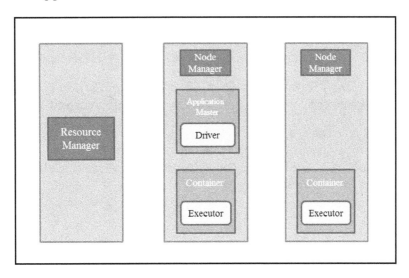

YARN cluster

In a YARN cluster, a client connects to RM, submits the request, and exits. RM launches the AM of the Spark application on one of the NM and the AM negotiates resources with the AM and then launches the driver thread. NMs launch containers that connect to AM. After containers initialize, AM launches executors in containers, which connect to the Driver in the AM to run the application.

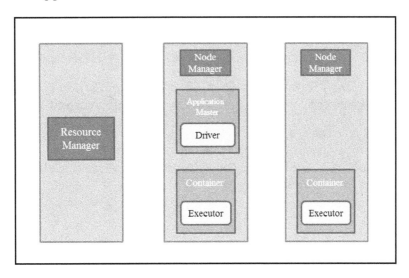

Logical Representation of Spark Application in YARN Cluster Mode

In the following command, we will deploy a Spark PI application on a YARN cluster:

```
cd $SPARK_HOME
./bin/spark-submit --master yarn --deploy-mode cluster --class
org.apache.spark.examples.SparkPi examples/jars/spark-
examples_2.11-2.1.1.jar
```

 To deploy Spark applications on YARN from a remote system, copy Hadoop configurations files on a remote system and set the environment variable HADOOP_CONF_DIR, which should point to the directory that contains Hadoop configure files.

Useful job configuration

Along with the job configurations mentioned in Spark standalone, here are a few useful configurations available in YARN mode:

- --num-executors: Spark on YARN cluster allows users to define the number of executors for the application. This option is not available yet in Spark standalone
- --queue: This option allows users to provide a queue name of YARN for submitting the application.

Apart from Spark standalone and YARN, Spark can also run on Mesos cluster manager as well.

Summary

In this chapter, we learned about the architecture of Spark application in distributed mode. We also discussed Spark applications running on Spark standalone and YARN cluster managers with examples.

In the next chapter, we will learn about advanced concepts of the Spark programming model. We will also discuss partitioning concepts on RDD along with advanced transformations and actions in Spark.

7
Spark Programming Model - Advanced

In the previous chapter, we discussed how Spark components get deployed on the cluster. It's now time to learn about the advanced concepts of the Spark programming model.

We will talk about the how RDD gets partitioned across the cluster, and some advanced transformations and actions that can be performed on an RDD. We will also discuss cluster-wide variables that can be accessed by various tasks being executed on different executors that are running on different worker nodes.

RDD partitioning

As we have seen in previous chapters, Spark loads data into an RDD. Since Spark runs in distributed mode, different executors can run on different worker machines and RDD is loaded in to the executor(s) memory. RDDs being a distributed dataset gets split across executors. These splits are called RDD partitions.

In other words, partitions are the splits of RDD loaded in different executors memory. The following diagram depicts the logical representation of RDD partitioned across various worker nodes:

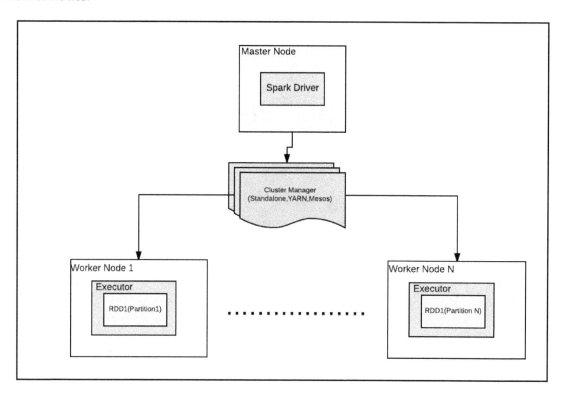

 More than one partition of an RDD can be loaded in an executor memory.

Spark partitions the RDD at the time of creation even if the user has not provided any partition count explicitly. However, the user can provide a partition count as well. Let's discuss it programmatically:

```
SparkConf conf = new
SparkConf().setMaster("local").setAppName("Partitioning Example");
JavaSparkContext jsc = new JavaSparkContext(conf);
JavaRDD<Integer> intRDD= jsc.parallelize(Arrays.asList(1, 2, 3, 4, 5, 6, 7,
8, 9, 10), 3);
```

In this example, an RDD of integers is created with 3 as the value for the `numPartitions` parameter. To verify the number of partitions, you can use:

```
intRDD.getNumPartitions()
```

If the user does not specify the value of `numPartitions`, the value of the configuration parameter `spark.default.parallelism` decides the number of partitions. As per Spark documentation (`https://spark.apache.org/docs/latest/configuration.html`), the value of this parameter depends upon the following factors:

- For distributed shuffle operations, like `reduceByKey` and `join`, the largest number of partitions in a parent RDD. For operations like parallelize with no parent RDDs, it depends on the cluster manager:
    - **Local mode**: Number of cores on the local machine
    - **Mesos fine grained mode**: 8
    - **Others**: The total number of cores on all executor nodes or two, whichever is the larger
- While loading data from the local file system or HDFS, by default Spark creates a number of partitions equal to the number of blocks. In the case of the local file system, the value of the parameter `hadoop fs.local.block.size`, which is 32 MB by default, is taken as the partition size. If the HDFS value of `dfs.blocksize`, which is 128 MB in Hadoop 2.x, this is considered as the partition size. However, a user can also specify the `numPartitions` value as follows:

    ```
    jsc.textFile("hdfs://localhost:8020/user/spark/data.csv",4)
    ```

 As a partition of an RDD is stored in the executor memory, the size of the partition is limited by the available memory of the executor process.

The major advantage of partitions lies in the parallelism of processing the data. A transformation that does not require shuffling, for example, `map`, can be executed parallelly on all the partitions of the RDD.

Apache Spark runs a maximum of one task per partition. So, to use Spark Cluster to its maximum efficiency, an RDD should be well partitioned. Therefore, on a Spark cluster of 256 cores, RDDs should consist of 250-255 partitions for the maximum utilization of the cluster. While reading a file of unsplittable format, such as a compressed format like `gz`, Apache Spark does not split it into partitions, so the whole file will be loaded into one partition. For example:

```
JavaRDD<String> textFile = jsc.textFile("test.gz",2);
System.out.println(textFile.getNumPartitions());
```

The preceding code will return 1 as count of the partitions even if 2 has been provided as the value of `numPartitions` parameter explicitly.

Repartitioning

After an RDD is loaded, the number of partitions of the RDD can be adjusted using a transformation called `repartition`:

```
JavaRDD<String> textFile = jsc.textFile("test.txt",3);
System.out.println("Before repartition:"+textFile.getNumPartitions());
JavaRDD<String> textFileRepartitioned = textFile.repartition(4);
System.out.println("After
repartition:"+textFileRepartitioned.getNumPartitions());
```

As per the preceding code example, the number of partitions before repartioning will be three and will increase to four after repartitioning. Repartition works for compressed files as well. So the number of partitions of a `gzip` file can be increased after reading using the repartition function:

```
JavaRDD<String> textFile = jsc.textFile("test.gz",3);
System.out.println("Before repartition:"+textFile.getNumPartitions());
JavaRDD<String> textFileRepartitioned = textFile.repartition(4);
System.out.println("After
repartition:"+textFileRepartitioned.getNumPartitions());
```

In this case, the number of partitions before repartition will be one, and after repartition will be four. Shuffling can occur while repartitioning as new partitions may get distributed over different nodes.

How Spark calculates the partition count for transformations with shuffling (wide transformations)

Transformations, like `reduceByKey`, `groupByKey`, `aggregateByKey` and so on, result in the shuffling of data, and data belonging to one key will be shuffled to the same executor. So, every transformation of this league provides an overloaded function, which allows the user to provide the partitioner of his/her choice.

If the user specifies the partitioner, the number of partitions created after the transformation will be based on that partitioner logic. However, if the user does not specify the partitioner, Apache Spark uses **Hash Partitioner** by default.

As per HashPartitioner, the resulted partition for a given key is decided by the following formula:

```
{hashCode of the key}%{number of partitions}
```

As Spark cannot decide the number of partitions by itself, therefore it keeps: *number of partitions = number of partitions of largest upstream RDD,* where the largest upstream RDD is the RDD with most number of partitions in the upstream DAG.

This helps Spark to avoid *Out Of Memory* errors as well because the number of partitions before after the transformation will be equal to the number of partitions of the largest upstream RDD; that is, the most number of partitions for a stage in that DAG.

Partitioner

As already stated, for any shuffle operation on a Pair RDD, the destination partition for a key is decided by the partitioner used during the shuffle. The partitioner used during the shuffling plays a major role in deciding the amount of data shuffling.

The basic requirement of a partitioner is that similar keys should land in the same partition. Apache Spark provides a transformation called `partitionBy` which helps to partition an RDD at any point as per the user's choice. Also, as stated previously, the user can also provide a partitioner of its own choice during the pair RDD transformation that required shuffling, like `reduceByKey`, `aggregateByKey`, `foldByKey`, and so on.

There are two built-in types of partitioner available in Spark. Spark also provides an option to specify a custom partitioner. The following are the partitioner implementations available in Spark:

1. Hash Partitioner
2. Range Partitioner

Hash Partitioner

Hash Partitioner partitions the keys based on the their **hashCode**. It determines the resulting partition using the following formula:

(hashCode of the key) % (total number of partitions)

where **hashCode** is a Java object **hashCode**

Let's partition an RDD of integers using HashPartitioner:

```
SparkConf conf = new
SparkConf().setMaster("local").setAppName("Partitioning");
JavaSparkContext jsc = new JavaSparkContext(conf);

JavaPairRDD<Integer, String> pairRdd = jsc.parallelizePairs(
Arrays.asList(new Tuple2<Integer, String>(1, "A"),new Tuple2<Integer,
String>(2, "B"),new Tuple2<Integer, String>(3, "C"),new Tuple2<Integer,
String>(4, "D"),new Tuple2<Integer, String>(5, "E"),new Tuple2<Integer,
String>(6, "F"), new Tuple2<Integer, String>(7, "G"),new Tuple2<Integer,
String>(8, "H")), 3);
```

We have initialized `JavaSparkContext` and created `pairRDD` with the key as an integer type, value as a string type, and with `numPartitions=3`.

If you print the number of partitions for RDD created previously, the result should be 3. Let's partition this RDD using `HashPartitioner`:

```
JavaPairRDD<Integer, String> hashPartitioned = pairRdd.partitionBy(new
HashPartitioner(2));
```

`org.apache.spark.HashPartitioner` provides a parameterized constructor, which accepts one parameter; that is, the number of partitions as follows:

```
HashPartitoner(int partitions)
```

Since, we have provided 2 as the value of the partition count, the resulted RDD will have two partitions which can be verified as follows:

```
System.out.println(hashPartitioned.getNumPartitions());
```

According to the HashPartitioner formulae - *(hashCode of the key) % (total number of partitions)*, the tuples with keys (2, 4, 6, 8) should be in partition 0, and tuples with keys (1, 3, 5, 7) should be in partition 1.

We can check the distribution of the keys among partitions as follows:

```
JavaRDD<String> mapPartitionsWithIndex =
hashPartitioned.mapPartitionsWithIndex((index, tupleIterator) ->
{List<String> list=new ArrayList<>();
while(tupleIterator.hasNext()){ list.add("Partition
number:"+index+",key:"+tupleIterator.next()._1());}
return list.iterator();}, true);
System.out.println(mapPartitionsWithIndex.collect());
```

 We will discuss the `mapPartitionsWithIndex` transformation in the next section (*Advanced transformations*)

Range Partitioner

Range Partitioner partitions the keys based on a range. All keys falling in the same range will land in the same partition. It is recommended that the data type follows the natural ordering, for example, integers, long, and so on.

`org.apache.spark.RangePartitioner` provides a parameterized constructor which accepts five parameters as follows:

```
RangePartitioner (int partitions, RDD <? extends scala.Product2< K , V >>
rdd, boolean ascending, scala.math.Ordering< K > evidence$1,
scala.reflect.ClassTag< K > evidence$2)
```

where:

Parameter 1: Number of partitions

Parameter 2: RDD to be partitioned

Parameter 3: Order of the range ascending/descending

Parameter 4: Ordering method for the key

Parameter 5: Class tag for the key

Let's partition `pairRDD` created previously using `RangePartitioner` as follows:

```
RangePartitioner rangePartitioner = new RangePartitioner(4,
org.apache.spark.api.java.JavaRDD.toRDD(pairRdd);, true,
scala.math.Ordering.Int$.MODULE$ ,
scala.reflect.ClassTag$.MODULE$.apply(Integer.class));
JavaPairRDD<Integer, String> rangePartitioned =
pairRdd.partitionBy(rangePartitioner);
```

Here, we have used Scala objects for ordering and class tag parameters. Also, a Java RDD needs to be converted to `org.apache.spark.rdd.RDD` to use it with `RangePartitioner`.

Since we have provided 4 as the value of the number of output partitions, the resulting RDD will contain four partitions, and as per the range partitioner, the logic keys distribution should be as follows:

(1,2) - Partition 0

(3,4) - Partition 1

(5,6) - Partition 2

(7,8) - Partition 3

The following code can be used to check the distribution of the keys:

```
JavaRDD<String> mapPartitionsWithIndex = rangePartitioned
.mapPartitionsWithIndex((index, tupleIterator) -> {List<String> list=new
ArrayList<>();
while(tupleIterator.hasNext()){ list.add("Partition
number:"+index+",key:"+tupleIterator.next()._1());}
return list.iterator();}, true);
System.out.println(mapPartitionsWithIndex.collect());
```

Custom Partitioner

Along with Hash Partitioner and Range Partitioner, Apache Spark provides an option to specify a custom partitioner if required. To create a **custom partitioner**, the user needs to extend the `org.apache.spark.Partitioner` class and provide the implementation of the required methods.

Consider that we have a pair RDD with key as a `StringType`. Our requirement is to partition all the tuples into two partitions based on the length of the keys - all the keys with an odd length should be in one partition, and the other partition should contain all the keys with an even length.

Let's create a custom partitioner based on these requirement:

```
import org.apache.spark.artitioner;
public class CustomPartitioner extends Partitioner{
   final int maxPartitions=2;
@Override
public int getPartition(Object key) {
   return (((String) key).length()%maxPartitions);
}
@Override
public int numPartitions() {
   return maxPartitions;
}}
```

Now, we will use this partitioner to partition the RDD with `StringType` keys:

```
JavaPairRDD<String, String> pairRdd =
jsc.parallelizePairs(Arrays.asList(new Tuple2<String, String>("India",
"Asia"),new Tuple2<String, String>("Germany", "Europe"),new Tuple2<String,
String>("Japan", "Asia"),new Tuple2<String, String>("France",
"Europe")),3);
JavaPairRDD<String, String> customPartitioned = pairRdd.partitionBy(new
CustomPartitioner());
```

To verify that the partition is working as expected, we will print the keys belonging to each partition as follows:

```
JavaRDD<String> mapPartitionsWithIndex = customPartitioned
.mapPartitionsWithIndex((index, tupleIterator) -> {List<String> list=new
ArrayList<>();
while(tupleIterator.hasNext()){ list.add("Partition
number:"+index+",key:"+tupleIterator.next()._1());}
return list.iterator();}, true);
System.out.println(mapPartitionsWithIndex.collect());
```

It will produce the following output which shows the partitioner is behaving as expected:

```
[Partition number:0,key:France, Partition number:1,key:India, Partition
number:1,key:Germany, Partition number:1,key:Japan]
```

In this section, we looked in detail at RDD partitioning, and we also learnt about different partitioners, including worked examples of each. In the next section, we will learn about some advanced transformations available in Spark.

Advanced transformations

As stated earlier in this book, if an RDD operation returns an RDD, then it is called a transformation. In Chapter 4, *Understanding the Spark Programming Model*, we learnt about commonly used useful transformations. Now we are going to look at some advanced level transformations.

mapPartitions

The working of this transformation is similar to map transformation. However, instead of acting upon each element of the RDD, it acts upon each partition of the RDD. So, the map function is executed once per RDD partition. Therefore, there will one-to-one mapping between partitions of the source RDD and the target RDD.

As a partition of an RDD is stored as a whole on a node, this transformation does not require shuffling.

In the following example, we will create an RDD of integers and increment all elements of the RDD by 1 using mapPartitions:

```
JavaRDD<Integer> intRDD =
jsc.parallelize(Arrays.asList(1,2,3,4,5,6,7,8,9,10),2);
```

Java 7:

```
intRDD.mapPartitions(new FlatMapFunction<Iterator<Integer>, Integer>() {
@Override
  public Iterator<Integer> call(Iterator<Integer> iterator) throws
Exception {
    List<Integer> intList =new ArrayList<>();
    while(iterator.hasNext())
    {
      intList.add(iterator.next()+1);\
    }
    return intList.iterator();
  }
});
```

Java 8:

```
intRDD.mapPartitions(iterator -> {
  List<Integer> intList =new ArrayList<>();
  while(iterator.hasNext())
  {
    intList.add(iterator.next()+1);
  }
  return intList.iterator();
});
```

 mapPartitions provide an iterator to access each element of the RDD belonging to the partition.

As stated in the previous chapter, the mapPartitions transformation is really useful if an interaction is required with external systems in the map phase, like reading from a database. Consider an instance where the RDD consists of 100 elements divided into three partitions. If, during the map phase, some data needs to be read from a database based on the value of the element, then running a map transformation will create 100 connections to the database. However, with mapPartitions only three connections will be created. A connection pool mechanism may be created to handle such scenarios. However mapPartitions implicitly provides an advantage in such situations. In the following example, we are reading rows from MySQL table based on every element of the RDD:

```
intRDD.mapPartitions(iterator -> {
  Class.forName("com.mysql.jdbc.Driver");
  Connection con=DriverManager.getConnection(
"jdbc:mysql://localhost:3306/test","root","root");
  Statement stmt=con.createStatement();
  List<String> names =new ArrayList<>();
  while(iterator.hasNext())
  {
    ResultSet rs=stmt.executeQuery("select name from emp where empId =
"+iterator.next()); if(rs.first())
    {names.add(rs.getString("empName"));
  }
}
return names.iterator();});
```

Since mapPartitions is being used, we can iterate over all elements of RDD using the same connection. Had it been a map transformation, one connection to MYSQL per element would have been created.

The `mapPartitions` transformation provides an overload where it helps the user to provide a Boolean parameter which decides whether the partitioning information should be preserved or not. The following is the Scala declaration for the same:

```
def mapPartitions[U](f: FlatMapFunction[JIterator[T], U],
preservesPartitioning: Boolean)
```

As per the Spark documentation, the value of this parameter should be false unless `mapPartitions` is being performed on a pair RDD and the input function does not modify the keys.

Partitioning information of an RDD is stored in the RDD object itself. An RDD class contains a reference to an instance of the partitioner class. This information is lost after `map` transformation is performed, which seems logical as the value of the element is being transformed. This holds true in the case of pair RDDs as well as Spark does not preserve partitioning information by default. The `mapPartitions` creates an instance of the `com.javachen.spark.examples.rdd.MapPartitionsRDD` class, to which the value of `preservesPartitioning` is passed as a constructor parameter, the default value of which is false.

The `map` transformation also instantiates `com.javachen.spark.examples.rdd.MapPartitionsRDD` with the default value of `preservePartitioning`, which is false. On the other hand, a filter transformation instantiates, `mapPartitions` RDD with `preservesPartitioning` value set to true. So partitioning information remains preserved in the case of filter transformation

mapPartitionsWithIndex

This is similar to `mapPartitions`. However, in this transformation, the value of the partition index is also available. We showed an example of this transformation in the first section of this chapter (RDD partitioning) while discussing partitioners.

In the following example, a `mapPartitionswithIndex` transformation is performed over int RDD to find out which elements belong to which partition:

Java 7:

```
intRDD.mapPartitionsWithIndex(new Function2<Integer, Iterator<Integer>,
Iterator<String>>() {
@Override
  public Iterator<String> call(Integer index, Iterator<Integer> iterator)
throws Exception {
    List<String> list =new ArrayList<String>();
```

```
      while(iterator.hasNext())
      {
        list.add("Element "+iterator.next()+" belongs to partition "+index);
      }
      return list.iterator();
   }
}, false);
```

Java 8:

```
intRDD.mapPartitionsWithIndex((index, iterator) -> {
   List<String> list = new ArrayList<String>();
   while (iterator.hasNext()) {
     list.add("Element " + iterator.next() + " belongs to partition " +
index);
   }
   return list.iterator();
}, false);
```

It also accepts a Boolean parameter which signifies the value of `preservesPartitioning`.

mapPartitionsToPair

This is the cumulative form of `mapPartitions` and `mapToPair`. Like `mapPartitions`, it runs `map` transformations on every partition of the RDD, and instead of `JavaRDD<T>`, this transformation returns `JaPairRDD <K,V>`.

In the following example, will convert `JavaPairRDD` of `<String, Integer>` type using `mapPartitionsToPair`:

Java 7:

```
JavaPairRDD<String, Integer> pairRDD = intRDD.mapPartitionsToPair(new
PairFlatMapFunction<Iterator<Integer>, String,Integer>() {
@Override
   public Iterator<Tuple2<String, Integer>> call(Iterator<Integer> t) throws
Exception {
     List<Tuple2<String,Integer>> list =new ArrayList<>();
   while(t.hasNext()) {
     int element=t.next();
     list.add(element%2==0?new Tuple2<String, Integer>("even",element): new
     Tuple2<String, Integer>("odd",element));
   }
   return list.iterator();
}});
```

Java 8:

```
JavaPairRDD<String, Integer> pairRDD = intRDD.mapPartitionsToPair(t -> {
  List<Tuple2<String,Integer>> list =new ArrayList<>();
  while(t.hasNext()){
    int element=t.next();
    list.add(element%2==0?new Tuple2<String, Integer>("even",element):
    new Tuple2<String, Integer>("odd",element));
  }
  return list.iterator();});
```

Like `mapPartitions` and `mapPartitionsWithIndex`, `mapPartitionsToPair` also provides an overoaded method that helps user to specify value for `preservePartioning`.

mapValues

`mapValues` is applicable only for pair RDDs. As its name indicates, this transformation only operates on the values of the pair RDDs instead of operating on the whole tuple.

Acting on a pair RDD, it runs a `map` operation on the RDD values. This transformation is really useful if the user is only interested in transforming the values on a pair RDD.

The following is an example of `mapValues` transformation:

Java 7:

```
pairRDD.mapValues(new Function<Integer, Integer>() {
@Override
  public Integer call(Integer v1) throws Exception {
    return v1*3;
  }
});
```

Java 8:

```
pairRDD.mapValues(v1 -> v1*3);
```

Another useful fact of `mapValues` is that it preserves the partitioning information; that is, it instantiates `com.javachen.spark.examples.rdd.MapPartitionsRDD` with the value of `preservesPartitioning` set to true, which makes sense since this transformation is only operating on values.

flatMapValues

This is similar to mapValues, but flatMapValues runs the flatMap function on the values of PairRDD.

Consider, we have a PairRDD containing the mapping of Month to List of expenses as follows:

```
JavaPairRDD<String, String> monExpRDD = jsc.parallelizePairs(
  Arrays.asList(new Tuple2<String, String>("Jan", "50,100,214,10"), new
Tuple2<String, String>("Feb","60,314,223,77")));
```

Our requirement is that, instead of keeping the expenses as the list, we need individual tuples containing the month as the key and the expense amount as the value. Let's use flatMapValues to fulfill the requirement:

Java 7:

```
JavaPairRDD<String, Integer> monExpflattened = monExpRDD.flatMapValues(new
Function<String, Iterable<Integer>>() {
@Override
  public Iterable<Integer> call(String v1) throws Exception {
    List<Integer> list =new ArrayList<>();
    String[] split = v1.split(",");
    for (String s:split)
    {
      list.add(Integer.parseInt(s));
    }
    return list;
  }
});
```

Java 8:

```
JavaPairRDD<String, Integer> monExpflattened =monExpRDD.flatMapValues(v ->
Arrays.asList(v.split(",")).stream().map(s ->
Integer.parseInt(s)).collect(Collectors.toList()));
```

repartitionAndSortWithinPartitions

repartitionAndSortWithinPartitions is an OrderedRDDFunctions, like SortByKey. It is a pairRDD functions. It first repartitions the pairRDD based on the given partitioner and sorts each partition by the key of pairRDD. repartitionAndSortWithinPartitions requires an instance of partitioner as an argument. The following is the declaration of this transformation:

```
repartitionAndSortWithinPartitions(Partitioner partitioner)
```

Let's repartition PairRDD of <Integer, String> using repartitionAndSortWithinPartitions. We will provide a instance of HashPartitioner as the argument:

```
JavaPairRDD<Integer, String> unPartitionedRDD =
jsc.parallelizePairs(Arrays.asList(new Tuple2<Integer, String>(8, "h"), new
Tuple2<Integer, String>(5, "e"), new Tuple2<Integer, String>(4, "d"),new
Tuple2<Integer, String>(2, "a"), new Tuple2<Integer, String>(7, "g"),new
Tuple2<Integer, String>(6, "f"),new Tuple2<Integer, String>(1, "a"),new
Tuple2<Integer, String>(3, "c")));
unPartitionedRDD.repartitionAndSortWithinPartitions(new
HashPartitioner(2));
```

By default, keys will be sorted according to their natural ordering. However, this transformation also provides an overloaded method which helps the user to provide a comparator to sort the keys based on requirement. This is also useful in the case where custom objects are used as keys:

```
repartitionAndSortWithinPartitions(Partitioner partitioner,Comparator<K>
comp)
```

coalesce

A coalesce transformation in Spark is used to reduce the number of partitions. If the partition count is too high, a user may need to reduce the number the partitions before running join operations. Joining two RDDs of n and m sizes respectively requires $n*m$ tasks. So, decreasing the partition count before joining RDDs can be a useful decision if the size of the partition (number of elements per partition) is small.

Repartition transformation can also be used to reduce the number of partitions of an RDD. However, repartition requires a full shuffle of data. coalesce, on the other hand, avoids full shuffle.

For example, an RDD has x number of partitions and the user performs coalesce to decrease the number of partitions to *(x-n)*, then only data of n partitions *(x-(x-n))* will be shuffled. This minimizes the data movement amongst nodes.

The coalesce transformation can be performed as follows:

```
pairRDD.coalesce(2)
```

foldByKey

`foldByKey` can be considered as `reduceByKey` with an initial zero value. Just like `reduceByKey`, it uses an associative function to merge values for each key, but it also uses an initial zero value:

```
foldByKey(V zeroValue,Function2<V,V,V> func);
```

As per the Spark documentation, the initial value should be neutral; that is, it may be added to the final result an arbitrary number of times, however it should not affect the final result. For example, *0* in the case of addition, *1* in the case of multiplication, empty list in the case of list concatenation.

The zero value acts as a mutable buffer. It is initialized per key once per partition. Once the key is encountered first in a partition and a zero value is initialized for it, it acts as a mutable buffer. Every value of the key belonging to the partition is merged in a mutable buffer. So, instead of creating a new object every time, as in the case of `reduceByKey`, this mutable object is used to fold the values of a key. It helps in garbage collection ifthe object creation is expensive.

This value should be a neutral value, but it can be used as quantitative value as well if some value needs to be added to a combined value of every key in every partition.

`foldByKey` can be used to run a word count as follows:

Java 7:

```
JavaRDD<String> stringRDD = jsc.parallelize(Arrays.asList("Hello Spark",
"Hello Java"));
JavaPairRDD<String, Integer> flatMapToPair = stringRDD.flatMapToPair(new
PairFlatMapFunction<String, String, Integer>() {
@Override
  public Iterator<Tuple2<String, Integer>> call(String t) throws Exception
{
    List<Tuple2<String,Integer>> list =new ArrayList<>();
    for (String s :t.split(" "))
```

```
    {
      list.add(new Tuple2<String, Integer>(s,1));
    }
    return list.iterator();
  }
});
JavaPairRDD<String, Integer> foldByKey = flatMapToPair.foldByKey(0,new
Function2<Integer, Integer, Integer>() {
@Override
  public Integer call(Integer v1, Integer v2) throws Exception {
    return v1+v2;
  }
});
```

Java 8:

```
JavaRDD<String> stringRDD = jsc.parallelize(Arrays.asList("Hello Spark",
"Hello Java"));
JavaPairRDD<String, Integer> flatMapToPair = stringRDD.flatMapToPair(s ->
Arrays.asList(s.split(" ")).stream() .map(token -> new Tuple2<String,
Integer>(token, 1)).collect(Collectors.toList()).iterator());
flatMapToPair.foldByKey(0,(v1, v2) -> v1+v2).collect();
foldByKey also provides following overloaded methods:
foldByKey(V zeroValue,Partitioner partitionerFunction2<V,V,V> func);
```

Since `aggregateByKey` involves data shuffling, this method allows user to provide instance of partitioner i.e Hash Partitioner, Merge Partitioner or custom partitioner based on requirement:

```
foldByKey(V zeroValue,int numPartitions,Function2<V,V,V> func);
```

Here, user can provide the number of partitions. In this case, `foldByKey` will create an instance of Hash Partitioner with the number of partitions the user provided and call the preceding variant.

aggregateByKey

`aggregateByKey` is similar to `reduceByKey/foldByKey`. However, it's behavior is more generalised. `reduceByKey/foldByKey` can be considered as a special case of `aggregateByKey`. `aggregateByKey` allows the user to return `pairRDD` with a different value type than the input RDD; that is, it can transform an RDD of (k1,v1) type to (k1,v2) type, which is not possible in the case of `reduceByKey/foldByKey`.

`aggregateByKey` accepts the following parameters:

```
aggregateByKey(V2 zeroValue, Function2<V2,V1,V2> seqFunction,
Function2<V2,V2,V2> combFunction)
```

The initial zero value is explained in the *foldByKey* section.

The function that aggregates the values of one partition can convert values of type v1 to v2. Function that merges values across partitions. Here v2 can be different or the same as v1, based on the requirement. Consider, we have a Pair RDD of type `<String, String>` as follows:

```
JavaPairRDD<String, String> pairRDD =
jsc.parallelizePairs(Arrays.asList(new Tuple2<String, String>("key1",
"Austria"), new Tuple2<String, String>("key2", "Australia"),new
Tuple2<String, String>("key3", "Antartica"), new Tuple2<String,
String>("key1", "Asia"),new Tuple2<String, String>("key2", "France"),new
Tuple2<String, String>("key3", "Canada"),new Tuple2<String, String>("key1",
"Argentina"),new Tuple2<String, String>("key2", "American Samoa"),new
Tuple2<String, String>("key3", "Germany")),3);
```

Our requirement is to find the count of values that start with A per key. We will use `aggregateByKey` to achieve this requirement as follows:

Java 7:

```
pairRDD.aggregateByKey(0, new Function2<Integer, String, Integer>() {
@Override
  public Integer call(Integer v1, String v2) throws Exception {
    if(v2.startsWith("A"))
    {
      v1+=1;
    }
  return v1;
}},
new Function2<Integer, Integer, Integer>() {
@Override
  public Integer call(Integer v1, Integer v2) throws Exception {
    return v1+v2;
  }});
```

Java 8:

```
pairRDD.aggregateByKey(0, (v1, v2) -> {
  if(v2.startsWith("A")){
    v1+=1;
  }
  return v1;
}, (v1, v2) -> v1+v2);
```

In the above example the value type of the input RDD is string, but the value type of the output RDD is an integer. Like `foldByKey`, `agregateByKey` also provides the following overloaded methods:

```
aggregateByKey(V2 zeroValue, Partitioner partitioner, Function2<V2,V1,V2>
seqFunction,Function2<V2,V2,V2> combFunction)

aggregateByKey(V2 zeroValue, int numPartitions, Function2<V2,V1,V2>
seqFunction,Function2<V2,V2,V2> combFunction)
```

> Refer to the *foldByKey* section to understand the use of a partitioner instance and `numPartitions` parameters.

combineByKey

This is the most generalised form function, which combines values of pair RDDs based on keys, such as `reduceByKey`, `groupByKey`, `foldByKey`, `aggregateByKey`, and so on. It is one step ahead of `aggregateByKey` because it lets the user create the initial combiner function as well. `combineByKey` transformation accepts the following three parameters:

- `createCombiner`: Function to create a combiner for a key; that is, it creates an initial value for a key when it is first encountered in a partition.
- `mergeValueWithinPartition`: Function that merges the value of a key to its existing combiner value within a partition. This function will only trigger when an initial combiner value is created for a key. In other words, for a key this function will only trigger if it exists more than once within a partition.
- `mergeCombiners`: Function that takes the combined values for keys created on each partition and merges them to create the final result.

  ```
  combineByKey(Function<V1,V2> createCombiner, Function2<V2,V1,V2>
  mergeValue,Function2<V2,V2,V2> mergeCombiners)
  ```

combineByKey transformation can be used to solve the problem described in the aggregateByKey section as follows:

Java 7:

```
JavaPairRDD<String, Integer> combineByKey = pairRDD.combineByKey(new
Function<String, Integer>() {
@Override
  public Integer call(String v1) throws Exception {
    if(v1.startsWith("A")) {
      return 1;
    }
    else{
      return 0;
    }}}, new Function2<Integer, String, Integer>() {
    @Override
        public Integer call(Integer v1, String v2) throws Exception {
          if(v2.startsWith("A")){
            v1+=1;
          }
        return v1;
        }}, new Function2<Integer, Integer, Integer>() {
        @Override
          public Integer call(Integer v1, Integer v2) throws Exception {
            return v1+v2;
          }
        });
```

Java 8:

```
pairRDD.combineByKey(v1 -> {
  if(v1.startsWith("A")){
    return 1;
  }
  else{
    return 0;
  }
}, (v1, v2) -> {
  if(v2.startsWith("A")){
    v1+=1;
  }
  return v1;
}, (v1, v2) -> v1+v2);
```

As per this code example, for every `<key,value>` tuple in RDD, if the key is encountered for the first time, then the `createCombiner` function will create the combiner and start the counter as *1* if the value in the tuple starts with `A` or as `0` otherwise. Then if a key exists more than once within a partition, the second function will trigger and increment the combiner value only if the value of the tuple starts with `A`.

Then, finally, the third function will sum the values across partitions for keys and produce the final result. Similar to `aggregateBykey/foldBykey`, `combineByKey` also provides an overloaded method, which allows the user to provide a partitioner instance or `numPartitions` as follows:

```
combineByKey(Function<V1,V2> createCombiner, Function2<V2,V1,V2>
mergeValue,Function2<V2,V2,V2> mergeCombiners, Partitioner partitioner)

combineByKey(Function<V1,V2> createCombiner, Function2<V2,V1,V2>
mergeValue,Function2<V2,V2,V2> mergeCombiners, int numPartitions)
```

Refer to the *foldByKey* section to learn about the usage of the partitioner instance and `numPartitions` parameters.

Along with the variants provided above, it provides another overloaded method which allows the user to specify the serializer for shuffle data along with a Boolean value that specifies `mapSideCombine` to be executed or not.

```
combineByKey(Function<V1,V2> createCombiner, Function2<V2,V1,V2>
mergeValue,Function2<V2,V2,V2> mergeCombiners, Partitioner partitioner,
boolean mapSideCombine,Serializer serializer)
```

`mapSideCombiner` helps to reduce the network IO by combining the data belonging to a key within a partition before shuffling the data. The user can turn it off if required. For example, `groupByKey` turns off `mapSideCombine`, however `reducyByKey/ FoldByKey/aggregateByKey` performs `mapSideCombine`. Therefore, `groupByKey` performs more network shuffle than the others.

In this section, we learnt about advanced level transformations, in the next section we will learn about about advanced level actions available in Spark.

Advanced actions

Upto now we have covered actions which focused on processing the entire data however big or small it may be. There are use cases where we might just need approximate values, or where we would like an asynchronous action which does not wait for the result, or even just the data from specific partitions. In this section,we will touch upon the appropriate actions that serve these specific requirements.

Approximate actions

In the previous chapter, we came across different methods in which RDD could be sampled to give a randomized output. This works fine as long as we want to debug or test our application. However, in other scenarios we might not want to get results which are accurate but which take a long time to execute, but rather require an approximate result within a certain percentage of error and in a time-bound manner. Spark has introduced approximate algorithms to cater to such needs, where the job can guarantee a result within a stipulated timeframe or/and within an error percentage. Some of the actions are:

- `countApprox`: Returns the approximate value of an RDD within a stipulated time, whether or not the job has completed or not. Usually if timeout (in milliseconds) is less, the error factor is higher.

  ```
  // countApprox(long timeout)
  JavaRDD<Integer> intRDD =
  sparkContext.parallelize(Arrays.asList(1,4,3,5,7));
  PartialResult<BoundedDouble> countAprx = intRDD.countApprox(2);
  System.out.println("Confidence::"+countAprx.getFinalValue().confide
  nce());
  System.out.println("high::"+countAprx.getFinalValue().high());
  System.out.println("Low::"+countAprx.getFinalValue().low());
  System.out.println("Mean::"+countAprx.getFinalValue().mean());
  System.out.println("Final::"+countAprx.getFinalValue().toString());
  ```

  There is another overridden version of `countApprox` which also takes into consideration the confidence of the approximate result, where confidence is the probability of the result being true to that percentage point. If the `countApprox` method has a confidence of 0.7, then one can expect 70% of the results to contain the true count. Also, while the value of timeout is in milliseconds, the value of confidence lies in the range [0,1].

  ```
  //countApprox(long timeout, double confidence)
  PartialResult<BoundedDouble> countAprox = intRDD.countApprox(1,
  0.95);
  ```

```
System.out.println("Confidence::"+countAprox.getFinalValue().confid
ence());
System.out.println("high::"+countAprox.getFinalValue().high());
System.out.println("Low::"+countAprox.getFinalValue().low());
System.out.println("Mean::"+countAprox.getFinalValue().mean());
System.out.println("Final::"+countAprox.getFinalValue().toString())
;
```

- countByKeyApprox: Applied on `pairRDD` which returns an approximate result within a timeout period. The return value is of type `PartialResult` and comes with different variations of the result such as `high()`, `low()`, `mean()`, and so on.

```
// countByKeyApprox(long timeout);
PartialResult<Map<String, BoundedDouble>> countByKeyApprx =
pairRDD.countByKeyApprox(1);
for( Entry<String, BoundedDouble> entrySet:
countByKeyApprx.getFinalValue().entrySet()){
  System.out.println("Confidence for "+entrySet.getKey()+"
  ::"+entrySet.getValue().confidence());
  System.out.println("high for "+entrySet.getKey()+"
  ::"+entrySet.getValue().high());
  System.out.println("Low for "+entrySet.getKey()+"
  ::"+entrySet.getValue().low());
  System.out.println("Mean for "+entrySet.getKey()+"
  ::"+entrySet.getValue().mean());
  System.out.println("Final val for "+entrySet.getKey()+"
  ::"+entrySet.getValue().toString());
}
```

If the accuracy of the result is more important than the time taken to generate the result, then another variation of `countByKeyApprox` can be used, which also takes into consideration the confidence which is a measure of correctness in the generated result.

```
//countByKeyApprox(long timeout, double confidence)
PartialResult<Map<String, BoundedDouble>> countByKeyApprox =
pairRDD.countByKeyApprox(1,0.75);
for( Entry<String, BoundedDouble> entrySet:
countByKeyApprox.getFinalValue().entrySet()){
  System.out.println("Confidence for "+entrySet.getKey()+"
  ::"+entrySet.getValue().confidence());
  System.out.println("high for "+entrySet.getKey()+"
  ::"+entrySet.getValue().high());
  System.out.println("Low for "+entrySet.getKey()+"
  ::"+entrySet.getValue().low());
  System.out.println("Mean for "+entrySet.getKey()+"
  ::"+entrySet.getValue().mean());
```

```
    System.out.println("Final val for "+entrySet.getKey()+"
    ::"+entrySet.getValue().toString());
}
```

- countByValueApprox : On pair RDD one can also approximate the count of values by using the countByValueApprox() action. This action returns the result within a stipulated timeout with considerable accuracy, which can be checked using the helper method confidence().

```
// countByKeyApprox(long timeout);
PartialResult<Map<Tuple2<String, Integer>, BoundedDouble>>
countByValueApprx = pairRDD.countByValueApprox(1);
for(Entry<Tuple2<String, Integer>, BoundedDouble> entrySet :
countByValueApprx.getFinalValue().entrySet()){
  System.out.println("Confidence for key "+entrySet.getKey()._1()
+"
  and value "+ entrySet.getKey()._2()+"
  ::"+entrySet.getValue().confidence());
  System.out.println("high for key "+entrySet.getKey()._1()+" and
value "+ entrySet.getKey()._2()+" ::"+entrySet.getValue().high());
  System.out.println("Low for key "+entrySet.getKey()._1()+" and
value "+
  entrySet.getKey()._2()+" ::"+entrySet.getValue().low());
  System.out.println("Mean for key "+entrySet.getKey()._1()+" and
value "+ entrySet.getKey()._2()+" ::"+entrySet.getValue().mean());
  System.out.println("Final val for key "+entrySet.getKey()._1()+"
and value"+ entrySet.getKey()._2()+"
::"+entrySet.getValue().toString());
}
```

Like other approximate actions, even countByValueApprox has another variant which caters to the confidence of the result:

```
// countByKeyApprox(long timeout, double confidence)
PartialResult<Map<Tuple2<String, Integer>, BoundedDouble>>
countByValueApprox = pairRDD.countByValueApprox(1,0.85);
for(Entry<Tuple2<String, Integer>, BoundedDouble> entrySet :
countByValueApprox.getFinalValue().entrySet()){
  System.out.println("Confidence for key "+entrySet.getKey()._1()
+" and
  value "+ entrySet.getKey()._2()+"
::"+entrySet.getValue().confidence());
  System.out.println("high for key "+entrySet.getKey()._1()+" and
value "+
  entrySet.getKey()._2()+" ::"+entrySet.getValue().high());
  System.out.println("Low for key "+entrySet.getKey()._1()+" and
value "+
```

```
    entrySet.getKey()._2()+" ::"+entrySet.getValue().low());
    System.out.println("Mean for key "+entrySet.getKey()._1()+" and
value "+
    entrySet.getKey()._2()+" ::"+entrySet.getValue().mean());
    System.out.println("Final val for key "+entrySet.getKey()._1()+"
and
    value "+ entrySet.getKey()._2()+"
::"+entrySet.getValue().toString());
    }
```

- countApproxDistinct : Based on the **HyperLogLog** algorithm, countApproxDistinct returns an estimate of distinct elements in the RDD. The input parameter for the action is called 'relativeSD' whose value must be greater than *0.000017* as smaller values create more counters and hence require more space. For a higher precision in the result, the computation time increases at a faster rate and there are possibilities when the actual results take less time to compute than higher precision approximate results.

```
long countApprxDistinct = intRDD.countApproxDistinct(0.95);
System.out.println("The approximate distinct element count is
::"+countApprxDistinct);
```

For pair RDDs, an approximate distinct count of values for each key can also be calculated using an action called countApproxDistinctByKey:

```
JavaPairRDD<String, Long> approxCountOfKey =
pairRDD.countApproxDistinctByKey(0.80);
approxCountOfKey.foreach(newVoidFunction<Tuple2<String,Long>>() {
@Override
  publicvoid call(Tuple2<String, Long> tuple) throws Exception {
    System.out.println("The approximate distinct vlaues for Key
    :"+tuple._1()+" is ::"+tuple._2());
  }
});
```

Asynchronous actions

Although most Spark actions are synchronous in nature, there are few actions that can be executed asynchronously. In certain scenarios one can execute different asynchronous actions on different RDDs simultaneously when the resources of a Spark cluster are not being utilized completely. There are countless scenarios where an asynchronous action can be utilized to its full potential as all asynchronous actions return `FutureAction`, which inherits its feature from the Future class of Java's concurrent package.

- `countAsync`: The `countAsync` action returns a `FutureAction` having a value of the total number of elements in the RDD. The `FutureAction` class has a few important helper methods, like `isDone()` to check if the action is complete, the `cancel()` method attempts to cancel the executing action, and the `get()` method waits if necessary for the computation to complete, and then retrieves its result.

  ```
  JavaFutureAction<Long> intCount = intRDD1.countAsync();
  System.out.println(" The async count for "+intCount);
  ```

- `collectAsync`: This is another asynchronous action that returns a future for retrieving all elements of this RDD. All the `FutureAction` helper methods discussed previously hold true for this action as well:

  ```
  JavaFutureAction<List<Integer>> intCol = intRDD2.collectAsync();
  for(Integer val:intCol.get()){
    System.out.println("The collect val is "+val);
  }
  ```

- `takeAsync`: An asynchronous action `takeAsync` retrieves the first n elements of the RDD in a `FutureAction`:

  ```
  JavaFutureAction<List<Integer>> takeAsync = intRDD.takeAsync(3);
  for( Integer val:takeAsync.get()) {
    System.out.println(" The async value of take is :: "+val);
  }
  ```

- `foreachAsync`: Applies a function to each element of the RDD asynchronously:

```
intRDD.foreachAsync(newVoidFunction<Integer>() {
@Override
  public void call(Integer t) throws Exception {
    System.out.println("The val is :"+t);
  }
});
```

Similarly, `foreachPartitionAsync` action applies a function to each partition of the RDD.

Miscellaneous actions

The following actions do not fall into any specific criteria but are helpful while dealing with partition specific actions:

- `lookup()`: The action `lookup()` fetches the list of values pertaining to a key in a pair RDD. This operation is done efficiently if the RDD has a known partitioner by only searching the partition that the key maps to:

```
List<Integer> lookupVal = pairRDD.lookup("a");
for(Integer val:lookupVal){
  System.out.println("The lookup val is ::"+val);
}
```

- `getNumPartitions`: `getNumPartitions` action returns the number of partitions in the RDD:

```
int numberOfPartitions = intRDD2.getNumPartitions();
System.out.println("The no of partitions in the RDD are
::"+numberOfPartitions);
```

- `collectPartitions`: The action `collectPartitions` returns an array that contains all the elements in specific partitions of the RDD:

```
List<Integer>[] collectPart = intRDD1.collectPartitions(newint[]{1,2});
System.out.println("The length of collectPart is "+collectPart.length);
for(List<Integer> i:collectPart){
  for(Integer it:i){
    System.out.println(" The val of collect is "+it);
  }
}
```

Shared variable

Spark segregates the job into the smallest possible operation, a closure, running on different nodes and each having a copy of all the variables of the Spark job. Any changes made to these variables do not get reflected in the driver program and so, to overcome this limitation, Spark provides two special variables: broadcast variables and accumulators (also called shared variables).

Broadcast variable

Broadcast variable is a read-only variable shared among each executor node. A variable, once broadcasted, gets copied to each executor's memory and can be referred to whenever needed in the execution of the program.

The broadcast variable is a very useful feature if some data needs to be referred to during the execution of tasks at various stages of the program. Like the distributed cache concept in Hadoop, where lookup data in a table can be placed for a map side join, the broadcast variable can be used in Spark to keep the look up data available in each executor's memory.

Properties of the broadcast variable

The following are the properties for the broadcast variable:

- **Broadcast variables are read-only:** Broadcast variables are immutable, that is, once initialized their value cannot be changed.
- **Broadcast variables get copied to executor memory at the time of creation:** A broadcast variable gets cached to the executor's memory only once, at the time of creation. Therefore, it increases the performance of Spark as the lookup values do not need to pass to transformation/action functions multiple times for referring.
- **Should fit in executor's memory:** The size of the broadcast variable should be small so that it can fit into an executor's memory. They are meant for the lookup values which are small in size and can be distributed over the cluster.

Let's start by creating a broadcast variable using `JavaSparkContext`:

```
SparkConf conf = new SparkConf().setMaster("local").setAppName("Broadcast
Example");
JavaSparkContext jsc = new JavaSparkContext(conf);
Broadcast<String> broadcastVar = jsc.broadcast("Hello Spark");
```

Code for creating broadcast variable using `SparkSession`:

```
SparkSession sparkSession =
SparkSession.builder().master("local").appName("My App")
.config("spark.sql.warehouse.dir", "file:////C:/Users/sgulati/spark-
warehouse").getOrCreate();
Broadcast<String> broadcastVar=
sparkSession.sparkContext().broadcast("Hello Spark",
scala.reflect.ClassTag$.MODULE$.apply(String.class));
```

The value of the broadcast variable can be read as follows:

```
broadcastVar.getValue();
```

Lifecycle of a broadcast variable

Broadcast variables are created using `SparkContext` and their lifecycle is managed by `BroadcastManager` and `ContextCleaner`. When a broadcast variable is created, it gets copied to each executor's memory.

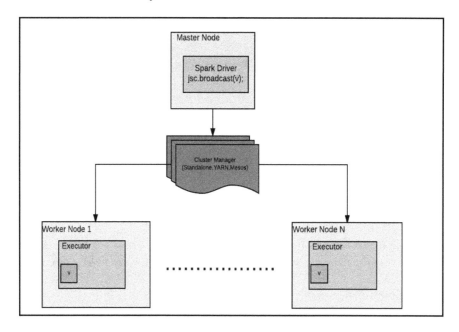

`BroadcastManager` is a service that gets initialized as soon as `SparkContext` is created. The `BroadcastManager` service initializes a `TorrentBroadcastFactory` (`https://jacek laskowski.gitbooks.io/mastering-apache-spark/content/spark-TorrentBroadcastF actory.html`) object, which is used to create a broadcast variable. `BroadcastManager` manages all the broadcast variables created, using `SparkContext` to keep track of them.

Once the broadcast variable is no longer needed, it should be removed from the executor's memory. There are two ways to do this:

- `unpersist()`: User can unpersist a broadcast variable when it is not needed any more. It can be done as follows:

  ```
  broadcastVar.unpersist();
  ```

  The `unpersist()` method removes the copies the broadcast variable from the executors memory asynchronously. However, this method provides an overload where the user can run `unpersist` synchronously as well.

  ```
  public void unpersist(boolean blocking)
  ```

  Therefore, `unpersist` can be done synchronously as follows:

  ```
  broadcastVar.unpersist(true);
  ```

  The `unpersist()` method removes the broadcast variable from the executors memory. However, it does not remove it from the driver's memory. If the broadcast variable is used again in the program after `unpersist()` is called, it will be resent to the executors.

- **Destroy**: The `destroy` method removes all the data and metadata related to the broadcast variable from executors and drivers asynchronously. Once, the broadcast variable has been destroyed, it cannot be called again. Any attempt to do so will throw an exception. It can be done as follows:

  ```
  broadcastVar.destroy();
  ```

  Similarly to the unpersist method, the destroy method also provides an overload, so it can be called synchronously as follows:

  ```
  broadcastVar.destroy(true);
  ```

  It is recommended to unpersist a broadcast variable before destroying it as it gets removed from the executors memory asynchronously first and does not block the Spark program execution.

Once a broadcast variable has been destroyed and garbage collected, all the data and metadata related to it is cleaned by `ContextCleaner`.

`ContextCleaner` is a Spark service which is responsible for cleaning up RDDs, broadcasts, accumulators, and so on. It also gets created with `SparkContext`. It maintains a weak reference to RDDs, broadcast variables, accumulators, and so on, and when the object is garbage collected it cleans up the data and metadata related to it using a daemon thread called Spark Context Cleaner thread.

Map-side join using broadcast variable

Anyone familiar with Hive concepts will be well aware of Map-side join concepts. In distributed systems, data is spread amongst different nodes. So when two distributed datasets are joined based on a key or column, the data needs to be shuffled over the network perform such operations as data belonging to same key should reach to the same node.

Map-side join comes into the picture when one of the datasets taking part in a join operation is small. To avoid shuffling the data over the network, the small dataset is loaded in the distributed cache memory and then the `map` operation is performed on the large dataset where it is joined with the small dataset loaded in memory. This type of join operation is known as a Map-side Join.

In Apache Spark, a Map-side join can be performed with the help of a broadcast variable. Consider we have the following datasets:

- User ID to Country ID mapping to all the users logged in to a popular website throughout the world in the last week. Country ID to country name mapping.
- Our requirement is to find the name of the country for every user ID. The straight forward solution to that problem is joining both datasets. However, as we know, the dataset containing the country ID to country name mapping should be small (as of 2017, there are less than two hundred countries in the world), so we can load it in memory. Let's look at it programmatically.

The two datasets are:

```
JavaPairRDD<String, String> userIdToCityId =
jsc.parallelizePairs(Arrays.asList(new Tuple2<String, String>("1", "101"),
new Tuple2<String, String>("2", "102"),new Tuple2<String, String>("3",
"107"), new Tuple2<String, String>("4", "103"), new Tuple2<String,
String>("11", "101"), new Tuple2<String, String>("12", "102"),new
Tuple2<String, String>("13", "107"), new Tuple2<String, String>("14",
```

```
"103")));

JavaPairRDD<String, String> cityIdToCityName =
jsc.parallelizePairs(Arrays.asList(new Tuple2<String, String>("101",
"India"), new Tuple2<String, String>("102", "UK"),new Tuple2<String,
String>("103", "Germany"), new Tuple2<String, String>("107", "USA")));
```

 We have kept datasets small for the purpose of this example. In reality, datasets will be loaded from external systems.

Now, if you join the datasets, shuffling is bound to happen. As already described in `Chapter 4`, *Understanding Spark Programming Model* a join transformation provides an overloaded method, using which the user can provide a custom partitioner for purpose of shuffling.

Instead of running the join operation, we will broadcast the dataset `cityIdToCityName` as follows:

```
Broadcast<Map<String, String>> citiesBroadcasted =
jsc.broadcast(cityIdToCityName.collectAsMap());
```

Now, we can simply run the `map` operation of RDD `userIdToCityId` to achieve our goal without the need of shuffling (as map transformation does not shuffle data) as follows:

```
JavaRDD<Tuple3<String, String, String>> joined = userIdToCityId.map(
v1 -> new Tuple3<String, String, String>(v1._1(), v1._2(),
citiesBroadcasted.value().get(v1._2()))));
System.out.println(joined.collect());
```

The output dataset will contain three fields in every row: `userId`, `countryid`, and the respective country name. In this section, we learnt about broadcast variables, their lifecycle and applications in the real world. In the next section we will learn about another cluster-wide shared variable called **Accumulator**.

Accumulators

Accumulators are shared variables which are used for aggregating values from executor nodes to driver node. Some characteristics of accumulators are:

1. Accumulators are write-only shared variables.
2. Operations that are associative and cumulative in nature are only supported by Accumulators.

3. The executor nodes do not have access to the accumulator's value but can only aggregate to the value.

4. The driver program has access to the accumulator's final value.

Although accumulators can be used both in transformation and action, Spark guarantees that it is only action in which accumulators will be run once. Accumulators used in a transformation could have duplicate values if there are any task failures or speculative execution, however rare that may be.

Spark has some built-in accumulators, such as `longAccumulator()`, `doubleAccumulator()`, and `collectionAccumulator()`, to perform basic aggregation over standards data types. Accumulators can also be understood in relation to what *counters* stood for in MapReduce. Let's work through the following example to understand accumulators. In our use case, we have an application log file with multiple exception entries and, depending on the count of occurrence of exceptions, a certain predefined task can be called. Now to approach such a problem we can use multiple techniques, and using accumulator can be one such way to solve it:

```
LongAccumulator longAccumulator =
sparkContext.sc().longAccumulator("ExceptionCounter");
JavaRDD<String> textFile =
sparkContext.textFile("src/main/resources/logFileWithException.log");
textFile.foreach(newVoidFunction<String>() {
@Override
  public void call(String line) throws Exception {
    if(line.contains("Exception")){
      longAccumulator.add(1);
        System.out.println("The intermediate value in loop
        "+longAccumulator.value());
      }
    }
});
System.out.println("The final value of Accumulator :
"+longAccumulator.value());
```

While `longAccumulator` and `doubleAccumulator` return long and double respectively, the `collectionAccumulator()` returns a list of added elements. So, we repeat our previous use case and use a `collectionAccumulator()` instead of `longAccumulator()`, and we get a list of elements each representing the added element:

```
CollectionAccumulator<Long> collectionAccumulator =
sparkContext.sc().collectionAccumulator();
textFile.foreach(newVoidFunction<String>() {
@Override
  publicvoid call(String line) throws Exception {
```

```
      if(line.contains("Exception")){
        collectionAccumulator.add(1L);
        System.out.println("The intermediate value in loop
        "+collectionAccumulator.value());
      }
    }
});
System.out.println("The final value of Accumulator :
"+collectionAccumulator.value());
```

Custom accumulators can also be written by sub-classing the AccumulatorV2 class. AccumulatorV2 is an abstract class that accumulates inputs of type IN, and produces output of type OUT. OUT should be a type that can be read atomically (for example, int, long), or thread-safely (for example, synchronized collections) because it will be read from other threads. Unlike built-in accumulators, custom accumulators need to be registered in SparkContext register() method and only then will they behave like a shared variable. Also there is a helper method isRegistered() in AccumulatorV2 class that returns a Boolean value to check if the custom accumulator has been registered or not. Let's reuse our previous use case again and build a custom accumulator that accepts a string value but returns a list of integers:

```
//Custom Accumulator
public class ListAccumulator extends AccumulatorV2<String,
CopyOnWriteArrayList<Integer>> {
  private static final long serialVersionUID = 1L;
  private CopyOnWriteArrayList<Integer> accList = null;
  public ListAccumulator() {
    accList = new CopyOnWriteArrayList<Integer>();
  }
  public ListAccumulator(CopyOnWriteArrayList<Integer> value) {
    if (value.size() != 0) {
      accList = new CopyOnWriteArrayList<Integer>(value);
    }
  }
  @Override
  public void add(String arg) {
    if (!arg.isEmpty())
      accList.add(Integer.parseInt(arg));
  }
  @Override
  public AccumulatorV2<String, CopyOnWriteArrayList<Integer>> copy() {
    return new ListAccumulator(value());
  }
  @Override
  public boolean isZero() {
    return accList.size() == 0 ? true : false;
```

```
  }
  @Override
  public void merge(AccumulatorV2<String, CopyOnWriteArrayList<Integer>>
  other)
  {
    add(other.value());
  }
  private void add(CopyOnWriteArrayList<Integer> value) {
    value().addAll(value);
  }
  @Override
  public void reset() {
    accList = new CopyOnWriteArrayList<Integer>();
  }
  @Override
  public CopyOnWriteArrayList<Integer> value() {
    return accList;
  }
}
```

Driver program

Following is the code to instantiate and call the accumulator from the Spark Job's main function:

```
ListAccumulator listAccumulator=new ListAccumulator();
sparkContext.sc().register(listAccumulator, "ListAccumulator");
textFile.foreach(newVoidFunction<String>() {
@Override
  public void call(String line) throws Exception {
    if(line.contains("Exception")){
      listAccumulator.add("1");
      System.out.println("The intermediate value in loop
      " + listAccumulator.value());
    }
  }
});
System.out.println("The final value of Accumulator :
"+listAccumulator.value());
```

Summary

This chapter covered various topics that govern the functioning of RDD-like partitioning and then used advanced transformations and actions to achieve specific requirements. We also looked at the limitations of sharing variables across executor nodes and how it can be achieved using broadcast variables and accumulators.

The next chapter introduces Spark SQL and related concepts like datafame, dataset, UDF and so on. We'll also discuss `SQLContext` and the newly introduced `SparkSession` and how its introduction has simplified the whole process of dealing with the Hive metastore.

8

Working with Spark SQL

This chapter will introduce Spark SQL and related concepts, like dataframe and dataset. Schema and advanced SQL functions will be discussed from the Apache Spark perspective; and writing custom **user-defined function** (**UDF**) and working with various data sources will also be touched upon.

This chapter uses Java APIs to create `SQLContext`/`SparkSession` and implement dataframes/datasets from Java RDD for raw data, such as CSV, and structured data, such as JSON.

SQLContext and HiveContext

Prior to Spark 2.0, `SparkContext` used to be the entry point for Spark applications, an `SQLContext` and `HiveContext` used to be the entry points to run Spark SQL. `HiveContext` is the superset of `SQLContext`. The `SQLContext` needs to be created to run Spark SQL on the RDD.

The `SQLContext` provides connectivity to various data sources. Data can be read from those data sources and Spark SQL can be executed to transform the data as per the requirement. It can be created using `SparkContext` as follows:

```
JavaSparkContext javaSparkContext = new JavaSparkContext(conf);
SQLContext sqlContext = new SQLContext(javaSparkContext);
```

The `SQLContext` creates a wrapper over `SparkContext` and provides SQL functionality and functions to work with structured data. It comes with the basic level of SQL functions.

The `HiveContext`, being a superset of `SQLContext`, provides a lot more functions. The `HiveContext` lets you write queries using Hive QL Parser ,which means all of the Hive functions can be accessed using `HiveContext`. For example, windowing functions can be executed using `javaSparkContext` HiveContext. Along with that it provides access to Hive UDFs. Similarly to `SQLContext`, `HiveContext` can be created using `SparkContext` as follows:

```
JavaSparkContext javaSparkContext = new JavaSparkContext(conf);
HiveContext hiveContext = new HiveContext(javaSparkContext);
```

The `HiveContext` does not require Hive to run. However, if needed, Hive tables can be queried using `HiveContext`. `hive-site.xml` is needed to access Hive tables. Also, all the data sources, which are accessible using `SQLContext`, can also be accessed using `HiveContext`.

`HiveContext` requires all hive dependencies to be included. So, if only basic SQL functions are required, then `SQLContext` will suffice. However, it's recommended to use `HiveContext` as it provides a wide range of functions.

In Spark 2.x both of these APIs are available. However, as per the documentation, they are deprecated. Spark 2.0 introduced a new entry point for all Spark applications called `SparkSession`.

```
javaSparkContextSparkSession
```

In Chapter 5, *Working with Data and Storage*, we used `SparkSession` to connect to Cassandra and to read data in various formats. In this section, we will discuss `SparkSession` in detail.

The `SparkSession` was introduced in Spark 2.0 as the single entry point for all Spark applications. Prior to Spark 2.0, `SparkContext` used to be the entry point for Spark applications: `SQLContext` and `HiveContext` were used for Spark SQL, `StreamingContext` was used for Spark streaming applications, and so on.

 We will explain Spark streaming in the next chapter.

In Spark 2.x, `SparkSession` can be used as the entry point for every Spark application. It combines all the functions of `SQLContext`, `HiveContext`, and `StreamingContext`. The `SparkSession` internally requires a `SparkContext` for computation.

Another key difference in `SparkSession` is that there can be multiple `SparkSession` instances in single a Spark application, which was not possible with `SparkContext`.

Initializing SparkSession

Let's create a `SparkSession` object. `SparkSession` follows the builder design pattern, therefore we can initialize `SparkSession` in the following way:

```
SparkSession sparkSession =SparkSession.builder()
.master("local")
.appName("Spark Session Example")
.getOrCreate();
```

You must have noticed that we have not created any `SparkContext` or `SparkConf` objects for initializing `SparkSession`. The `SparkConf` and `SparkContext` are encapsulated in `SparkSession`. No explicit initialization of these objects is required with `SparkSession`.

The `SparkConf` and `SparkContext` can be accessed using the `SparkSession` object as follows:

```
SparkContext sparkContext = sparkSession.sparkContext();
SparkConf conf = sparkSession.sparkContext().getConf();
```

You can run Spark SQL using `SparkSession`. However, Hive SQL support is not enabled by default. To enable it `SparkSession` can be initialized as follows:

```
SparkSession sparkSession = SparkSession.builder()
.master("local")
.appName("Spark Session Example")
.enableHiveSupport()
.getOrCreate();
```

As described in Chapter 3, *Lets Spark*, runtime configurations can be set in the `SparkConf` object before initializing `SparkContext`. Since we do not need to create `SparkConf` explicitly for creating `SparkSession`, there are configurational parameters for the Spark application that can be provided in `SparkSession` as follows:

```
SparkSession sparkSession = SparkSession.builder()
.master("local")
.appName("Spark Session Example")
.config("spark.driver.memory", "2G")
.getOrCreate();
```

After initializing a Spark object, runtime configurations can be altered as well as follows:

```
sparkSession.conf().set("spark.driver.memory", "3G");
```

Reading CSV using SparkSession

In Chapter 5, *Working with Data and Storage*, we read CSV using SparkSession in the form of a Java RDD. However, this time we will read the CSV in the form of a dataset. Consider, you have a CSV with the following content:

```
emp_id,emp_name,emp_dept
1,Foo,Engineering
2,Bar,Admin
```

The SparkSession can be used to read this CSV file as follows:

```
Dataset<Row> csv =
sparkSession.read().format("csv").option("header","true").load("C:\\Users\\
sgulati\\Documents\\my_docs\\book\\testdata\\emp.csv");
```

Similarly to the collect() function on RDD, a dataset provides the show() function, which can be used to read the content of the dataset:

```
csv.show();
```

Executing this function will show the content of the CSV files along with the headers which seems similar to a relational table. The content of a dataset can be transformed/filtered using Spark SQL which will be discussed in the next sections.

Dataframe and dataset

Dataframes were introduced in Spark 1.3. Dataframe built on the concept of providing schemas over the data. An RDD basically consists of raw data. Although it provides various functions to process the data, it is a collection of Java objects and is involved in the overhead of garbage collection and serialization. Also, Spark SQL concepts can only be leveraged if it contains some schema. So, earlier version of a Spark provide another version of RDD called SchemaRDD.

SchemaRDD

As its name suggests, it is an RDD with schema. As it contains schema, run relation queries can be run on the data along with basic RDD functions. The `SchemaRDD` can be registered as a table so that SQL queries can be executed on it using Spark SQL. It was available in earlier version of a Spark. However, with Spark Version 1.3, the `SchemaRDD` was deprecated and dataframe was introduced.

Dataframe

In spite of being an evolved version of `SchemaRDD`, dataframe comes with big differences to RDDs. It was introduced as the part of Project *Tungsten* that allows data to be stored off-heap in binary format. This helps in unloading the garbage collection overhead.

A dataframe comes with the concept of always having schema with data (the Spark framework manages the schema and only passes data between the nodes). As Spark understands the schema and data is stored off-heap in binary format, there is no need to encode data using Java (or Kryo) serialization, which reduces the serialization effort as well.

Also, the dataframe API introduced the concept of building *optimized query* plans that can be executed with the Spark Catalyst optimizer. As dataframe, like RDD, also follows lazy evaluation, it allows the creation of an optimized query plan before execution. Finally, the operation happens on RDDs only, but it is transparent to the user. Consider, the following query:

```
select a.name, b.title from a,b where a.id=b.id where b.title ='Architect'
```

Here, instead of joining tables and then filtering the data based on title, the data will be first filtered and then joined as per the optimized query plan. This helps to reduce network shuffle.

With all this advancement, dataframe has some shortcomings. Dataframe does not provide compile-time safety. Consider the following example of dataframe from Spark 1.6:

```
JavaRDD<Employee> empRDD = jsc.parallelize(Arrays.asList(new
Employee("Foo", 1),new Employee("Bar", 2)));
SQLContext sqlContext = new SQLContext(jsc);

DataFrame df = sqlContext.createDataFrame(empRDD, Employee.class);
```

Here we created a dataframe of `Employee` objects using `sqlContext`. The constructor of `Employee` objects accepts two parameters: name, ID.

JavaBean should contain a default constructor and should be serializable to be used as elements for RDD, dataframe, or dataset.

Notice that `DataFrame` does not contain any type. To filter elements, a filter operation can be executed on `DataFrame` as follows:

```
DataFrame filter = df.filter("id >1");
```

Here, the complier has no option to identify whether the column name specified in the filter condition exists or not. If it does not, it will throw exceptions at runtime.

Another disadvantage of dataframe is that it was Scala centric. All APIs are not available in Java or Python.

Dataset

Dataset was introduced in Spark 1.6. It is the combination of RDD and dataframe. Dataset brings compile time safety, the object oriented programming style of RDD, and the advances of dataframes together. Therefore, it is an immutable strongly typed object which uses schema to describe the data. It uses the efficient off-heap storage mechanism, Tungsten, and creates optimized query plans that get executed with Spark Catalyst optimizer.

Datasets also introduced the concept of encoders. Encoders work as translators among JVM objects and Spark internal binary format. The tabular representation of data with schema is stored in Spark binary format. Encoders allow operations on serialized data. Spark comes with various inbuilt encoders, along with an encoder API for JavaBean. Encoders allow the access of individual attributes without the need to de-sterilize an entire object. Thus, it reduces serialization efforts and load.

Creating a dataset using encoders

A dataset can be created using `empRDD` as follows:

```
Dataset<Employee> dsEmp = = sparkSession.createDataset(empRDD.rdd(),
org.apache.spark.sql.Encoders.bean(Employee.class));
```

Notice, a dataset is a strongly typed object. We've created a dataset object which contains elements of `Employee`.

We can run the following operation on dataset to filter employees with *ID > 1*:

```
Dataset<Employee> filter = dsEmp.filter(emp->emp.getId()>1);
filter.show();
```

Another advantage of a dataset is that it provides both Scala and Java APIs, which allows Java engineers to work efficiently with datasets.

Creating a dataset using StructType

In the previous section, we discussed the creation of a dataset from RDD with the help of encoders. Similarly in Chapter 5, *Working with Data and Storage*, we also discussed a couple of different ways in which we can create dataframes , an alias for dataset (row), from JSON, CSV, and XML files. There is another way in which we can dynamically create a schema and hence form an object of dataset (row). The first step involves converting RDD(T) to RDD(row) using the factory pattern method of class RowFactory. Then we identify the number of fields in the data and create a schema of StructType representing the structure of RDD(row) and finally apply a schema to the createDataFrame method in SparkSession.

As an example, let's assume we have a text file whose first row represents the name of the column and the rest of the rows represents data:

```
//Create a RDD
JavaRDD<String> deptRDD = sparkSession.sparkContext()
                        .textFile("src/main/resources/dept.txt", 1)
                        .toJavaRDD();

//Convert the RDD to RDD<Rows>
JavaRDD<Row> deptRows = deptRDD.filter(str->
!str.contains("deptno")).map(new Function<String, Row>() {
  private static final long serialVersionUID = 1L;
  @Override
  public Row call(String rowString) throws Exception {
    String[] cols = rowString.split(",");
    return RowFactory.create(cols[0].trim(),
cols[1].trim(),cols[2].trim());
  }
});

//Create schema
String[] schemaArr=deptRDD.first().split(",");
List<StructField> structFieldList = new ArrayList<>();
for (String fieldName : schemaArr) {
  StructField structField = DataTypes.createStructField(fieldName,
```

```
DataTypes.StringType, true);
  structFieldList.add(structField);
}
StructType schema = DataTypes.createStructType(structFieldList);

Dataset<Row> deptDf = sparkSession.createDataFrame(deptRows, schema);
deptDf.printSchema();
deptDf.show();
```

Unified dataframe and dataset API

With the evolution of Spark 2.x, the untyped characteristics of dataframe and the typed characteristics of dataset have been merged into dataset. So, fundamentally a dataframe is an alias of a collection of generic objects of a dataset (row), where row is a generic untyped JVM object. In Java, a dataframe is represented as a dataset (row). The unification of dataframe with dataset allows us to operate upon the data in multiple ways such as:

- **Using strongly typed APIs**: Java functions provide type safety while working on dataset, also referred as a typed transformation:

  ```
  dsEmp.filter(newFilterFunction<Employee>() {
    @Override
    publicboolean call(Employee emp) throws Exception {
      return emp.getEmpId() > 1;
    }
  }).show();

  //Using Java 8
  dsEmp.filter(emp -> emp.getEmpId()>1).show();
  ```

- **Using untyped APIs**: An untyped transformation provides SQL-like column specific names, and the operation can be used to operate upon data:

  ```
  dsEmp.filter("empID > 1").show();
  ```

- **Using DSL**: Dataframes/dataset provide a domain-specific language for structured data manipulation. In Java, one can use the function `col()` by importing the Spark SQL package `org.apache.spark.sql.functions.col` which provides a statically typed function on untyped column names of a dataframe.

  ```
  dsEmp.filter(col("empId").gt(1)).show();
  ```

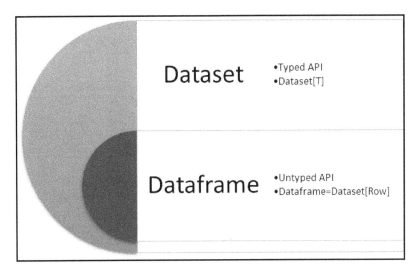

Figure 8.1: Unified dataset API Spark 2.x

Data persistence

By default, data is persisted using Parquet file format in Spark unless the configuration `spark.sql.sources.default` it set to any other format. Fully qualified file format names should be used as a data source except for file formats (JSON, **Parquet**, JDBC, ORC, **LIBSVM**, CSV, and text) which are natively supported as of Spark 2.1 . Though native file formats have built-in support with dtasets, some limitation exits, such as: for saving the data in text file format only single column is supported; similarly for saving ORC file format, Hive support should be enabled while creating `SparkSession`. Data can be persisted using either of the options provided by a dataset.

```
deptDf.write().mode(SaveMode.Overwrite).json("DirectoryLocation");
deptDf.write().mode("overwrite").format("csv").save("src/main/resources/out
put/deptText");
deptDf.write().mode(SaveMode.Overwrite).format("csv").save("DirectoryLocati
on ");
```

Data persistence mode is a very important aspect of how data is saved on the disk if existing data already exists. `SaveMode` provides four different options to handle such scenarios, default being `error` which throws an exception if the data is already present, as shown in the following table:

SaveMode	Any language	Meaning
`SaveMode.ErrorIfExists`	`error`	When saving a dataframe to a data source, if data already exists, an exception is expected to be thrown.
`SaveMode.Append`	`append`	When saving a dataframe to a data source, if data/table already exists, the contents of the dataframe are expected to be appended to existing data.
`SaveMode.Overwrite`	`overwrite`	When saving a dataframe to a data source, if a data/table already exists, the existing data is expected to be overwritten by the contents of the dataframe.
`SaveMode.Ignore`	`ignore`	When saving a dataframe to a data source, if data already exists, the save operation is expected to not save the contents of the dataframe and to not change the existing data. This is similar to a `CREATE TABLE IF NOT EXISTS` in SQL.

Spark SQL operations

Working in Spark SQL primarily happens in three stages: the creation of dataset, applying SQL operations, and finally persisting the dataset. We have so far been able to create a dataset from RDD and other data sources (refer to `Chapter 5`, *Working with Data and Storage*) and also persist the dataset as discussed in the previous section. Now let's look at some of the ways in which SQL operations can be applied to a dataset.

Untyped dataset operation

Once we have created the dataset, then Spark provides a couple of handy functions which perform basic SQL operation and analysis, such as the following:

- `show()`: This displays the top 20 rows of the dataset in a tabular form. Strings of more than 20 characters will be truncated, and all cells will be aligned right:

  ```
  emp_ds.show();
  ```

  Another variant of the `show()` function allows the user to enable or disable the 20 characters limit in the `show()` function by passing a Boolean as false to disable truncation of the string:

  ```
  emp_ds.show(false);
  ```

- `printSchema()`: This function prints the schema to the console in a tree format:

  ```
  emp_ds.printSchema();
  ```

- `select()`: This selects a set of columns as passed as an argument from the dataset:

  ```
  emp_ds.select("empName" ,"empId").show();
  ```

  By statically importing the function `org.apache.spark.sql.functions.col`, one can add extra features to columns by using helper functions associated with `col()`, such as creating an alias, incrementing the value of the column, casting to a specific datatype, and so on:

  ```
  emp_ds.select(col("empName").name("Employee Name")
  ,col("empId").cast(DataTypes.IntegerType).name("Employee
  Id")).show();
  ```

- `filter()`: This function is used to select rows meeting the criteria passed as an argument to the `filter()` function:

  ```
  emp_ds.sort(col("empId").asc()).filter(col("salary").gt("250
  0"));
  ```

- `groupBy()`: This groups the dataset using the specified columns, so that one can run aggregation on them:

```
emp_ds.select("job").groupBy(col("job")).count().show();
```

- `join()`: This joins with another dataframe using the given join expression. The function accepts three parameters: the first being another dataset; the second being the column on which the data will be joined; and the third being joinType--inner, outer, left_outer, right_outer, and leftsemi. The following performs a left-outer join between `emp_ds` and `deptDf`:

```
emp_ds.as("A").join(deptDf.as("B"),emp_ds.col("deptno").equalTo(dep
tDf.col("deptno")),"left").select("A.empId","A.empName","A.job","A.
manager","A.hiredate","A.salary","A.comm","A.deptno","B.dname","B.l
oc").show();
```

Temporary view

Spark SQL provides all the capabilities of processing a SQL query by using a temporary view. All the data and metadata information of a temporary view is dropped once the session or application ends. The result of queries in a temporary view is returned as `Dataset<Row>`.

```
deptDf.createOrReplaceTempView("dept");
Dataset<Row> result = sparkSession.sql("select dname,loc from dept where
deptno > 20" );
result.show();
```

Temporary views are accessible within the same session and will throw an error if accessed from another session. The following example will throw an exception `Table or view not found:  dept`, since we are trying to access the temporary view from a new session.

```
deptDf.createOrReplaceTempView("dept");
Dataset<Row> result = sparkSession.sql("select loc,count(loc) from dept
where deptno > 10 group by loc" );
```

In the following section we will discuss how we can avoid such an error and also share data across sessions using a global temporary view.

Global temporary view

Global temporary views are primarily used to share within a session and then get automatically dropped once the session ends. These session-scoped views also serve as a temporary table on which SQL queries can be made and are stored in database `global_temp`. The database name can be changed by modifying the SQL configuration `spark.sql.globalTempDatabase`. However, qualified names should be used to access `GlobalTempView(database.tableName)` or else it throws an error `Table or view not found`:

```
deptDf.createGlobalTempView("dept_global_view");
sparkSession.newSession().sql("SELECT deptno,dname,loc, rank() OVER
(PARTITION BY loc ORDER BY deptno ) FROM
global_temp.dept_global_view").show();
```

While using Thrift Server with a multi-session (`spark.sql.hive.thriftServer.singleSession = false`), a global temporary view can be used to access data from a different session. Prior to Spark 2.1, the only way to share data across sessions was to persist the data and then access it using catalog.

Spark UDF

The UDF is a special way of enhancing the features of SQL in Spark SQL. It operates on a single row and returns a single output value corresponding to the single row. Some of the most common UDFs used are concatenating a string, formatting dates, changing case of string values, and so on. Apart from default UDFs, one can create custom UDFs and register them in Spark SQL with an alias. The alias can then be used as standard function in SQL queries.

Some of the points that need to be taken care of while writing a UDF include:

- In Java, depending on the number of input parameters, the UDF class implements changes so that the UDF having only one input parameter implements UDF1, with two input parameters the class changes to UDF2, and so on
- One can opt for arrays or struct as input parameters to avoid the limitation of having a maximum 22 input parameters

- Once the UDF class has been written and instantiated, it registers the instance in Spark SQL session
- Registered UDFs cannot be used with the **Domain Specific Language** (**DSL**) of a dataframe. The query optimization engine catalyst treats UDFs as a black box without offering any optimization

As an example, let's create a UDF that calculates the number of days between today and the date passed:

```
publicclass CalcDaysUDF implements UDF2<String,String, Long> {
  private static final long serialVersionUID = 1L;
  @Override
  public Long call(String dateString,String format) throws Exception {
    SimpleDateFormat myFormat = new SimpleDateFormat(format);
    Date date1 = myFormat.parse(dateString);
    Date date2 = new Date();
    long diff = date2.getTime() – date1.getTime();
    return TimeUnit.DAYS.convert(diff, TimeUnit.MILLISECONDS);
  }
}
```

Now let's call this class in a SQL query:

```
UDF2 calcDays=new CalcDaysUDF();
//Registering the UDFs in Spark Session created above
sparkSession.udf().register("calcDays", calcDays, DataTypes.LongType);
emp_ds.createOrReplaceTempView("emp_ds");
sparkSession.sql("select calcDays(hiredate,'dd-MM-yyyy') from
emp_ds").show();
```

Spark UDAF

The **user defined aggregate function** (**UDAF**) operates upon more than one row while returning single value results. UDAF normally works in conjunction with a group by clause where some analysis or aggregation may be required on a set of data identified using the group by clause. In Spark, two different types of UDAF can be created untyped and type-safe UDAF.

Untyped UDAF

A custom untyped UDAF can be written extending `UserDefinedAggregateFunction` and then defining the following functions:

- `public StructType inputSchema()`: The datatype of the input argument(s) of the aggregate function is defined in this method.

- `public DataType dataType()`: The return value of the UDAF will correspond to the datatype defined in this method.

- `public boolean deterministic()`: If the function is deterministic, that is, given the same input, always return the same output and it should return true or false.

- `public StructType bufferSchema()`: The internal fields that are required to compute aggregation are defined in this method, such as for calculating the average, one would need sum and count. For a UDAF with two intermediate values of `DoubleType` and `LongType`, the returned `StructType` will be as follows :

  ```
  new StructType() .add("sumVal", DoubleType) .add("countVal",
  LongType)
  ```

  The names of the field defined in `StructType` are used to identify the buffer values.

- `public void initialize(MutableAggregationBuffer arg0)`: The method initializes the values of the fields defined in the `bufferSchema()` method. The rule for initializing the values is that, while applying the merge function on two initial buffers, it should return the same initial buffer, that is, `merge(initialBuffer, initialBuffer)` should equal `initialBuffer`. On each node, the `initialize()` method is called once for each group of rows.

- `public void update(MutableAggregationBuffer arg0, Row arg1)`: The update method updates the values of `bufferSchema()` with new input data from input. Since UDAF operates over multiple rows, this method gets called once per input row.

- `public void merge(MutableAggregationBuffer arg0, Row arg1)`: The `merge` function aggregates two partial `bufferSchema` while returning the updated value in `MutableAggregationBuffer`.

- `public Object evaluate(Row arg0)`: The `evaluate` method operates upon the aggregated `bufferSchema` to return the final output value of datatype defined in method `dataType()`.

As an example, let's understand how average gets calculated in Spark SQL:

```
publicclass AverageUDAF extends UserDefinedAggregateFunction {
  private static final long serialVersionUID = 1L;
  @Override
  public StructType inputSchema() {
    returnnew StructType(new StructField[] { new StructField("counter",
DataTypes.DoubleType, true, Metadata.empty())});
  }

  @Override
  public DataType dataType() {
    return DataTypes.DoubleType;
  }
  @Override
  publicboolean deterministic() {
    return false;
  }

  @Override
  public StructType bufferSchema() {
    returnnew StructType() .add("sumVal", DataTypes.DoubleType)
.add("countVal", DataTypes.DoubleType);
  }

  @Override
  publicvoid initialize(MutableAggregationBuffer bufferAgg) {
    bufferAgg.update(0, 0.0);
    bufferAgg.update(1, 0.0);
  }

  @Override
  publicvoid update(MutableAggregationBuffer bufferAgg, Row row) {
    bufferAgg.update(0, bufferAgg.getDouble(0)+row.getDouble(0));
    bufferAgg.update(1, bufferAgg.getDouble(1)+2.0);
  }

  @Override
  publicvoid merge(MutableAggregationBuffer bufferAgg, Row row) {
    bufferAgg.update(0, bufferAgg.getDouble(0)+row.getDouble(0));
    bufferAgg.update(1, bufferAgg.getDouble(1)+row.getDouble(1));
  }

  @Override
  public Object evaluate(Row row) {
    return row.getDouble(0)/row.getDouble(1);
  }
}
```

Calling the UDAF function from Spark is similar to UDF, that is, instantiate the UDAF function, register to `SparkSession`, and finally call the alias of UDAF used while registering in `SparkSession`:

```
//Instantiate UDAF
AverageUDAF calcAvg= new AverageUDAF();
//Register UDAF to SparkSession
sparkSession.udf().register("calAvg", calcAvg);
//Use UDAF
sparkSession.sql("select deptno,calAvg(salary) from emp_ds group by deptno
").show();
```

Type-safe UDAF:

Type-safe UDAF in Spark can be implemented by extending the abstract class `Aggregator` and applying it to datasets. It is loosely based on `Aggregator` from algebird: `https://github.com/twitter/algebird`. The following methods needs to be defined after extending the `Aggregator` class:

- `public Encoder<Average> bufferEncoder()`: Encoder is for the intermediate value type and is similar to the untyped UDAF function `bufferSchema()`.
- `public Encoder<Double> outputEncoder()`: Specifies the encoder for the final output value type, that is, the output of the UDAF function and similar to untyped the UDAF function `dataType()`.
- `public Average zero()`: The `zero()` method should satisfy the property that any *b + zero = b*. It is similar to the untyped UDAF function `initialize()`.
- `public Average reduce(Average buffer, Employee employee)`: Aggregates two values of the same kind and returns the updated value. It is similar to the untyped UDAF function `update()`.
- `public Average merge(Average b1, Average b2)`: Merges two intermediate values and is similar to the untyped UDAF function `merge()`.
- `public Double finish(Average reduction)`: Calculates the final output of UDAF and is similar to the untyped UDAF function `evaluate()`.

Drawing a similarity between the previous untyped UDAF to calculate the average, let's follow the same objective of calculating the average but using a type-safe UDAF.

Create a class with variables whose final values for a given iteration will determine the output of the UDAF, such as, in the case of average, the two variables are `sum` and `count`:

```
publicclass Average implements Serializable {
  private static final long serialVersionUID = 1L;
  private double sumVal;
  privatelong countVal;
  public Average() {
  }
  public Average(long sumVal, long countVal) {
    super();
    this.sumVal = sumVal;
    this.countVal = countVal;
  }

  publicdouble getSumVal() {
    return sumVal;
  }
  publicvoid setSumVal(double sumVal) {
    this.sumVal = sumVal;
  }
  publiclong getCountVal() {
    return countVal;
  }
  publicvoid setCountVal(long countVal) {
    this.countVal = countVal;
  }
}
```

Create a UDAF class extending the `Aggregator` class of package `org.apache.spark.sql.expressions.Aggregator`:

```
publicclass Average implements Serializable {
  private static final long serialVersionUID = 1L;
  private double sumVal;
  privatelong countVal;
  public Average() {
  }
  public Average(long sumVal, long countVal) {
    super();
    this.sumVal = sumVal;
    this.countVal = countVal;
  }

  publicdouble getSumVal() {
    return sumVal;
  }
  publicvoid setSumVal(double sumVal) {
```

```
      this.sumVal = sumVal;
  }
  publiclong getCountVal() {
    return countVal;
  }
  publicvoid setCountVal(long countVal) {
    this.countVal = countVal;
  }
}publicclass TypeSafeUDAF extends Aggregator<Employee, Average, Double>
implements Serializable{
  private static final long serialVersionUID = 1L;

  public Average zero() {
    returnnew Average(0L, 0L);
  }

  public Average reduce(Average buffer, Employee employee) {
    double newSum = buffer.getSumVal() + employee.getSalary();
    long newCount = buffer.getCountVal() + 1;
    buffer.setSumVal(newSum);
    buffer.setCountVal(newCount);
    return buffer;
  }

  public Average merge(Average b1, Average b2) {
    double mergedSum = b1.getSumVal() + b2.getSumVal();
    long mergedCount = b1.getCountVal() + b2.getCountVal();
    b1.setSumVal(mergedSum);
    b1.setCountVal(mergedCount);
    return b1;
  }

  public Double finish(Average reduction) {
    return ((double) reduction.getSumVal()) / reduction.getCountVal();
  }
  public Encoder<Average> bufferEncoder() {
    return Encoders.bean(Average.class);
  }
  public Encoder<Double> outputEncoder() {
    return Encoders.DOUBLE();
  }
}
```

Instantiate the UDAF class, convert the instance to a typed column giving it an alias as the column name, and then pass it to the dataset:

```
TypeSafeUDAF typeSafeUDAF=new TypeSafeUDAF();
Dataset<Employee> emf = emp_ds.as(Encoders.bean(Employee.class));
TypedColumn<Employee, Double> averageSalary =
typeSafeUDAF.toColumn().name("averageTypeSafe");
Dataset<Double> result = emf.select(averageSalary);
```

Hive integration

Spark is integrated really well with Hive, though it does not include much of its dependencies and expects them to be available in its classpath. The following steps explain how to integrate Spark with Hive:

1. Place `hive-site.xml`, `core-site.xml`, and `hdfs-site.xml` files in the `SPARK_HOME/conf` folder.

2. Instantiate `SparkSession` with Hive support and, if `hive-site.xml` is not configured, then the context automatically creates `metastore_db` in the current directory and creates a `warehouse` directory configured by `spark.sql.warehouse.dir`, which defaults to the directory `spark-warehouse`.

```
SparkSession sparkSession = SparkSession
  .builder()
  .master("local")
  .config("spark.sql.warehouse.dir","Path of Warehouse")
  .appName("DatasetOperations")
  .enableHiveSupport()
  .getOrCreate();
```

3. Once we have created a `SparkSession` with Hive support enabled, we can proceed to use it with the added benefits of query support from Hive. One way to identify the difference between Hive query function support and Spark query function support is by checking all the functions supported by Hive.

```
sparkSession.sql("show functions").show(false);
```

4. If we know the name of the function, then we can also use the `describe` function with the name of the function as follows:

```
sparkSession.sql("DESCRIBE FUNCTION add_months").show(false);
```

5. One can also look for an extended description for usage details of the function:

```
sparkSession.sql("DESCRIBE FUNCTION EXTENDED
add_months").show(false);
```

Table Persistence

The `saveAsTable` function can be used to persist datasets in the Hive metastore as a table. By default, Spark creates a managed table at the path mentioned in configuration `spark.sql.warehouse.di`. The various options of `SaveMode` and format remain the same, as discussed in the previous section.

```
deptDf.write().mode(SaveMode.Overwrite).format("csv").saveAsTable("Departme
nt");
```

Summary

In this chapter, we discussed `SparkSession`, which is the single entry point for Spark in 2.x versions. We talked about the unification of dataset and dataframe APIs. Then, we created a dataset using RDD and discussed various dataset operations with examples. We also learnt how to execute Spark SQL operations on a dataset by creating temporary views. Last but not least, we learnt how to create UDFs in Spark SQL with examples.

In the next chapter, we will learn how to process real-time streams with Spark.

9

Near Real-Time Processing with Spark Streaming

So far in this book, we have discussed batch analytics with Spark using the core libraries and Spark SQL. In this chapter, we will learn about another vertical of Spark that is processing near real-time streams of data. Spark comes with a library known as Spark Streaming, which provides the capability to process data in near real time. This extension of Spark makes it a true general purpose system.

This chapter will the explain internals of Spark Streaming, reading streams of data in Spark from various data sources with examples, and newer extensions of stream processing in Spark known as **structured streaming**.

Introducing Spark Streaming

With the advancement and expansion of big data technologies, most of the companies have shifted their focus towards data-driven decision making. It has now become an essential and integral part of the business. In the current world, not only the analytics is important, but also how early it is made available is important. Offline data analytics, as known as batch analytics, help in providing analytics on the history data. On the other hand, online data analytics showcase what is happening in real time. It helps organizations to take decisions as early as possible to keep themselves ahead of their competitors. Online analytics/near real time analytics is done by reading incoming streams of data, for example user activities for e-commerce websites, and process those streams to get valuable results.

The Spark Streaming API is a library that allows you to process data from live streams at near real time. It provides high scalability, fault tolerance, high throughput, and so on. It also brings stateful APIs over the live data stream out of the box and provides connectors to various data sources, for example, Kafka, Twitter, and Kinesis for reading live data.

Spark Streaming introduced an abstraction known as discretized stream as known as DStream. Incoming streams of data are converted into DStreams, which is internally created as a sequence of RDDs. This enables seamless integration of Spark Streaming with Spark Core components and other extensions such as Spark SQL, MLlib, and so on.

DStream in Spark Streaming is represented by a stream of data divided in small batches as known as micro batches. The Spark Streaming API transforms the stream of data into micro batches and feeds it to the Spark engine for processing.

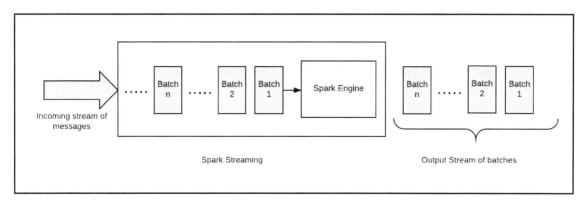

Thus Spark Streaming clubs advantage of batch processing with streaming. Instead of processing an event at a time, a small batch of events is processed at once. This allows Spark to keep a unified programming paradigm for both batch and real-time streaming verticals.

Before proceeding with a Spark Streaming example, let's discuss the concept of micro batching in detail:

Understanding micro batching

Micro batching is defined as the procedure in which the incoming stream of messages is processed by dividing them into group of small batches. This helps to achieve the performance benefits of batch processing; however, at the same time, it helps to keep the latency of processing of each message minimal.

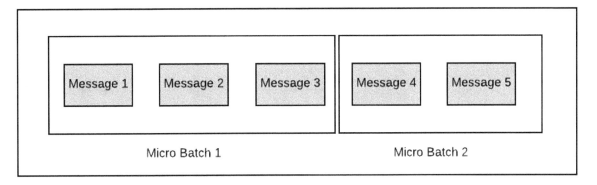

Here, an incoming stream of messages is treated as a flow of small batches of messages and each batch is passed to a processing engine, which outputs a processed stream of batches.

In Spark Streaming, a micro batch is created based on time instead of size, that is, events received in a certain time interval, usually in milliseconds, are grouped together into a batch. This assures that any message does not have to wait much before processing and helps to keep latency of processing under control.

Another advantage of micro batching is that it helps to keep the volume of control message lower. For example, if a system requires an acknowledgement is to be sent by the processing engine for every message processed then, in case of micro batching, one acknowledgement is to be sent per batch of messages rather than per message.

Micro batching comes with a disadvantage as well. In failure scenarios, the whole batch needs to be replayed even if only one message within the batch has failed.

Getting started with Spark Streaming jobs

Unlike all the previous batch jobs, streaming jobs are unique in its sense that it is a continuous running job and Spark Streaming is no exception to this rule despite being called micro batched. Before discussing any further let's first write a hello world program in Spark Streaming and what better to start with than a word count problem on a streaming source, a socket. In the following example, we will count the number of words each micro batch has:

```
SparkConf sparkConf = new
SparkConf().setAppName("WordCountSocketEx").setMaster("local[*]");
JavaStreamingContext streamingContext = new JavaStreamingContext(sparkConf,
Durations.seconds(1));

JavaReceiverInputDStream<String> StreamingLines =
```

```
streamingContext.socketTextStream( "IP_OF_THE_SOCKET",
Integer.parseInt("PORT_OF_THE_SOCKET"), StorageLevels.MEMORY_AND_DISK_SER);
JavaDStream<String> words = StreamingLines.flatMap( str ->
Arrays.asList(str.split(" ")).iterator() );
JavaPairDStream<String, Integer> wordCounts = words.mapToPair(str-> new
Tuple2<>(str, 1)).reduceByKey((count1,count2) ->count1+count2 );
wordCounts.print();
streamingContext.start();
streamingContext.awaitTermination();
```

In the example, a couple of points that need to be observed while writing a streaming job are as follows:

- For any streaming job, create a `StreamingContext`, in case of Java it's `JavaStreamingContext`.
- Each streaming context accepts two parameters, `SparkConf` and `batchDuration`. Batch duration determines the interval of micro batching and hence should be chosen very carefully.
- Any Spark Streaming job does not start computation until and unless the `start()` method of streaming context is called.
- Also call the method `awaitTermination()` or `stop()` explicitly to stop the streaming job.
- Never set the master URL as `local` or `local[1]` as that transpires into running only one thread per job. While DStream-based receivers (sockets, Kafka, Flume, Kinesis, and so on), require one thread to execute the receiver while the other can be used for processing the DStream data. Hence it is always suggested to use `local[n]` configuration with n being greater than one or better still one can use `local[*]`. Similar logic can be extended to Streaming jobs running on clusters as well, the number of cores allocated to the Spark Streaming application must be more than the number of receivers.
- Also add the following Maven dependency for working with Spark Streaming:

```
<dependency>
  <groupId>org.apache.spark</groupId>
  <artifactId>spark-streaming_2.11</artifactId>
  <version>2.1.1</version>
</dependency>
```

 To stream data on a socket one can use the utility/command on Linux-based machines called Netcat. Use the following command to create a server-side socket for streaming data:
```
$nc -lk <Port Number>
```

Streaming sources

Streaming sources are segregated into two categories in Spark Streaming, that is, basic source and advance source. All those sources that are directly available through `StreamingContext`, such as filesystem and socket streams are called **basic sources** while sources that require dependency linkages, as in the case of Kafka, Flume, and so on are called **advanced sources**. Streaming sources can also be defined on the basis of reliability; if an acknowledgement is sent to the source system after receiving and replicating the messages then such receivers are called **reliable receivers**, such as the Kafka API. Similarly if the system does not send an acknowledgement to the source system then they are termed as unreliable.

Some common streaming sources apart from socket streaming, which were discussed in previous examples, are explained in the next section.

fileStream

Data files from any directory can be read from a directory using the `fileStream()` API of `StreamingContext`. The `fileStream()` API accepts four values, that is, the directory being watched for the files to be streamed, the `key` class, the `value` class, and the `InputFormat` class. For files compatible with Hadoop and having text data can use the following syntax for streaming data:

```
streamingContext.fileStream(inputDirectory, LongWritable.class, Text.class,
TextInputFormat.class)
```

There is another simpler API that hides all the key, value, and text input format details and comes in handy while reading simple text files:

```
streamingContext.textFileStream(inputDirectory);
```

One important point of difference from previous examples of socket streaming is that since for streaming filesystems data one does not need receivers and hence an extra thread is not required for running receiver process. Some key points to remember while processing file stream data is that only files that have been moved after the Spark job have be launched in running state is considered, also the file should not be changed once it has been moved to the streaming directory.

Kafka

Kafka is a publish-subscribe messaging system that provides a reliable Spark Streaming source. With the latest Kafka direct API, it provides one-to-one mapping between Kafka's partition and the DStream generated RDDs partition along with access to metadata and offset. Since, Kafka is an advanced streaming source as far as Spark Streaming is concerned, one needs to add its dependency in the build tool of the streaming application. The following is the artifact that should be added in the build tool of one's choice before starting with Kafka integration:

```
groupId = org.apache.spark
artifactId = spark-streaming-kafka-0-10_2.11
version = 2.1.1
```

After adding the dependency, one also needs basic information about the Kafka setup, such as the server(s) on which Kafka is hosted (`bootstrap.servers`) and some of the basic configurations describing the message, such as sterilizer, group ID, and so on. The following are a few common properties used to describe a Kafka connection:

- `bootstrap.servers`: This describes the host and port of Kafka server(s) separated by a comma.
- `key.deserializer`: This is the name of the class to deserialize the key of the messages from Kafka.
- `value.deserializer`: This refers to the class that deserializes the value of the message. Usually, since the message is text and hence `StringSerializer` class suffice the need.
- `group.id`: This uniquely identifies the group of consumer processes to which a message consumer belongs.
- `auto.offset.reset`: This is used when we being to consume messages from a topic in Kafka, but does not have initial offset in Kafka or if the current offset does not exist anymore on the server then one of the following options helps Kafka strategies on deciding the offset:
    - `earliest`: This automatically reset the offset to the earliest offset
    - `latest`: This automatically reset the offset to the latest offset
    - `none`: This throws exception to the consumer if no previous offset is found for the consumer's

Before moving any further let's fist have an understanding as to how a basic Kafka consumer will be written in Spark Streaming. As a use case we will try and consume tweets from a Kafka streaming source and count the hashtags within each micro batch interval:

```
JavaSparkContext sc = new JavaSparkContext(conf);
        JavaStreamingContext streamingContext = new
JavaStreamingContext(sc, Durations.minutes(2));
        Map<String, Object> kafkaParams = new HashMap<>();
        kafkaParams.put("bootstrap.servers", "10.0.75.1:9092");
        kafkaParams.put("key.deserializer", StringDeserializer.class);
        kafkaParams.put("value.deserializer", StringDeserializer.class);
        kafkaParams.put("group.id",
"use_a_separate_group_id_for_each_strea");
        kafkaParams.put("auto.offset.reset", "latest");
        Collection<String> topics = Arrays.asList("mytopic",
"anothertopic");
SparkConf sparkConf = new
SparkConf().setAppName("WordCountSocketEx").setMaster("local[*]");
        final JavaInputDStream<ConsumerRecord<String, String>> stream =
KafkaUtils.createDirectStream(streamingContext,LocationStrategies.PreferCon
sistent(),
                        ConsumerStrategies.<String,
String>Subscribe(topics, kafkaParams));

        JavaPairDStream<String, String> pairRDD = stream.mapToPair(record->
new Tuple2<>(record.key(), record.value()));
        pairRDD.foreachRDD(pRDD-> { pRDD.foreach(tuple->
System.out.println(new Date()+" :: Kafka msg key ::"+tuple._1() +" the val
is ::"+tuple._2()));});
        JavaDStream<String> tweetRDD = pairRDD.map(x-> x._2()).map(new
TweetText());
        tweetRDD.foreachRDD(tRDD -> tRDD.foreach(x->System.out.println(new
Date()+" :: "+x)));
        JavaDStream<String> hashtagRDD = tweetRDD.flatMap(twt->
Arrays.stream(twt.split(" ")).filter(str->
str.contains("#")).collect(Collectors.toList()).iterator() );
        hashtagRDD.foreachRDD(tRDD ->
tRDD.foreach(x->System.out.println(x)));
        JavaPairDStream<String, Long> cntByVal = hashtagRDD.countByValue();
        cntByVal.foreachRDD(tRDD -> tRDD.foreach(x->System.out.println(new
Date()+" ::The count tag is ::"+x._1() +" and the val is ::"+x._2())));
```

As discussed in the previous section, for any streaming application we need a `StreamingContext` and the same is true for Kafka as well. After creating `StreamingContext` one should define the configuration parameter for the Kafka connector and group them together in a Map, similarly group all topics in a collection List. Now we use `KafkaUtils` helper method `createDirectStream()` to create a DStream object by passing `StreamingContext`, `LocationStrategy`, and `ConsumerStrategy`, which encompass a collection of topics and consumer configuration map. This is sufficient to consume Kafka messages as DStreams, where each message from Kafka has a key and value pair. However, we are more interested in the value part of the message that contains tweets, so we filter the tweet text and then split the word having whitespace and finally counting each word containing hashtag.

This section covered basics of streaming sources. Some aspects of consuming messages from Kafka needs more detail and understanding of the use case as well and hence is out of scope in current context. Nevertheless Kafka and Spark documentation covers in detail on how offset strategies can be custom implemented and state can be recovered from a failure using check pointing (refer to the *Fault tolerance and reliability* section) and other mechanisms. In the next section, we will learn about stream transformation such as stateful and stateless operations.

Streaming transformations

As in the previous word count example, we saw that words from each line were being counted once and for the next set of records the counter was reset again. But what if we want to add the previous state count to the new set of words in the following batch to come? Can we do that and how? The answer to the first part of the question is, in Spark Streaming there are two kinds of transformation, stateful and stateless transformation, so if we want to preserve the previous state then one will have to opt for stateful transformation rather than the stateless transformation that we achieved in the previous example.

Stream processing can be stateless or stateful based on the requirement. Some stream processing problems may require maintaining a state over a period of time, others may not.

Consider that an airline company wants to process data consistiting of the temperature reading of all active a flights at real time. If the airline wants to just print or store the reading received from flight at real time than no state needs to be maintained and it is considered as stateless stream processing. Another scenario is that every 10 minutes, the airline wants to find out the average of temperature readings of the last one hour for every active flight. In this case, a window of one hour can be defined with a sliding interval of 10 minutes. Hence, in this scenario state needs to be maintained and it can be considered as stateful stream processing within a window time frame.

Suppose if an airline wants to find the average temperature reading of an entire journey of every flight, that is, from the time the flight takes off to the time it lands then an external state needs to be maintained since the duration of journey will be different for different flights and also flights can be delayed as well. Hence, no particular window duration can be defined. Such streaming use case is considered stateful stream processing too whose state is maintained throughout the session of execution of a Spark Streaming job.

Let's develop these use cases using Spark Streaming.

Consider, after taking off flights are sending data in the following JSON format:

```
{"flightId":"tz302","timestamp":1494423926816,"temperature":21.12,"landed":
false}
where flightId = unique id of the flight
timestamp = time at which event is generated
temperature = temperature reading at the time of event generation
landed =  boolean flag which defines whether flight has been landed or
still on the way

Following POJO will be used to map messages to Java Object for further
processing

public class FlightDetails implements Serializable {
    private String flightId;
    private double temp;
    private boolean landed;
private long temperature;
}
```

 In this example, we will be reading messages from a socket. In real-world scenarios, messages should be pushed to durable message brokers/queues such as Kafka, Kinesis, and so on.

Stateless transformation

The simplest stateless transformation is a map function where each passing element is treated independent of each other. In the following example, we will read incoming messages from a stream and map it to FlightDetails objects as follows:

```
JavaReceiverInputDStream<String> inStream=
jssc.socketTextStream("localhost", 9999);
JavaDStream<FlightDetails> flightDetailsStream = inStream.map(x -> {
            ObjectMapper mapper = new ObjectMapper();
            return mapper.readValue(x, FlightDetails.class);
});
```

Incoming messages can be printed or be stored hdfs as follows:

```
flightDetailsStream.print();
flightDetailsStream.foreachRDD((VoidFunction<JavaRDD<FlightDetails>>) rdd
-> rdd.saveAsTextFile("hdfs://namenode:port/path"));
```

Some common stateless transformation are shown in the following table:

Transformation	Description
flatMap(func)	Returns a DStream of flattened data; that is, each input item can return more than one output item
filter(func)	Filters the record satisfying the function passed as an argument
join(otherStream, [numTasks])	For a DStream having a pair RDDs of *(K, V)* and *(K, X)* it returns a new DStream having pair RDDs *(k, (V,X))*
union(otherStream)	A DStream is retuned having union of element of two different DStreams
count()	Returns a new DStream of single element RDDs by counting the number of elements in each RDD of the source DStream
reduce(func)	The aggregate function reduces the elements of a DStream while returning a new DStream of single element RDDs
reduceByKey(func, [numTasks])	For a pair DStream RDD, it returns a new DStream of *(K, V)* pairs where the values for each key are aggregated using the given reduce function

Stateful transformation

Stateful transformation maintains the state across a period of time, which is greater than the micro batch interval and can be as long as an entire session of Spark Streaming jobs. This is achieved by creating checkpoints on streaming applications, though strictly speaking, windowing (refer to the Windowing section) may not require checkpoints, but other operations on windowing may. Let's find out how we can checkpoint our streaming application.

Checkpointing

In `Chapter 4`, *Understanding Spark Programming Model*, we discussed various techniques of caching/persisting RDDs to avoid all the re-computation in cases of failures. The same techniques can be followed with a DStream type as well. However, as streaming applications are meant to run all the time, an application may fail because of system failures or network failures as well. To make the Spark Streaming application capable of recovering from such failures, it should be checkpointed to all external locations, most likely a fault tolerant storage such as HDFS and so on.

Spark Streaming allows us to checkpoint the following types of information:

- **Metadata checkpointing**: This helps to checkpoint the metadata of the Spark Streaming application such as configurations provided to the application while submitting, the batches of data that are in processing, and a set of operations defined to be executed to incoming DStreams, and so on.
- **Data checkpointing/generated DStream checkpointing**: This helps to checkpoint generated DStreams in case of stateful operations as generated DStreams can be combination of various transformed DStreams across multiple batches and this chain keeps on increasing in a streaming application. So it must be checkpointed.

Checkpoint generated DStreams, in the case of stateful transformations, are mandatory in Spark Streaming. However, users can also create checkpoints in case of stateless transformations to checkpoint metadata of the Spark Streaming application or to avoid re-computation. Even RDDs can be checkpointed.

To enable checkpointing in Spark Streaming applications, the following method can be called on the Spark Streaming context:

```
jssc.checkpoint("/path/of/the/checkpoint_directory");
```

It is suggested to keep checkpoints in a fault tolerant filesystem, preferably HDFS.

Two types of transformation, that is, windowing based, and full session based can be implemented with state in Spark Streaming. Full session stateful transformation maintains session throughout the life cycle of any Spark Streaming job and one of the most popular methods that maintains the state throughout the life cycle is `updateStateByKey`. However, Apache Spark 1.6 introduced an efficient alternative to `updateStateBykey` that is not only better in performance, but is easier to code as well.

Let's calculate the average temperature of flights for the entire journey of the flight. As different flights have different journey times and keeping the flight delay situation in mind, we will solve this use case using the `mapWithState` stateful stream processing.

The `mapWithState` transformation can be executed on the `PairDStream` type, so let's convert our `flightDetailsStream` to the `PairStream` type with the key as `flightId` and the value as `flightDetailsObject`:

```
JavaPairDStream<String, FlightDetails> flightDetailsPairStream =
flightDetailsStream.mapToPair(f -> new Tuple2<String,
FlightDetails>(f.getFlightId(), f));
```

The `mapWithState` transformation accepts an object of `org.apache.spark.streaming.StateSpec`, which is of an abstract type.

The implementation of which requires an implementation of:

```
org.apache.spark.api.java.function.Function3 or
org.apache.spark.api.java.function.Function4 type.
```

The following is the implementation of a `Function3` interface that will be used to create a `StateSpec` object:

```
Function3<String, Optional<FlightDetails>, State<List<FlightDetails>>,
Tuple2<String, Double>> mappingFunc = (flightId, curFlightDetail, state) ->
{
                //fetch existing state else create  new list.
                List<FlightDetails> details = state.exists() ?
state.get() : new ArrayList<>();
                boolean isLanded = false;
           /*if optionsla object is present, add it in the list and check
set the boolean flag 'islanded' to true if flight has landed*/
                if (curFlightDetail.isPresent()) {
                details.add(curFlightDetail.get());
                if (curFlightDetail.get().isLanded()) {
                    isLanded = true;
                }
            }
//Calculate average value of the all temperature values
```

```
            Double avgSpeed = details.stream().mapToDouble(f ->
f.getTemperature()).average().orElse(0.0);

        /*Remove the state if flight has landed else update the state with
the updated list of FlightDetails objects */
        if (isLanded) {
                state.remove();
        } else {
                state.update(details);
        }
        //Return the current average
return new Tuple2<String, Double>(flightId, avgSpeed);
};
```

As shown in the preceding code example, `Function3` contains four parameters that will be used to create a `StateSpec` object:

- `KeyType`: Type of key of `PairStream`, which is `String` in our case.
- `Optional<ValueType>`: Optional object of `ValueType`, which is `FlightDetails` in our case. This parameter is optional since a batch may or may not contain data for a particular key.
- `org.apache.spark.streaming.State<T>`: We are storing the state as `List<FightDetails>`.
- `MappedType`: This is the final type the user wants to output. As we want to evaluate the average temperature, we have kept it as a `Double` type.

 Please do read the comments added in the code to understand the working of the `Function3` implementation.

Now, we will execute the stateful transformation of `flightDetailsPairStream` as follows:

```
JavaMapWithStateDStream<String, FlightDetails, List<FlightDetails>,
Tuple2<String, Double>> mapWithState =
flightDetailsPairStream.mapWithState(StateSpec.function(mappingFunc));

mapWithState.print();
```

 As defined in the previous section, the following statements need to be added at the end of every streaming application to start streaming context:
```
jssc.start();
jssc.awaitTermination();
```

Every time a message is received for the flight average of the temperature until that time is calculated and printed and once the flight lands the final average is calculated and the state will be removed.

In real-world scenarios, it is possible that devices that are emitting messages fail because of some reason. So to handle such scenarios, timeout can be configured to remove the state if any message is not received in some specific duration.

Timeout can be configured while defining `StateSpec` objects as follows:

```
flightDetailsPairStream.mapWithState(StateSpec.function(mappingFunc).timeou
t(Durations.minutes(5)));
```

This signifies that if a device does not send a message in five minutes then state will be removed. The user can set the timeout limit based on the requirement.

Windowing

In Spark Streaming, an incoming stream of messages are grouped based on an interval, called a batch interval, and the system receives the data in batches of batch interval. So if we have created a `StreamingContext` having a batch interval of say two minutes then the input DStream will generate RDDs from the received data at an interval of two minutes each and will process them independently. However, for use cases such as calculating word count on the last eight minutes of data every two minutes or maybe finding maximum value of stocks in the last half an hour of reading every six minutes one would require state of RDDs from the previous batch interval. To solve these kinds of use cases where state of a RDD from any batch interval is maintained for a certain finite interval we use window-based stateful transformations.

A window is defined using two parameters, which is `windowDuration` and `slideInterval`. As shown in the following diagram, window of length 8 minutes is defined, which is sliding every two minutes. In this case, the incoming stream of messages will be collected for 8 minutes at first and then at the tenth minute, the messages received in the first two minutes will be discarded and a window will be formed with messages received between second to tenth minute and this process will keep on repeating every two minutes.

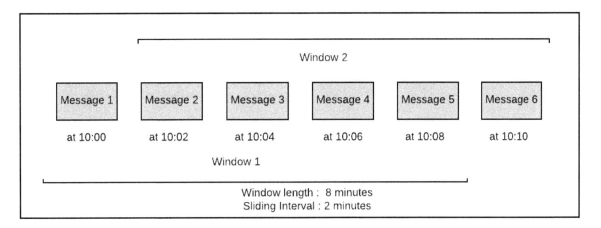

Hence, as per the diagram, **Window 1** will contain **Message 1** to **Message 5** and **Window 2** will contain **Message 2** to **Message 6**, and so on, which is radically different from stateless transformation where a message that belongs to one batch does not fall in the other batch.

All windowing processes do not necessarily need to maintain any external checkpoint and the state can be kept in memory, however, there are chances of losing data in case of driver failure. Sliding window on the incoming stream can be defined on JavaDStream RDD by calling the following function:

```
window(Duration windowDuration, Duration slideDuration)
```

So in a windowing process, a window of fixed duration keeps on sliding as per slide interval value, but it must be noted that the window duration and slide duration must be a multiple of batch interval as the received data is divided in batches of batch interval.

Window duration and slide interval of window stream is shown in the following table:

Window stream (batch interval 2 minute)	Description
`jDStream.window(Durations.minutes(8))`	Valid window stream
`jDStream.window(Durations.minutes(8),Durations.minutes(2))`	Valid window stream
`jDStream.window(Durations.minutes(12),Durations.minutes(8))`	Valid window stream

`jDStream.window(Durations.minutes(2),Durations.minutes(2))`	Valid window stream
`jDStream.window(Durations.minutes(12),Durations.minutes(12))`	Valid window stream
`jDStream.window(Durations.minutes(5),Durations.minutes(2))`	Invalid window stream as window duration is not a multiple of batch interval
`jDStream.window(Durations.minutes(10),Durations.minutes(1))`	Invalid window stream as slide duration is not a multiple of batch interval

Now let's define a window on incoming streams of data to find out average temperature of every active flight (flights that are sending data) in the last one hour and this result should be computed every 10 minutes:

```
JavaDStream<FlightDetails> window =
flightDetailsStream.window(Durations.minutes(60),Durations.minutes(10));
```

We can execute, transformation on the window to find the average temperature of every active flight as follows:

```
JavaPairDStream<String, Double> transfomedWindow = window.mapToPair(f->new
Tuple2<String,Double>(f.getFlightId(),f.getTemperature())).
      mapValues(t->new Tuple2<Double,Integer>(t,1))
      .reduceByKey((t1, t2) -> new Tuple2<Double,
Integer>(t1._1()+t2._1(), t1._2()+t2._2())).mapValues(t -> t._1()/t._2());
  transfomedWindow.cache();
transfomedWindow.print();
```

This transformation will be executed every time the window slides, that is, every 10 minutes in this case.

It is always suggested to checkpoint the DStream in a windowing operation just to avoid recomputing in case of failures as there are chances of losing data in case of failures in streaming applications.

 As defined in the previous section, the following statements need to be added at the end of every streaming application to start the streaming context:
```
jssc.start();
jssc.awaitTermination();
```

In this section, we learned about stateless and stateful transformations in Spark Streaming. In the next section, we will perform exercises with Spark Streaming by connecting to various sources for reading streams of data.

Transform operation

So far we have done transformation of DStreams, but not all operations of RDD are available in the DStream API. The transform operation overcomes such a limitation and allows RDD operations on the DStream. Assume a scenario where the DStream data can be joined with RDD and then some analytical operations can be applied on them. This exposes streaming data to a whole set of atypical operation available in the RDD and hence makes it extremely powerful.

As an example let's assume that we have a list of words whose weightage should be preferential when compared with other words. So now if we run our word count example, if the words from RDD exist in DStream then the count should reflect the summed up value from the RDD and the DStream:

```
JavaStreamingContext streamingContext = new JavaStreamingContext(sparkConf,
Durations.seconds(1));
```

```java
List<Tuple2<String, Integer>> tuples = Arrays.asList(new Tuple2<>("hello",
10), new Tuple2<>("world", 10));
JavaPairRDD<String, Integer> initialRDD =
streamingContext.sparkContext().parallelizePairs(tuples);

JavaReceiverInputDStream<String> StreamingLines =
streamingContext.socketTextStream( "IP_OF_THE_SOCKET",
Integer.parseInt("PORT"), StorageLevels.MEMORY_AND_DISK_SER);

JavaDStream<String> words = StreamingLines.flatMap( str ->
Arrays.asList(str.split(" ")).iterator() );

JavaPairDStream<String, Integer> wordCounts = words.mapToPair(str-> new
Tuple2<>(str, 1)).reduceByKey((count1,count2) ->count1+count2 );

wordCounts.print();

JavaPairDStream<String, Integer> joinedDstream =
wordCounts.transformToPair(newFunction<JavaPairRDD<String, Integer>,
JavaPairRDD<String, Integer>>() {
  @Override
  public JavaPairRDD<String, Integer> call(JavaPairRDD<String, Integer>
rdd) throws Exception {
    JavaPairRDD<String, Integer> modRDD = rdd.join(initialRDD).mapToPair(
      newPairFunction<Tuple2<String, Tuple2<Integer, Integer>>, String,
Integer>() {
        @Override
        public Tuple2<String, Integer> call(
          Tuple2<String, Tuple2<Integer, Integer>> joinedTuple) throws
Exception {
            returnnew Tuple2<>(joinedTuple._1(),(joinedTuple._2()._1() +
joinedTuple._2()._2()));
        }
      });
      return modRDD;
  }
});
joinedDstream.print();
streamingContext.start();
streamingContext.awaitTermination();
```

In this example, we have used `transformToPair` to join our DStream to the RDD and using the `mapToPair` function, which is available for RDDs, we sum up the values if the key words match. These kinds of transform operations show the versatility so Spark exposes the same set of data to different Spark modules and hence solving inter domain use cases without writing multiple jobs.

Fault tolerance and reliability

Streaming jobs are designed to run continuously and failure in the job can result in loss of data, state, or both. Making streaming jobs fault tolerant becomes one of the essential goals of writing the streaming job in the first place. Any streaming job comes with some guarantees either by design or by implementing certain configuration features, which mandates how many times a message will be processed by the system:

- **At most once guarantee**: Records in such systems can either be processed once or not at all. These systems are least reliable as far as streaming solution is concerned.
- **At least once guarantee**: The system will process the record at least once and hence by design there will be no loss of messages, but then messages can be processed multiple times giving the problem of duplication. This scenario however is better than the previous case and there are use cases where duplicate data may not cause any problem or can easily be deduced.
- **Exactly once guarantee**: Records here will be processed exactly once with an assurance that neither the data will be lost nor the data will be processed multiple times. This is an achievable ideal scenario any streaming job vouch for either by design or by configuration changes.

Now with these three possible guarantees let's understand the failure scenarios in a Spark Streaming job and if possible how each one can be recovered. Any Spark job on a high level comprises of three stages, that is, data receiver, transformation, and output with the possibility of failure occurring at any stage. In order for a streaming job to guarantee end to end exactly once processing each stage of the job should provide the same guarantee too. Stages of Spark Streaming job is as follows:

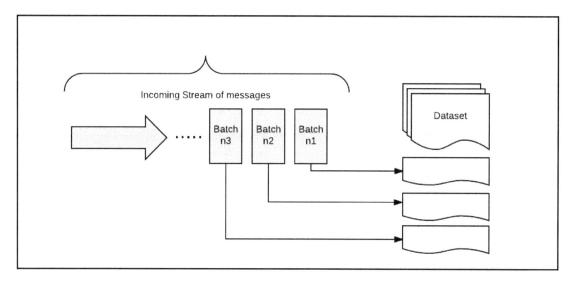

Data receiver stage

Failure at the data receiver stage can occur because of multiple reasons of different receivers and, accordingly, the processing guarantee varies from exactly once to at least once.

File streams

If a streaming job processes the data from a filesystem, which is fault tolerant, such as HDFS, GlusterFS, MapR-FS, and so on, then Spark Streaming will always give a guarantee of processing the data exactly once since it is always able to recover the data from filesystem.

Advanced streaming sources

For receiver-based sources, fault tolerance of a streaming job depends on two factors, which are failure scenario and type of receiver. A receiver receives the data and replicates them on two Spark executors to achieve fault tolerance and hence if one of the executors fails then the tasks and receivers are executed on another node by Spark without any data loss. However, if the driver fails then by design all the executors fail and the computed data and other meta information gets lost. To achieve fault tolerance on a driver node checkpointing of DStreams should be done, which saves the DAG of DStreams to fault-tolerant storage of the checkpoint. When the failed driver gets restarted it looks for meta information from the checkpoint location to launch new executors and restart the receivers. However, to restart a failed Driver, mentioning the checkpoint folder location is not enough. Automatic driver restart configuration needs to be used while submitting the job on a cluster, for example, in YARN the job should be run in cluster mode and number of retries set in configuration `yarn.resourcemanager.am.max-attempts`. Similarly in Spark standalone mode one should submit the Spark job with cluster mode and `-- supervise` while in Mesos marathon can restart applications or use the `--supervise` flag.

Apart from setting cluster configuration, the restarted job should be able to figure out if the streaming job has to recover the `StreamingContext` from the checkpoint or create a new one. This can be achieved by writing the code with following guidelines:

- The setup code should be written in a function that returns a `StreamingContext`.
- Within the same function, also mention the `checkpoint` directory as an argument to the method `checkpoint()` on `StreamingContext`.
- Set up a context by using the factory method `getOrCreate()` on `StreamingContext` and passing the arguments as the `checkpoint` directory and the name of the function returning `StreamingContext`. When the streaming job gets restarted it first looks into the `checkpoint` directory first to create the `StremaingContext` and if it does not exist in the said folder then it creates a new one.

In the previous sections, we went through an example of writing a streaming word count job accepting data from a socket. We can extend the same example to make the streaming job recoverable in case of driver failure by refactoring the code and moving the streaming logic to a function that returns `StreamingContext`. We have also made the job stateful by adding a `mapWithState` function that holds a word and its count during the entire session:

```
protectedstatic JavaStreamingContext createContext(String ip, int port,
String checkpointDirectory) {
```

```
  SparkConf sparkConf = new
SparkConf().setAppName("WordCountRecoverableEx");
  JavaStreamingContext streamingContext = new
JavaStreamingContext(sparkConf, Durations.seconds(1));
  streamingContext.checkpoint(checkpointDirectory);
  // Initial state RDD input to mapWithState
  @SuppressWarnings("unchecked")
  List<Tuple2<String, Integer>> tuples = Arrays.asList(new
Tuple2<>("hello", 1), new Tuple2<>("world", 1));
  JavaPairRDD<String, Integer> initialRDD =
streamingContext.sparkContext().parallelizePairs(tuples);
  JavaReceiverInputDStream<String> StreamingLines =
streamingContext.socketTextStream(ip,port,
  StorageLevels.MEMORY_AND_DISK_SER);
  JavaDStream<String> words = StreamingLines.flatMap(str ->
Arrays.asList(str.split(" ")).iterator());
  JavaPairDStream<String, Integer> wordCounts = words.mapToPair(str -> new
Tuple2<>(str, 1)).reduceByKey((count1, count2) -> count1 + count2);

  // Update the cumulative count function
  Function3<String, Optional<Integer>, State<Integer>, Tuple2<String,
Integer>> mappingFunc = newFunction3<String, Optional<Integer>,
State<Integer>, Tuple2<String, Integer>>() {
    i
    public Tuple2<String, Integer> call(String word,
Optional<In@Overrideteger> one, State<Integer> state) {
      int sum = one.orElse(0) + (state.exists() ? state.get() : 0);
      Tuple2<String, Integer> output = new Tup;le2<>(word, sum);
      state.update(sum);
      return output;
    }
  };
  // DStream made of get cumulative counts that get updated in every batch
  JavaMapWithStateDStream<String, Integer, Integer, Tuple2<String,
Integer>> stateDstream =
wordCounts.mapWithState(StateSpec.function(mappingFunc).initialState(initia
lRDD));
  stateDstream.print();
  return streamingContext;
}
```

The `createContext()` method can now be called from the main method as follows:

```
Function0<JavaStreamingContext> createContextFunc =
newFunction0<JavaStreamingContext>() {
  @Override
  public JavaStreamingContext call() {
    returncreateContext(ip, port, checkpointDirectory);
  }
};
JavaStreamingContext ssc =
JavaStreamingContext.getOrCreate(checkpointDirectory, createContextFunc);
ssc.start();
ssc.awaitTermination();
```

Although enabling checkpoints by the following previous guidelines does guarantee recovery of Spark driver, in-memory blocks of buffered data are lost on the driver restart. Reliable receivers send acknowledgements to the source hence in case if a receiver fails while buffering the data itself then no acknowledgement will be sent to the source. When the receiver recovers, the source will again send the data that will be consumed and acknowledged by the receivers. But a scenario can arise when the acknowledgement has been sent, but while the message is being processed, the driver fails and by design all other executors also get killed and hence the data being operated upon gets lost. On the other hand, unreliable receivers do not send acknowledgement in the first place and hence the data may be lost when the receiver recovers from failure. To overcome this problem Spark Streaming introduced a feature called **write ahead log** (**WAL**), which writes the data to the checkpoint directory first and then the streaming processing starts. In case of driver recovery with WAL enabled, the data is read from `checkpoint` directory and any loss of data by driver is avoided. Though this process slightly degrades the performance, it makes driver recovery data loss free. WAL can be enabled by setting the following Spark configuration to `true`:

```
sparkConf.set("spark.streaming.receiver.writeAheadLog.enable", "true")
```

WAL, along with checkpoints, ensures at least once semantics (no data loss), but not *exactly once* processing guarantee. Let's analyze a scenario where the receiver writes the data in WAL, but fails while trying to update Kafka offset. After a while the receiver recovers from failure and first processes the messages from WAL and then requests for a new set of data from Kafka, but since the offset was not updated in Kafka when the receiver failed hence Kafka will again send the same set of data and the message will be processed again. Though in some use cases this may not be of any concern while in others some mechanism has to be developed to process such duplicate records.

To overcome duplicity of data and ensure exactly once semantics, Spark Streaming introduced, Kafka Direct API, as described in the streaming sources section, which does away with WAL and treats Kafka as a filesystem while consuming data from the topic. Some salient features of Kafka Direct API are:

- It ensures exactly once semantics
- Data is not consumed using Kafka receivers, but a simple consumer API is used by executors to consume data directly from Kafka
- WAL is not used in case of failure, data is re-consumed in case of recovering from any failure directly from Kafka
- Spark driver calculates the offset range to be consumed in the next micro batch interval and then it is Spark executor, which uses simple consumer API to consume those offsets

Transformation stage

Once the data has been received by a DStreams, it transforms them to RDDs and they are then processed using the Spark core engine. As far as processing of data in Spark core is concerned it is exactly once as the transformation on received input RDD will always have the same set of records and hence the same output.

Output stage

By default, output operations guarantee at least once processing of streaming messages. Operations where we are writing the output to disk is sufficient as even if the data gets written more than once it will only overwrite the data already written to disk and hence it gives an impression of processing the data only once. Care should be taken in case of operations where we iterate over each elements of DStream such as `foreachRDD` because in case of failure the same data can be traversed again we do not have any automatic mechanisms to deal with it. There are a couple of guidelines that one can follow to achieve exactly once semantics:

- **Idempotent operation**: The simplest way to ensure exactly once semantics in output operation is to make sure the operations is idempotent, as is the case in `saveAs***Files` operations, the same data gets written to files multiple times, overwriting the previous failed attempts.
- **Transactional updates**: If an identifier can be identified per micro batch then the successive operation can be made transactional by keeping a check if the identifier is getting repeated or not and if it does get repeated then determining how to handle them. The discretion of choosing the identifier is open to the design of writing streaming code, however, one of the popular approaches is to use batch time available in `foreachRDD` and the partition index of the RDD to create an identifier.

Structured Streaming

Structured is a brand new edition in Apache Spark's streaming processing vertical. It is a stream processing engine built on top of the Spark SQL engine. With the introduction of structured streaming, a unification bond of batch processing and stream processing as it allows us to develop a stream processing is enabled application similar to the batch processing application. At the same time, it is scalable and fault tolerant as well.

As per Apache Spark's documentation, *Structured Streaming provides fast, scalable, fault-tolerant, end-to-end exactly-once stream processing without the user having to reason about streaming.*

Instead of using DStream in structured streaming, the dataset API can be used and it is the responsibility of the Spark SQL engine to keep the dataset updated as new streaming data arrives. As the dataset API is used, all the Spark SQL operations are available. Therefore, users can use SQL queries on the stream data using the optimized Spark SQL engine and it provides an easier way of aggregations on the streaming data.

Alpha version of structured streaming is released in Spark 2.1 and it is not ready for production deployment yet.

Let's understand the concept of structured streaming with examples. We will use structured streaming to solve the average flight temperature problem that we solved using stateful processing.

Recap of the use case

Before moving further lets first recall the use case, we wanted to calculate the average temperature of flights for the entire journey of the flight by processing the data received at real time. So at any time a message is received average temperature of the corresponding flight since the first message received needs to be calculated.

The message format of the data having temperature information is as follows:

```
{"flightId":"tz302","timestamp":1494423926816,"temperature":21.12,"landed":
false}
where flightId = unique id of the flight
timestamp = time at which event is generated
temperature = temperature reading at the time of event generation
landed = boolean flag which defines whether flight has been landed or still
on the way
```

The **plain old java object** (**POJO**) class for mapping messages to Java objects for further processing:

```
public class FlightDetails implements Serializable {
  private String flightId;
  private double temp;
  private boolean landed;
  private long temperature;
}
```

Let's move towards implementing this solution for the given problem using structured streaming.

 In this example, we will be reading messages from a socket. In real-world scenarios, messages should be pushed to durable message brokers/queues such as Kafka, Kinesis, and so on.

The first step after initiating `SparkSession` is to read data from an incoming source, which is socket in our case:

```
Dataset<Row> inStream =
sparkSession.readStream().format("socket").option("host",
"127.0.0.1").option("port", 9999).load();
```

As shown in the preceding code, instead of receiving incoming messages as DStream, those are available in the form of a dataset. Consider it as an unbounded dataset. Every message received in the stream is added to this dataset.

Logical representation of input stream as unbounded dataset is shown in the following diagram:

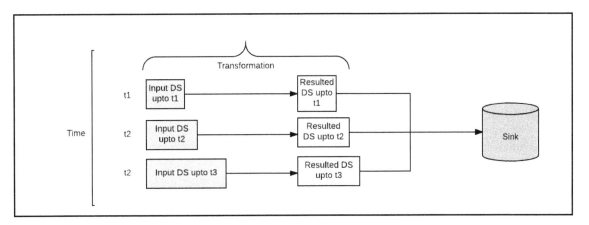

 As a dataset is a type-safe RDD with schema and RDD is immutable, so every time a new dataset is joined with the old one and a merged dataset is created.

The next step is to map row type to `FlightDetails` objects:

```
Dataset<FlightDetails> dsFlightDetails =
inStream.as(Encoders.STRING()).map(x -> {
    ObjectMapper mapper = new ObjectMapper();
    return mapper.readValue(x, FlightDetails.class);
}, Encoders.bean(FlightDetails.class));
```

So as per the preceding code, the incoming messages are encoded to `STRING` type and then mapped to `FlightDetails` object. Thus we are using Spark encoders to convert `Dataset<Row>` to `Dataset<FlightDetails>`.

To get our desired result, we can register temp view on the dataset and can run SQL using `SparkSession` as follows:

```
dsFlightDetails.createOrReplaceTempView("flight_details");
Dataset<Row> avdFlightDetails = sparkSession.sql("select flightId,
avg(temperature) from flight_details group by flightId");
```

It looks exactly similar to the running Spark SQL on batch data Thus, this framework makes streaming computation quite easy and helps users perform from batch and streaming computation the same way. Therefore, it reduces the steepness of learning curve for users.

The resulted dataset can be written to the external sink, using the following action:

```
StreamingQuery query = avdFlightDetails.writeStream()
  .outputMode("complete")
  .format("console")
  .start();
query.awaitTermination();
```

Here, we are writing output to the console.

Every time an incoming message is received, input messages are appended to existing dataset items and a new dataset is created. SQL queries on the dataset ID are created, which creates a new resultant dataset and then the resulted dataset can further be transformed or written to sink.

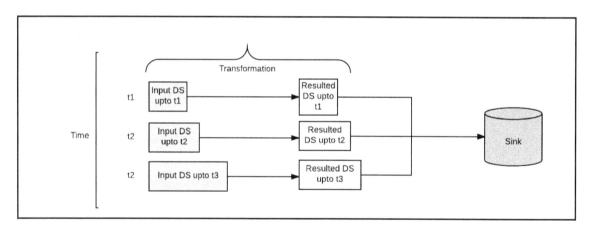

Structured streaming - programming model

As shown in the previous code example, an output mode is required while writing resulted dataset to the sink. The following are the various output modes available with structured streaming:

- `append`: Only new items appended to the resulted dataset will be written to the sink.
- `update`: Only those items that are updated in the resulted dataset will be written to the sink.
- `complete`: All items in the resulted dataset will be written to the sink. Handling duplicates in the case is the responsibility of the user.

If a user is performing some aggregation during the transformation of the incoming dataset, for example `avg` in the preceding example, then `append` mode cannot be used. `update` or `complete` modes will be applicable in such scenarios.

Built-in input sources and sinks

Structured streaming library provides some built-in input sources and sinks that can be easily plugged in without the use of any external library.

Input sources

The following are the built-in sources available in the structured streaming library:

- **Socket source**: As shown in the preceding example, socket source is provided using which data can be read from a socket in UTF-8 format.
- **File source**: This allows us to read files placed in a directory as a stream of data. Various files types such as text, CSV, JSON, and Parquet are supported.
- **Kafka source**: Kafka consumer is provided to read data from Kafka broker. This is very useful for production use cases. Kafka Broker Versions 0.10.0 or higher are supported.

Built-in Sinks

Some of the common built-in sinks are as follows:

- **Console sink**: As shown in the preceding example, this sink helps to print output to the console. It is very useful for debugging purposes:

```
writeStream
.format("console")
.outputMode("complete")
.start()
```

- **Memory sink**: This sink helps us to write data into memory in the form of in-memory table. Like the console sink, it is also helpful for debugging purposes:

```
writeStream
.format("memory")
.queryName("tableName")
.outputMode("append")
.start()
```

- **File sink**: This sink helps to store output to an external location in the form of a file:

```
writeStream
.format("csv") // can be "orc", "json", "csv", etc.
.option("path", "path/to/destination/dir")
.outputMode( "complete")
.start()
```

Summary

This chapter focused on handling streaming data from sources such as Kafka, socket, and filesystem. We also covered various stateful and stateless transformation of DStream along with checkpointing of data. But chekpointing of data alone does not guarantee fault tolerance and hence we discussed other approaches to make Spark Streaming job fault tolerant. We also talked about the transform operation, which comes in handy where operations of RDD API is not available in DStreams. Spark 2.0 introduced structured streaming as a separate module, however, because of its similarity with Spark Streaming, we discussed the newly introduced APIs of structured streaming also.

In the next chapter, we will focus on introducing the concepts of machine learning and then move towards its implementation using Apache Spark MLlib libraries. We will also discuss some real-world problems using Spark MLlib.

10
Machine Learning Analytics with Spark MLlib

So far, we have discussed batch and streaming applications and also SQL operations using Spark. In this chapter, we will discuss Spark modules on machine learning. We will briefly discuss what machine learning is and then move ahead with Spark's implementation of machine learning.

We will primarily focus on the `spark.ml` package of Spark that works on dataframe as an input data type. We will cover topics like pipeline and then move ahead with operations on features.

Introduction to machine learning

Spark MLlib is a general purpose machine learning library that gives all the benefits of Spark, that is, distributed computing, scalability, and fault tolerance along with easy inter-operability among different Spark modules and other libraries. Machine learning is not a new concept and certainly not solely developed by Spark, what makes Spark MLlib stand out on its own is its ease of use and generalization in developing any ML algorithm using pipeline. Again, pipeline as a concept has been used by the scikit-learn library and Apache Spark has done a brilliant job by using the same concept, but in a distributed mode. Generally, Spark's machine learning module ships:

1. Common machine learning algorithms.
2. Tools to load, extract, transform, and select features.

3. The ability to chain multiple operations using pipeline.
4. The ability to save and load algorithms, models, and pipelines.
5. The capability of performing linear algebra and statistical operations.

Over the years just like machine learning, Spark's implementation of it has also gone through a huge transformation. The initial release of Spark used the `spark.mllib` package that had RDD-based APIs, however, with Spark 2.0 a new package called `spark.ml` was introduced that operated upon dataframe. This shift from RDD to dataframe had many advantages, such as:

- All the benefits of Tungsten and Catalyst optimizer can be applied to MLlib operations
- Various data sources that are accessible via dataframe can now be directly utilized in MLlib
- Feature extraction and transformation can utilize Spark SQL operations
- Dataframe-based API also provides uniformity both within MLlib operations and across Spark modules and in a very user friendly manner

At an abstract level Spark's ML package implementation can be thought of as a set of UDF operations over datafame.

Before moving further with Spark's implementation of machine learning, let's first understand machine learning as a field of study and its related concepts.

Concepts of machine learning

A reductionist approach to defining machine learning in general would be, a programming paradigm where existing data helps in either generalizing the results as in classification algorithms or make some predictions. One of the pioneers of machine learning, *Andrew Ng*, defines machine learning as the *Science of how computers learn without being explicitly programmed*. Whichever assertion resonates with you, one thing which is clear that machine learning encompasses areas and solves problems from health diagnostics to space exploration and the way you connect with your friends online to the way your food is getting delivered to your doorstep.

Every day, system intelligence is being added to the services that make machines more intelligent while showing us ways to optimize and improve. Machine learning very broadly can be categorized into four categories:

- **Supervised learning**: Algorithms that learn from existing datasets output (label) and then utilize them to predict output values or labels for unlabeled datasets constitute supervised learning. Some of the examples of supervised learning are regression and classification models. Regression models are used to predict values while classification models are used for categorizing things such as spam emails.

- **Unsupervised learning**: Unsupervised learning is exploratory in nature and machine learning is used to find patterns or correlations among the input dataset. Examples of unsupervised learning are K-means clustering and **Principal Component Analysis (PCA)**.

- **Semi-supervised learning**: It involves a hybrid approach of both supervised and unsupervised learning for solving a problem. The technique is to process a small set of labeled data along with a large set of unlabeled data to derive an output. Speech and image based processing utilizes this approach to solve their domain specific problems.

- **Reinforced learning**: Reinforced learning is used in artificial intelligence and its related fields. It allows machines and software agents to automatically determine the ideal behavior within a specific context, in order to maximize its performance.

Machine learning also has some terminologies that are specific to its domain and it is worth discussing them:

- **Feature**: For any observation feature represents a set of traits that describes the entity quantitatively. For example, for a car the feature can be its color, car model, number of seats, and so on.

- **Label**: Label is a dependent entity whose outcome is related to the values of a feature. Such as in case of features of a car depending on the car model and number of seats and the label could be the maker of the car.

So far, we have got acquainted with basic terminologies around machine learning; however, Spark's implementation of machine learning adds a few more concepts that are required other than the topics already discussed previously. Although the `spark.mllib` package is currently in maintenance mode and may get deprecated by Spark 3.0 as planned, yet one of the key components of the RDD-based API that needs an introduction is MLib's datatype.

Datatypes

Though dataframes have become the deFacto way of doing ML operations, we will still go over basic knowledge of traditional RDD-based Spark MLlib datatypes as follows:

- **Local vector**: Local vectors are stored on a single machine having values as double and indices of each such values are stored as an integer starting with zero. Local vectors can further be sub classified into dense and sparse vectors. A double array representing its values is called d**ense vector** while s**parse vector** contains two arrays representing indices and values separately.

  For example, a vector (2.0, 0.0, 5.0, 3.0) can be represented as a:

  - Dense vector as *[2.0, 0.0, 5.0, 3.0]*
  - Sparse vector as *[4, (0,2,3), (2.0,5.0,3.0)]*

- **Labeled point**: A dense or sparse local vector having a label or a response value is called a labeled point. They are used in supervised learning more prominently in classification and regression-based algorithms. Labeled point values are stored in a double datatype.

Algorithm	Values
Binary classification	*0 or 1*
Multiclass classification	*0, 1, 2...*
Regression	*Double*

- **Local matrix**: A matrix that is stored on a single machine having values as a double datatype and row and column indices being represented as integer is called local matrix. It can further be segregated into the dense matrix whose values are stored in a single double array in column major order while sparse matrix stores non zero values in **Compressed Sparse Column** (**CSC**) format in column major order.

- **Distributed matrix**: A distributed matrix is stored in one or more RDDs and hence is distributed in nature. Also the row and column indices of distributed matrix are of type long while the values are of double type. Conversion of a distributed matrix to any other type may require shuffling and hence is an expensive operation. Distributed matrices have been further classified into the following sub categories:

  - **Row matrix**: *Row-oriented distributed matrix without meaningful row indices*-RDD of sequence of vector without rows indices

- **Indexed row matrix**: like a row matrix, but with meaningful row indices
- **Coordinate matrix**: elements values are explicit defined by using `IndexedRow(row_index, col_index, value)`
- **Block matrix**: included set of `matrix block (row_index, col_index, matrix)`

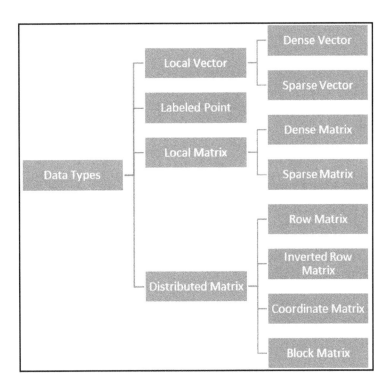

Spark 2.0 introduced the paradigm shift in the way machine learning algorithms are implemented in Spark. They not only changed the RDD-based operation to dataframe based operations by introducing a new package spark.ml, but also focused on solving problems using pipelines. Some of the important concepts surrounding pipelines and its associated terminologies are discussed in the following sections.

Machine learning work flow

Machine learning work flow in general involves two set of operations: one involving training the model and the other testing the trained model with newer datasets.

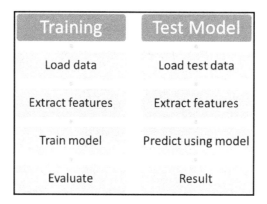

The ML workflow requires iterations over the same set of training data over and over again while only changing the tuning parameters. The objective of such an iterative process is to achieve minima in error while evaluating the values on training data and only then the model is fed with test data to give resultant output. In order to combine all these sequences of data pre-processing, feature extraction, model fitting, and validation stages in a ML workflow, spark introduced *Pipelines*.

Pipelines

The pipeline API is part of the `spark.ml` package and it consists of a sequence of stages such as data cleaning, Feature extraction, model training, model validation, model testing, and so on. It provides the ability to chain all these different stages in a sequence for developing any machine learning algorithm. First let's get acquainted with common terminologies used in ML workflow using pipelines:

- **Dataframe**: Unlike the `spark.mllib` package, where the datatype was RDD based, in `spark.ml` the datatype is dataframe. Every pipeline expects input data to be dataframe, which can again be created from various Data sources discussed in `Chapter 8`, *Working with Spark SQL*, such as from filesystems, external databases, and other data generation sources.

- **Transformers**: A transformer transforms a dataframe into another dataframe by either adding a few more columns in the existing dataset or changing the dataframe values itself and thereby giving the resultant in a new dataframe. Some examples of transformers are:
  - Binarizer transformer converts input columns of a dataframe into *0* or *1* depending on a threshold value
  - A machine learning model accepts feature vector from dataframe and then appends the predicted label as a new column to the resultant dataframe

A transformer applies the `transform()` method to convert dataframes:

- **Estimator**: An estimator is any machine learning algorithm that trains or fits on the training data to produce a model, which again is a transformer. The model then transforms the test data producing resultant value(s) in the output dataframe. For example:
  - K-means is an estimator that accepts training dataframe to produce K-means model
  - Decision tree is an estimator that produces a decision tree model

    An estimator has a `fit()` method that is to be invoked on learning dataframe in order to generate a model that can transform the input data.

- **Pipeline**: A pipeline chains together multiple stages of machine learning workflow each comprising of a transfromer or an estimator. The sequence of job chaining is specific to an algorithm or use case and hence the order of `PipelineStages`, that is, transformer and estimator, as being passed to a pipeline is important.

Now that we understand these common terminologies, let's write our first Machine Learning algorithm and understand how these parameters are related to each other. For simplicity we will try and understand a very basic regression model called **linear regression**. Please be forewarned that the results will not be perfect as our intention here is to only understand major components in an *ML workflow*.

A simple linear regression model can be represented as an equation of the form:

$$y = ax + b$$

Where x is a variable or in ML parlance a feature vector and a is the slope of the line. b is a constant that represents the intercept on the y axis when $x=0$.

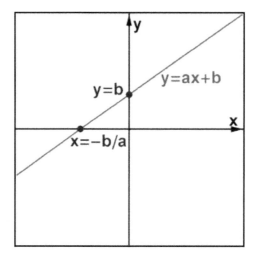

Using this model of linear regression, we will try and predict the values of **total impression**, which is sum total of like, comment, and share that a Facebook post will get depending on feature vector parameters such as Post Month, Post Weekday, Post Hour, and so on.

The dataset can be downloaded from http://archive.ics.uci.edu/ml/datasets/Facebook+metrics and it has around 500 records. To keep the model simple, we will select only a few columns from the preceding dataset and call it formattedDF. From the feature vector formattedDF we will split the dataset into two, one being train dataset and the other being test dataset. Also since, the linear regression model accepts single feature vectors we will use VectorAssembler, a transformer that combines multiple raw features into a single feature vector. We will then pass the instance of VectorAssembler to a pipeline along with the instance of LinearRegression, which together returns a transformer instance lrPipeline. The pipeline instance lrPipeline is then trained using the fit() method on the training data. The fit() method returns a PipelineModel on which test data can be tested:

```
Dataset<Row> formattedDF = ds.select(col("Page total
    likes"),col("Category"),col("Post Month"),col("Post
    Weekday"),col("Post Hour"),col("Paid"),col("Lifetime People who
```

```
have liked your Page and engaged with your post"),col("Total
  Interactions"));
formattedDF.show();
//Split the sample into Training and Test data
Dataset<Row>[] data=    formattedDF.na().drop().randomSplit(new
  double[]{0.7,0.3});
System.out.println("We have training examples count :: "+
  data[0].count()+" and test examples count ::"+data[1].count());
String[] featuresCols = formattedDF.drop("Total
  Interactions").columns();
//This concatenates all feature columns into a single feature
  vector in a new column "rawFeatures".
VectorAssembler vectorAssembler = new
  VectorAssembler().setInputCols(featuresCols).
  setOutputCol("rawFeatures");
//StandardScaler scaler = new StandardScaler().setInputCol
  ("rawFeatures").setOutputCol("features").setWithStd
  (true).setWithMean(false);
LinearRegression lr = new LinearRegression().setLabelCol("Total
   Interactions").setFeaturesCol("rawFeatures")
                        .setMaxIter(10)
                        .setRegParam(0.3)
                        .setElasticNetParam(0.8);

// Chain vectorAssembler and lr in a Pipeline
Pipeline lrPipeline = new Pipeline().setStages(new PipelineStage[]
   {vectorAssembler, lr});
// Train model.
PipelineModel lrModel = lrPipeline.fit(data[0]);
// Make predictions.
Dataset<Row> lrPredictions = lrModel.transform(data[1]);
// Select example rows to display.
lrPredictions.show(20);
```

Before moving further, you should notice that the result of prediction has not been very accurate. This is because:

- Our ML model was very simplistic, even the definition of linear regression considered the simplest possibility Linear Regression and that being a linear equation
- The sample size was very limited to around *500* records in total and *350* records as training data
- We did not include an exhaustive list of parameters as feature vector
- We also did not focus on model selection or parameter tuning

Now let's discuss the solution for each reason mentioned:

1. Our understanding of using ML algorithms should be very precise, for example, there are two variants for Linear regression that exist in Spark, as of Spark 2.0, one is called **linear regression** while the other is called **generalized linear regression**. And it doesn't end there, under generalized linear regression comes various implementation options such as Gaussian, Binomial, Poisson, Gamma, and Tweedie. So what becomes of paramount importance is which type of ML algorithm is being used and if there are any subtypes associated with the ML algorithm. If it does, then which variant would be best suited for our use case. There is no straightforward answer to this question; however, domain knowledge of data science would certainly help in arriving at a better conclusion while deciding the model suited.

2. The choice of sample should be exhaustive enough to cover most if not all the possible scenarios of the features.

3. The choice of machine learning algorithm plays an important role; however, equally important is the choice of parameters representing the feature vector. For example, in the preceding use case we have not covered the gender of the user who has posted the message, but as some studies suggest that gender of user also plays an important role in generating impressions, that is, comment, like, or share. Another important aspect is adding or removing human bias factors in the feature vector. Microsoft has launched two self-learning chat bots *Tay* and *Zo*, but they have failed miserably since they are supposed to learn from their interaction of which the company has no control over. This has been a matter for concern to them and this whole scenario should be a concern for any ML algorithm developer who needs to make a conscious decision to add human bias in feature vectors or not.

4. Each ML workflow has its own set of tuning parameters that can be tweaked to generate one set of results or the other. Which combination of parameters suits ones needs for any use case depends both on experience and our ability to juggle around various parameters and then evaluating the results.

In this section, we discussed ML workflow using pipeline and chaining of various components to implement them. In the following section, we will discuss various techniques to extract, transform, and select features.

Operations on feature vectors

Though the `spark.ml` package uses the dataframe for ML workflows, depending on the use case one might need to extract data from raw dataframe or transform the dataframe in a format as required by the ML algorithms or at times one might just need a few selected parameters as feature vectors. All these different types of operations require usage of specially developed APIs that can be clubbed into the following categories.

Feature extractors

When the data present in a raw dataframe are not explicitly present in the form an ML algorithm expects we use feature extractors to extract those features. Common feature extractors are:

- **CountVectorizer**: A `CountVectorizer` converts a collection of text documents into a vector representing the word count of text documents. `CountVectorizer` works in two different ways depending how the value of the dictionary gets populated. Let's first assume that the user has no prior information of the type of data that will populate the dataset of text; in such a scenario the dictionary gets prepared based on occurrence of term frequency across the dataset. `VocabSize` defines the number of words a dictionary can hold while the optional parameter `minDF` restricts the entry of words in the dictionary if occurrence of the word within the document is less than the value of `minDF`:

```
List<Row> data = Arrays.asList(
  RowFactory.create(Arrays.asList("w1", "w2", "w3")),
  RowFactory.create(Arrays.asList("w1", "w2", "w4", "w5", "w2"))
);
StructType schema = new StructType(new StructField [] {
  new StructField("text", new ArrayType(DataTypes.StringType,
true), false, Metadata.empty())
                });
              Dataset<Row> df = spark.createDataFrame(data,
schema);

              CountVectorizerModel cvModel = new
CountVectorizer()
              .setInputCol("text")
              .setOutputCol("feature")
              .setVocabSize(5)
              .setMinDF(2)
              .fit(df);
```

```
                      System.out.println("The words in the Vocabulary
are :: "+ Arrays.toString(cvModel.vocabulary()));


                      cvModel.transform(df).show(false);
```

```
The output of above code is:
The words in the Vocabulary are :: [w2, w1]
+-------------------+-------------------+
|text               |feature            |
+-------------------+-------------------+
|[w1, w2, w3]       |(2,[0,1],[1.0,1.0])|
|[w1, w2, w4, w5, w2]|(2,[0,1],[2.0,1.0])|
+-------------------+-------------------+
```

When the dictionary is not defined CountVectorizer iterates over the dataset twice to prepare the dictionary based on frequency and size. The process of preparing the feature vector can be optimized if one knows the value of the words that constitute the dictionary and hence save one iteration. In this scenario, an *a-priori* dictionary is built at the time of instantiating CountVectorizer, so if on the same dataset as demonstrated in the previous example if we run the following transformation:

```
CountVectorizerModel cvMod = new CountVectorizerModel(new
String[]{"w1", "w2", "w3"})
                              .setInputCol("text")
                              .setOutputCol("feature");
           System.out.println("The words in the Vocabulary
are :: "+ Arrays.toString(cvMod.vocabulary()));
                 cvMod.transform(df).show(false);
```

We get the following output:

The words in the Vocabulary are: [w1, w2, w3]

```
+-------------------+-------------------------+
|text               |feature                  |
+-------------------+-------------------------+
|[w1, w2, w3]       |(3,[0,1,2],[1.0,1.0,1.0])|
|[w1, w2, w4, w5, w2]|(3,[0,1],[1.0,2.0])      |
+-------------------+-------------------------+
```

- **Term Frequency-Inverse Document Frequency (TF-IDF)**: It is used as a feature extraction technique. TF-IDF is used to compute the weight of individual words in a document rather than entire datasets. By weight here it implies the statistical evaluation to gauge the importance of a word within a document in a collection or dataset. As the frequency of words increase in the document, so does its importance, but then in TF-IDF it is offset by the frequency of the word in the entire collection or dataset. TF-IDF comprises of two parts, namely:

- **Term Frequency (TF)**: It is a statistical measure of frequency a term occurs in a document. For example, if in a document spark occurs five times and the total number of words in that document is 20, then:

    TF= Number of frequency of word in a document / Total number of words in a document.

    =5/20=0.25

    In the Spark ML library one can use `HashingTF` or `CountVectorizer` to calculate TF:

- **Inverse Document Frequency (IDF)** measures the importance of a term in the collection or a dataset as a whole. It takes care of the fact that certain terms, such as *is*, *are*, *the*, and so on, despite occurring more, have little importance as far as the dataset is concerned. So if the word spark occurs in 100 documents out of the consideration dataset of *100,000* documents, then:

```
IDF= loge(Total number of documents/Number of documents with the
    specific term or word)
  = loge(10000/100) = 4.6
    Hence the value of TF-IDF = TF*IDF
      = 0.25*4.6=1.15
```

    In Spark, IDF is an estimator that generates an `IDFModel` by using the `fit()` method on a dataset. A feature vector created by `HashingTF` or `CountVerctorizer` is then passed to it using the `transform()` method, which rescales or offsets the original vector values:

```
List<Row> data = Arrays.asList(
                RowFactory.create(0.0, "Spark"),
                RowFactory.create(0.0, "Spark"),
                RowFactory.create(0.5, "MLIB"),
                RowFactory.create(0.6, "MLIB"),
                RowFactory.create(0.7, "MLIB"),
                RowFactory.create(1.0, "ML")
        );
```

```
        StructType schema = new StructType(new StructField[]{
            new StructField("label", DataTypes.DoubleType, false,
Metadata.empty()),
            new StructField("words", DataTypes.StringType, false,
Metadata.empty())
            });
        Dataset<Row> rowData = spark.createDataFrame(data,
schema);

        Tokenizer tokenizer = new
Tokenizer().setInputCol("words").setOutputCol("tokenizedWords");
        Dataset<Row> tokenizedData =
        tokenizer.transform(rowData);

        int numFeatures = 20;
        HashingTF hashingTF = new HashingTF()
                .setInputCol("tokenizedWords")
                .setOutputCol("rawFeatures")
                .setNumFeatures(numFeatures);
        Dataset<Row> featurizedData =
hashingTF.transform(tokenizedData);

        IDF idf = new
IDF().setInputCol("rawFeatures").setOutputCol("features");
                IDFModel idfModel = idf.fit(featurizedData);

        Dataset<Row> rescaledData =
idfModel.transform(featurizedData);
        rescaledData.select("label", "features").show(false);
```

Word2Vec being an estimator produces a Word2VecModel by accepting dataset values composed of sentences or a sequence of words together being represented as a document. The model generates a fixed-size vector by transforming the document into the vector using the average of all words in the document. Word2Vec is popularly used for prediction, document similarity calculation, and so on:

```
List<Row> data = Arrays.asList(
                RowFactory.create(Arrays.asList("Learning
Apache Spark".split(" "))),
                RowFactory.create(Arrays.asList("Spark has API
for Java, Scala, and Python".split(" "))),
                RowFactory.create(Arrays.asList("API in above
laguage are very richly developed".split(" ")))
                );
                StructType schema = new StructType(new
StructField[]{
```

```
                    new StructField("text", new
ArrayType(DataTypes.StringType, true), false, Metadata.empty())
                    });
                    Dataset<Row> documentDF =
spark.createDataFrame(data, schema);

                    Word2Vec word2Vec = new Word2Vec()
                      .setInputCol("text")
                      .setOutputCol("result")
                      .setVectorSize(10)
                      .setMinCount(0);

                    Word2VecModel model = word2Vec.fit(documentDF);
                    Dataset<Row> result =
model.transform(documentDF);

            result.show(false);
```

Features		
	Extraction	CountVectorizer
		TF-IDF
		Word2Vec
	Transformation	Tokenizer
		StopWordsRemover
		n-gram
		VectorAssembler
		and so on.
	Selection	ChiSqSelector
		RFormula
		VectorSlicer

Feature transformers

Feature transformers are transformers that transform the data by scaling, converting, or modifying the features of parent dataframes. Some of the common feature transformers are:

- **Tokenizer**: Tokenizer transforms sentences or a document by splitting them into individual words. As in the following example, sentences of the dataframe will be split into words:

```
List<Row> data = Arrays.asList(
                    RowFactory.create(0, "Learning Apache Spark"),
                    RowFactory.create(1, "Spark has API for Java,
Scala, and Python"),
                    RowFactory.create(2, "API in above laguage are
very richly developed")
                    );

            StructType schema = new StructType(new
StructField[]{
                new StructField("id", DataTypes.IntegerType,
false, Metadata.empty()),
                    new StructField("sentence",
DataTypes.StringType, false, Metadata.empty())
                });

            Dataset<Row> sentenceDataFrame =
spark.createDataFrame(data, schema);

            Tokenizer tokenizer = new
Tokenizer().setInputCol("sentence").setOutputCol("words");

            Dataset<Row> tokenized =
tokenizer.transform(sentenceDataFrame);
            tokenized.show(false);
```

Tokenizer provides a very straightforward purpose of splitting sentences on the basis of whitespaces and hence at times its usability gets restricted because of its simplicity. RegexTokenizer can be used to overcome this limitation of splitting the words on the basis of regular expression.

- `StopWordsRemover`: This is a transformer that expunges the commonly used words from a document as they don't contribute much to the content of the document, but rather to the context such as words like `is,a,the`, and so on. By default, the language for stop word removal is English, however, that can be changed using the method `loadDefaultStopWords` (languages), where supported language are English, French, Italian, Russian, and so on. A custom list of stop words can also be specified using the `stopWords` parameter:

```
List<Row> data = Arrays.asList(
                    RowFactory.create(Arrays.asList("This", "is",
"a", "book", "on","Spark")),
                    RowFactory.create(Arrays.asList("The",
"language", "used", "is", "Java"))
                );

                StructType schema = new StructType(new
StructField[]{
                    new StructField(
                      "raw",
DataTypes.createArrayType(DataTypes.StringType), false,
Metadata.empty())
                });

                StopWordsRemover remover = new
StopWordsRemover()
                                .setInputCol("raw")
                                .setOutputCol("filtered");
                Dataset<Row> dataset =
spark.createDataFrame(data, schema);
                remover.transform(dataset).show(false);

The output of the sample code is
+-------------------------------+---------------------+
|raw                            |filtered
|
+-------------------------------+---------------------+
|[This, is, a, book, on, Spark] |[book, Spark]        |
|[The, language, used, is, Java]|[language, used, Java]|
+-------------------------------+---------------------+
```

- `VectorAssembler`: This is used as a transformer to combine multiple columns in a dataframe to a single vector column. In certain algorithms such as linear regression, logistic regression, or decision trees the inputs dataset is expected to have a single feature vector and it is at such scenarios `VectorAssembler` plays its part. `VectorAssembler`, however, has some limitations as per the datatype of input columns and accepts all numeric, Boolean, and Vector datatypes:

```
Dataset<Row> featSet =
emp_ds.select(col("empId"),col("salary"),col("deptno"))
        String[] featuresCols = featSet.columns();
          VectorAssembler vectorAssembler = new
VectorAssembler().setInputCols(featuresCols).setOutputCol("rawFeatu
res");
        Dataset<Row> output = vectorAssembler.transform(featSet);
        output.show(false);
```

Feature selectors

A dataframe may have columns that may not be required or at times may not be important enough to contribute in any way in label calculation. Feature selectors are transformers that help in selecting a subset of features from a larger set of features. Common feature selectors are:

- `ChiSqSelector`: `ChiSqSelector` selects features from a feature vector using chi-squared test of independence. Details of chi-squared test of independence is beyond the scope of this book, however, simply put the selector dynamically chooses the best number of features depending on the value of the `NumTopFeatures` parameter that would affect the predictive output of ML algorithms:

```
List<Row> data = Arrays.asList(
                RowFactory.create(1, Vectors.dense(0.1, 0.0,
1.0, 20.0), 0.0),
                RowFactory.create(2, Vectors.dense(0.2, 1.0,
13.0, 40.0), 1.0),
                RowFactory.create(3, Vectors.dense(0.3, 2.0,
21.0, 1.1), 0.0)
            );
                StructType schema = new StructType(new
StructField[]{
                new StructField("id", DataTypes.IntegerType,
false, Metadata.empty()),
                new StructField("rawfeatures", new
VectorUDT(), false, Metadata.empty()),
```

```
                    new StructField("label", DataTypes.DoubleType,
false, Metadata.empty())
                        });

                    Dataset<Row> df = spark.createDataFrame(data,
schema);

                    ChiSqSelector selector = new ChiSqSelector()
                        .setNumTopFeatures(1)
                        .setFeaturesCol("rawfeatures")
                        .setLabelCol("label")
                        .setOutputCol("features");

                    Dataset<Row> result =
selector.fit(df).transform(df);
                        result.show();
```

- `VectorSlicer`: It is a transformer that accepts a feature vector and returns a feature vector that is a subset of original feature vectors. Such kinds of transformations are required when the original feature vector has features that are not relevant for the algorithms being applied on the dataset. Column indices or names can be passed to `VectorSlicer` for choosing the subset feature vector, however, for using names to filter out features one is supposed to set features name firsthand by using the `setNames()` method:

```
  Dataset<Row> featSet =
emp_ds.select(col("empId"),col("salary"),col("deptno"));
                    String[] featuresCols = featSet.columns();
                    Dataset<Row> vecAssembler = new
VectorAssembler().setInputCols(featuresCols).setOutputCol("rawFeatu
res").transform(featSet);
                    VectorSlicer vectorSlicer = new
VectorSlicer().setInputCol("rawFeatures").setOutputCol("features");
                    vectorSlicer.setIndices(new int[]{1, 2});
                    Dataset<Row> output =
vectorSlicer.transform(vecAssembler);
                    output.show(false);
```

Summary

In this chapter, we discussed machine learning as a field of study and its various sub classifications. We then progressed ahead to discuss various parlance associated with machine learning and how machine learning has been implemented in Apache Spark. We also covered the datatypes that are used in the `spark.mllib` package and then discussed job chaining using pipeline. Terminologies around pipeline were also discussed in detail along with use cases. Finally, *operations on features what a feeling* discussed.

In the following chapter, we will look into another module of Spark, that is, GraphX, and we will discover types of GraphX RDD and various operations associated with them. We will also discuss use cases around GraphX implementation.

11
Learning Spark GraphX

In this chapter, we will discuss the Spark `GraphX` library, which helps to perform graph-based computation on the top of Spark. The purpose of this chapter is to make the reader familiar with the `GraphX` library. We will discuss how graphs are stored in Spark along with inbuilt operations that can be executed on graphs. We will also talk about some graph-based algorithms that are available in the `Graphx` library.

Introduction to GraphX

As per the Apache Spark documentation: "*GraphX is Apache Spark's API for graphs and graph-parallel computation*". Graph based computations have become very popular with the advancement of technologies. Whether it is finding the shortest path between two points, matching DNA, or social media, graph computations have become ubiquitous.

Graph consists of a vertex and edges, where a vertex defines entities or nodes and edges defines the relationships from entities. Edges can be one directional or bidirectional based on the requirement. For example, an edge describing friendship relations between two users on Facebook is bidirectional; however, an edge describing follower relations between two users on Twitter may or may not be bidirectional because one can follow another person on Twitter without being followed by that person.

The Spark `Graphx` library helps to run graph-based computations on top of Spark. It provides a graph-based abstraction on the Spark RDD called a *Property Graph*, which is a directed multigraph where every vertex and edge is associated with a property. The `GraphX` library provides various sets of transformations to run graph. It also comes with basic graph-based algorithms: for example, **PageRank**, **Triangle Count**, and so on, which helps to run graph-based analytics.

Let's start exploring the `Graphx` library!

Introduction to Property Graph

It is the basic abstraction of the `Graphx` API. Property is a directed multi-graph where every vertex and edge is associated with a property. Each vertex in the Property Graph is also associated with a unique 64-bit long identifier (`VertexId`). A directed multi-graph is defined as a directed graph where there can be multiple edges (`relationships`) between the same vertices, such as A can be a friend and team mate of B.

The following is a logical representation of a Property Graph:

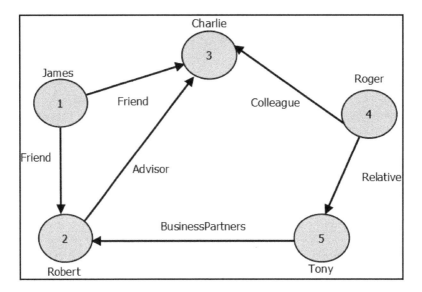

Logical representation of Property Graph

Here, we have a Property Graph consisting of five vertices. Each vertex in the graph consists of a `VertexId` and a `property`, which is a string object in this case, and every edge is also associated with a property, which is a string object as well, which describes the relation between the vertices.

Spark stores vertices and edges in different RDDs as follows:

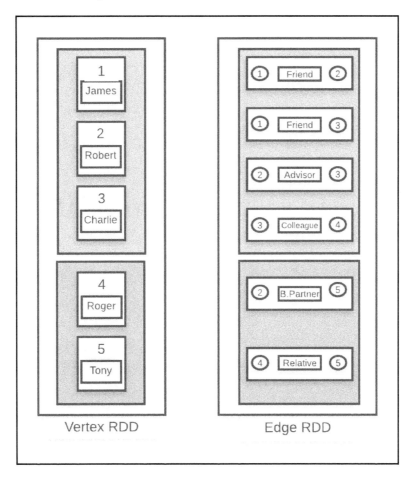

Storage representation of Property Graph

Every element of the RDD of vertices contains a `VertexId` and an associated property and every element of the RDD of edges contains the ID of source vertex, ID of the destination vertex, and the associated property. The blue and green blocks represent the partitions of RDDs.

The following are some properties of the graph abstraction:

- As Property Graphs are stored as RDDs, they possess all the properties of the RDD such as partitioned and distributed, immutable, fault tolerant, lazy evaluation, and so on
- As vertices and edges are stored as separate RDDs, it makes it feasible to transform either vertices or edges without transforming the other
- During transformation, unaffected structure, attributes, and indices parts of the graph can be reused while creating new graphs
- IDs of vertices are used to partition the RDD range among different nodes

Getting started with the GraphX API

In this section, we will create a graph using the `GraphX` API. Here we will first create vertex and edge RDDs and then we will use them to create the graph.

 As of Spark 2.1.x, the `GraphX` library only provides a stable Scala API. The Java API of GraphX is still in ALPHA version. In this chapter, we will call Scala APIs of GraphX in Java wherever required to perform the graph operations provided in the `GraphX` library.

Let's start with creating a graph using the example provided in the previous section. The following are the ways of creating the graph.

Using vertex and edge RDDs

1. First we define the vertex and edge RDD as follows:

```
List<Tuple2<Object, string>> vertices = new ArrayList<>();

vertices.add(new Tuple2<Object, string>(1l, "James"));
vertices.add(new Tuple2<Object, string>(2l, "Robert"));
vertices.add(new Tuple2<Object, string>(3l, "Charlie"));
vertices.add(new Tuple2<Object, string>(4l, "Roger"));
vertices.add(new Tuple2<Object, string>(5l, "Tony"));

List<Edge<string>> edges = new ArrayList<>();

edges.add(new Edge<string>(1, 2, "Friend"));
edges.add(new Edge<string>(2, 3, "Advisor"));
```

```
edges.add(new Edge<string>(1, 3, "Friend"));
edges.add(new Edge<string>(4, 3, "colleague"));
edges.add(new Edge<string>(4, 5, "Relative"));
edges.add(new Edge<string>(5, 2, "BusinessPartners"));

JavaRDD<Tuple2<Object, string>> verticesRDD =
javaSparkContext.parallelize(vertices);
JavaRDD<Edge<string>> edgesRDD =
javaSparkContext.parallelize(edges);
```

org.apache.spark.graphx.Graph API requires
scala.reflect.ClassTag objects for vertex type and edge type. These are
Scala objects, which are singleton by nature.

2. These can be defined by calling the Scala APIs in Java as follows:

```
ClassTag<string> stringTag =
scala.reflect.ClassTag$.MODULE$.apply(string.class);
```

As properties associated with both vertices and edges are of string, so the
preceding ClassTag object can be used in both.

3. Using these RDDs, Graph() can be created as follows:

```
Graph<string, string> graph = Graph.apply(verticesRDD.rdd(),
edgesRDD.rdd(), "",
StorageLevel.MEMORY_ONLY(),StorageLevel.MEMORY_ONLY(), stringTag,
stringTag);
```

4. Vertices and edges can be printed using the collect() action as follows:

```
graph.vertices().toJavaRDD().collect().forEach(System.out::println)
;
graph.edges().toJavaRDD().collect().forEach(System.out::println);
```

From edges

Graphs can also be created using only edges as follows:

```
Graph<string, string> graph = Graph.fromEdges(edgeRDD.rdd(),
"",StorageLevel.MEMORY_ONLY(), StorageLevel.MEMORY_ONLY(), stringTag,
stringTag);
```

However in this case, there is no property associated with vertices. Map transformation needs to execute on vertices to associate the property with vertices. We will discuss map transformation on graphs in the next section.

EdgeTriplet

In addition to the `Edge` class, there is another abstraction that the `GraphX` library provides, which is known as `EdgeTriplet`. `EdgeTriplet` extends the `Edge` class and adds properties of source OS destination vertices as well.

So in addition to fields of the `Edge` class such as ID of source vertex, ID of the destination vertex and edge property, it also contains properties of the source and destination vertices.

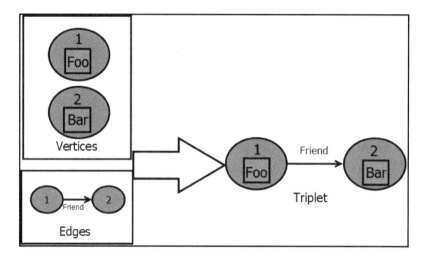

Logical representation of EdgeTriplet

The `triplets()` function on the graph provides the `EdgeTriplets` of the graph as follows:

```
RDD<EdgeTriplet<string, string>> triplets = graph.triplets();
```

All `EdgeTriplet` elements of the graph can be printed as follows:

```
graph.triplets().toJavaRDD().collect().forEach(System.out::println);
```

Graph operations

The `Graphx` library provides various inbuilt operations that can be executed on Property Graphs. In this section, we will discuss those operations.

mapVertices

Similar to map transformation on RDD, `mapVertices` allows users to transform the vertices of graphs. The following is the signature of the `mapVertices` method:

```
mapVertices(scala.Function2<Object,VD,VD2> map, scala.reflect.ClassTag<VD2>
evidence$3, scala.Predef.$eq$colon$eq<VD,VD2> eq)
```

To implement `scala.Function2` in Java, `scala.runtime.AbstractFunction2` can be used because implementing `scala.Function2` in Java requires users to implement a large number of abstract methods and this generates a lot of byte code.

`AbstractFunction0`, `AbstractFunction1`, `AbstractFunction2`, ... were introduced to reduce the byte code generated by anonymous functions such as `scala.Function0`, `scala.Function1`, `scala.Function2`, ... That is why they are kept in the `scala.runtime` package. We can leverage them while calling graph operations in Java. However, as these are abstract classes, we cannot implement these as Lambdas:

```
public class AbsFunc1 extends scala.runtime.AbstractFunction2<Object,
string, string> implements Serializable {
@Override
  public string apply(Object arg0, string arg1) {
    return "Vertex:"+arg1;
  }
}
```

Here the property vertex is transformed by adding `Vertex:` string in front of every vertex name. `Notice`, that `AbsFunc1()` `implements` `Serializable` as well which is mandatory as Spark, being a distributed processing system, requires objects to be serialized.

As described in the previous section, `scala.reflect.ClassTag` can be created in Java as follows:

```
ClassTag<string> stringTag =
scala.reflect.ClassTag$.MODULE$.apply(string.class);
```

`scala.Predef.$eq$colon$eq` is also a Scala object which can be defined in Java as follows:

```
$eq$colon$eq<string, string> tpEquals =
scala.Predef.$eq$colon$eq$.MODULE$.tpEquals();
```

Hence, `mapVertices()` can be executed as follows:

```
Graph<string, string> mapVertices = graph.mapVertices(new AbsFunc1(),
stringTag, tpEquals);
```

To verify, all vertices can be printed as follows:

```
mapVertices.vertices().toJavaRDD().collect().forEach(System.out::println);
```

`mapvertices()` is equivalent to executing maps on the vertices RDD in terms of the transformed output values of vertices, that is:

```
JavaRDD<string> map = graph.vertices().toJavaRDD().map(x->"Vertex:"+x);
```

However, do notice that it does not preserve graph indices or structures. It is returning JavaRDD, which needs to be used to construct the graph again. So, `mapVertices()` is recommended.

mapEdges

Similar to `mapVertices`, `mapEdges` is used to transform edges. The following is the signature of `mapEdges`:

```
mapEdges(scala.Function1<Edge<ED>,ED2> map, scala.reflect.ClassTag<ED2>
evidence$4)
```

The graph object created previously has edges with the property of string type. In this example, we will transform the edge property to integer value equal in length to the string. The following is the definition of the transformation function:

```
public class AbsFunc1 extends AbstractFunction1<Edge<string>,Integer>
implements Serializable {
@Override
public Integer apply(Edge<string> edge) {
  return edge.attr().length();
}
```

Therefore, `mapEdges` can be executed as:

```
graph.mapEdges(new AbsFunc1(),
scala.reflect.ClassTag$.MODULE$.apply(Integer.class));
```

mapTriplets

Similar to `mapVertices` and `mapEdges`, `mapTriplets` is used to transform edge triplets. The following is the signature of the method:

```
mapTriplets(scala.Function1<EdgeTriplet<VD,ED>,ED2> map,
scala.reflect.ClassTag<ED2> evidence$6)
```

Here, we will perform the same operation as we executed in the `mapEdges` section; that is, `transform` the edge property to integer value. The following is the definition of the transformation function:

```
public class AbsFunc1 extends
AbstractFunction1<EdgeTriplet<string,string>,Integer> implements
Serializable {
  @Override
  public Integer apply(EdgeTriplet<string,string> triplet) {
    return triplet.attr().length();
  }
}
```

The `mapTriplets` transformation can be executed as follows:

```
 graph.mapTriplets(new AbsFunc1(),
scala.reflect.ClassTag$.MODULE$.apply(Integer.class));
```

reverse

`reverse()` transformation is used to reverse the direction of edges in the graph. This operation just reverses the source and destination indices of the edges without updating any vertex and edge properties. It can be executed as follows:

```
Graph<string, string> reversedGraph = graph.reverse();
```

To verify, print the `edgetriplet`:

```
reversedGraph.triplets().toJavaRDD().collect().forEach(System.out::println)
;
```

subgraph

As its name suggests, the subgraph operations return a subpart of the graph. This operation returns the graph with vertices and edges that satisfy the user-defined criteria. In this example, we will fetch the subpart of the graph where the edge property is Friend.

The following is the signature of the subgraph method:

```
subgraph(scala.Function1<EdgeTriplet<VD,ED>,Object>    epred,
scala.Function2<Object,VD,Object> vpred)
```

The first parameter is used to filter the edges and the second parameter is used to filter vertices based on the user-defined criteria. As we want to filter the graph where the edge property is Friend, we do not need to specify any filter condition in the second parameter. The following is the implementation of both parameters:

```
public class AbsFunc1 extends AbstractFunction1<EdgeTriplet<string,string>,
Object> implements Serializable {
@Override
  public Object apply(EdgeTriplet<string, string> arg0) {
    return arg0.attr().equals("Friend");
  }
}
public class AbsFunc2 extends AbstractFunction2<Object, string, Object>
implements Serializable {
  @Override
  public Object apply(Object arg0, string arg1) {
    return true;
  }
}
```

Hence, the subgraph operation can be executed as follows:

```
Graph<string, string> subgraph = graph.subgraph(new AbsFunc1(), new
AbsFunc2());
subgraph.triplets().toJavaRDD().collect().forEach(System.out::println);
```

The logical output of the preceding operation on the graph is as follows:

Logical representation of output of the subgraph operation

aggregateMessages

Aggregating data about vertices is very common in graph-based computations. For example, finding the total number of friends on Facebook for a user or finding the total number of followers on Twitter. `aggregateMessages` transformation is the primary aggregate function of GraphX. The following is the signature of the method:

```
aggregateMessages (scala.Function1< EdgeContext < VD , ED ,
A>,scala.runtime.BoxedUnit> sendMsg, scala.Function2<A, A, A> mergeMsg,
TripletFields tripletFields, scala.reflect.ClassTag<A> evidence$11)
```

`aggregateMessages` works as a map reduce function. The `sendMessage` function can be considered as a `mapFunction`, which helps to send a message from the source to the destination or vice versa. It takes the `EdgeContext` object as parameter, which exposes methods to send messages between source and destination vertices. `mergeMsg` function can be considered as a reduce function, which helps to aggregate the messages sent using the `sendMessage` function.

The Triplets object can be used to specify which part of `EdgeContext`, such as source attributes or destination attributes, is used in the `sendMsg` function to optimize the behavior. The default value of this parameter is `TripletFields.All`.

In this example, we will count that a vertex is the destination of how many directed edges. It is similar to counting how many followers a user has on Twitter.

The following is the definition of the `sendMsg` function:

```
public class AbsFunc1 extends
AbstractFunction1<EdgeContext<string,string,Integer>, BoxedUnit> implements
Serializable {
  @Override
  public BoxedUnit apply(EdgeContext<string, string, Integer> arg0) {
    arg0.sendToDst(1);
    return BoxedUnit.UNIT;
  }
}
```

Here we are sending a message with the value `1` from the source to the destination vertex.

The `mergeMsg` function can be defined as follows:

```
public class AbsFunc1 extends scala.runtime.AbstractFunction2<Integer,
Integer, Integer> implements Serializable {
  @Override
  public Integer apply(Integer i1, Integer i2) {
    return i1+i2;
  }
}
```

In this function, we are performing a sum on all the messages received at a vertex. This can be visualized as a word count program in map reduce.

Using the preceding user-defined functions, the `aggregateMessages` operation can be executed as follows:

```
VertexRDD<Integer> aggregateMessages = graph.aggregateMessages(new
AbsFunc4(), new AbsFunc5(), TripletFields.All,
scala.reflect.ClassTag$.MODULE$.apply(Integer.class));
aggregateMessages.toJavaRDD().collect().forEach(System.out::println);
```

As shown in the preceding example, it returns a type of `VertexRDD`, which contains the vertex ID and aggregated result. The vertices that are not the destination for any directed edge are not included in the resultant RDD.

outerJoinVertices

Joining datasets is a very popular operation in analytics systems. The `outerJoinVertices` operation is used to join graphs with external RDDs. Joining graphs to external datasets can be really useful at times when some external properties need to be merged in the graph.

The following is the signature of the `outerJoinVertices` transformation:

```
outerJoinVertices ( RDD <scala.Tuple2<Object,U>> other,
scala.Function3<Object, VD, scala.Option<U>, VD2> mapFunc,
scala.reflect.ClassTag<U> evidence$13, scala.reflect.ClassTag<VD2>
evidence$14, scala.Predef.$eq$colon$eq<VD,VD2> eq)
```

Here, the first parameter is the dataset to join with. The vertex ID of the graph vertices is joined with the Tuple object/key elements. The second parameter is the user-defined join function. As the name of the operation suggests, it works as an outer join operation. Therefore, the join function takes a `scala.Option` option that will be empty if there is no match found for the vertex ID in the external dataset.

The remaining parameters are Scala objects, `ClassTag`, and `eq`; we have already defined them in the previous section. Let's define the external RDD. The vertex property is the graph defined in the preceding sections as random names. Here we will define an RDD that will have last names for those names:

```
List<Tuple2<Object, string>> dataToJoin = new ArrayList<>();
dataToJoin.add(new Tuple2<Object, string>(1l,"Wilson"));
dataToJoin.add(new Tuple2<Object, string>(2l,"Harmon"));
dataToJoin.add(new Tuple2<Object, string>(3l,"Johnson"));
dataToJoin.add(new Tuple2<Object, string>(4l,"Peterson"));
dataToJoin.add(new Tuple2<Object, string>(5l,"Adams"));
JavaRDD<Tuple2<Object, string>> dataToJoinRdd =
javaSparkContext.parallelize(dataToJoin);
```

The following is the user-defined function defining the operation executed with the outer join of vertices:

```
public class AbsFunc1 extends AbstractFunction3<Object, string,
Option<string>, string> implements Serializable {
@Override
  public string apply(Object o, string s1, Option<string> s2) {
    if (s2.isEmpty()) {
      return s1 ;
    }
    else {
      return s1 + " " + s2.get();
    }
  }
}
```

If a match is not found then it is returning the first name itself.

Therefore, the `outerJoinVertices` operation can be executed as follows:

```
Graph<string, string> outerJoinVertices =
graph.outerJoinVertices(dataToJoinRdd.rdd(), new AbsFunc1(),
scala.reflect.ClassTag$.MODULE$.apply(string.class),
scala.reflect.ClassTag$.MODULE$.apply(string.class),
scala.Predef.$eq$colon$eq$.MODULE$.tpEquals());
outerJoinVertices.vertices().toJavaRDD().collect().forEach(System.out::prin
tln);
```

In this section, we learned about various graph-based operations. In the next section, we will implement some graph algorithms using the `GraphX` library.

Graph algorithms

The Spark `Graphx` library provides built-in implementations for some very popular graph algorithms. These implementations help to perform various graph-based analytics in a simplified manner. The `org.apache.Spark.graphx.GraphOps` API allows for executing these operations on the graph. In this section, we will run graph-based analytics using the following implementations:

PageRank

PageRank is one of the most popular algorithms in graph theory. It is used to rank the vertices based on their importance. The importance of a vertex is calculated by the number of edges directed to the vertex. For example, a user is highly ranked on Twitter based on their followers, that is, the number of directed edges to that user vertex.

The PageRank algorithm was developed by Google founders *Larry Page* and *Sergey Brin* to measure the importance of web pages. Thus, the best example of PageRank implementation is the Google Search Engine. Google ranks pages based on their importance. For example, if page X contains hyperlinks to page Y then page Y has importance to page X as its rank increases. Google uses this algorithm very efficiently to rank pages and outputs highly ranked pages first based on keywords in a user's search query.

Spark Graphx provides the following two ways to execute PageRank.

Static PageRank

`staticPageRank` runs for a defined number of iterations to calculate the page rank. Here is the signature of static PageRank operations:

```
staticPageRank (int numIter, double resetProb)
```

This method requires two arguments. The first argument is the number of iterations needed to be executed to calculate the page rank and the second parameter is the reset probability that is used to calculate the *damping factor* in PageRank and its value should be `0.0<resetProb<1.0`. Please refer to `http://infolab.stanford.edu/~backrub/google.html` to get details about the damping factor.

The static page rank on the graph can be executed as follows:

```
Graph<Object, Object> graphWithStaticRanking =
graph.ops().staticPageRank(1,0.20);
```

This operation results in a graph that contains vertices with their ranking. To find the ranks, vertices' elements can be printed as follows:

```
graphWithStaticRanking.vertices().toJavaRDD().collect().forEach(System.out:
:println);
```

Considering the graph example provided in this chapter, **vertex 3** should be ranked as the highest.

Dynamic PageRank

Instead of taking a defined number of iterations as an input, dynamic PageRank requires users to provides a tolerance value (double). The number of iterations in this case is dynamic as ranks will keep on calculating until the rank value is changing more than the specified tolerance value. Here is the signature of the method:

```
pageRank(double tol, double resetProb)
```

Thus dynamic PageRank can be executed as follows:

```
graph.ops().pageRank(0.00001,0.20)
```

As per the preceding example, dynamic PageRank will keep on running until the change in the rank value is more than *0.00001*.

Triangle counting

The **triangle count** is another common algorithm in graph theory. Triangle in graph theory is a three node graph where each vertex is connected to each other. For example, if A and B are friends on Facebook and C is their mutual friend and A, B, C form a triangle, the graph with more triangles is tightly connected.

Triangle counting on Spark clusters requires the graph to be partitioned:

```
graph.partitionBy(PartitionStrategy.CanonicalRandomVertexCut$.MODULE$);
```

Here we have used the CanonicalRandomVertexCut strategy to partition the graph. The TriangleCount operation on a graph can be executed as follows:

```
Graph<Object, string> triangleCountedGraph = graph.ops().triangleCount();
```

This operation returns a graph with every vertex containing the count that is equal to the number of triangles it is associated to. Referring to the logical representation of the graph, provided in the *Property Graph* section, the graph contains one triangle, which is as follows:

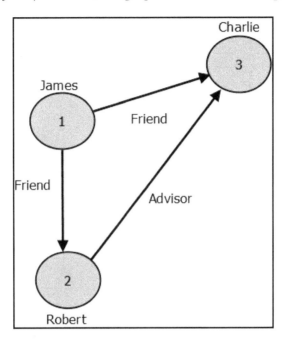

Logical representation of Triangle of vertices

To verify, we can print vertices' properties as follows:

```
triangleCountedGraph.vertices().toJavaRDD().collect().forEach(System.out::p
rintln);
```

The result should show that nodes 1, 2, and 3 have one associated triangle and no associated triangle to nodes 4 and 5.

Connected components

In graph theory, the connected component is the subgraph that is any two vertices that are reachable using edge paths. The whole graph can be a single connected component as well. Consider the following example, which is an extension of examples provided in the *Property Graph* section:

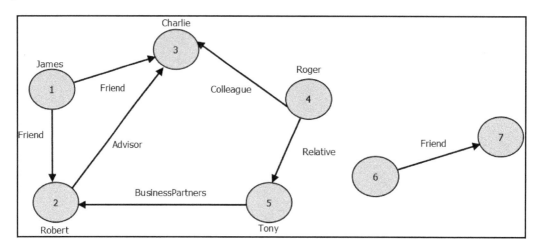

Logical representation of a graph with two connected components

Here, we have two connected components. Nodes 1 to 5 form a connected component where every node is connected to each other using some edge path. Similarly, nodes 6 and 7 form another connected component.

The `connectedComponents` operations label each of the other nodes in the connected components of a graph with the vertex ID of its lowest-numbered vertex. Therefore, considering the example provided previously, nodes 1 to 5 will be labeled as 1 and nodes 6 and 7 will be labeled as 6.

The `connectedComponents` operation in a Spark graph can be executed as follows:

```
Graph<Object, string> connectedComponentsGraph =
graph.ops().connectedComponents();
```

This operation will return a graph where the vertex property is the respective label of the vertex, which can be verified as follows:

```
connectedComponentsGraph.vertices().toJavaRDD().collect().forEach(System.ou
t::println);
```

Summary

In this chapter, we discussed the Spark `Graphx` library. We started with graph abstraction provided in the `Graphx` library known as the *Property Graph* and then we discussed various graph operations provided by the `Graphx` library with code examples. Finally, we discussed built-in graph algorithms provided by the `Graphx` library along with code examples.

The motive of this book is to explain concepts of Spark in detail and provide their implementations in Java and this is what we have focused while writing each chapter of this book. We would like to thank all the readers of this book and hope that this book has served the purpose of learning that you aspired for. Your feedback is precious for us so please feel free to provide your feedback, at Packt Publishing for this book. As said, once you know how to walk you can always make efforts to run, we hope that this book will help readers to walk on the road of Apache Spark and guide them to achieve their goals.

Index

R

Range Partitioner 199
RDD cache 145, 146
RDD of integers
  sum of even numbers, finding 79
RDD of strings
  filtering 76
RDD partitioning 193, 194, 195, 196
RDD persistence 145, 146
RDD transformations
  about 115
  Cartesian transformation 124
  distinct 123
  file transformation 117
  flatMap() transformation 118
  flatMapToPair() transformation 120
  intersection transformation 122
  map transformation 115, 116
  mapToPair() transformation 119
  union() transformation 121, 122
reduceByKey() transformation 126, 127
reinforced learning 285
reliability 271
reliable receivers 257
repartitionAndSortWithinPartitions transformation
  208
repartitioning 196
Representational state transfer (REST) 99
Resilient Distributed Datasets (RDDs)
  about 25
  benefits 29
  lazy evaluation 28
  logical representation 26
  number of words, counting in file 80
  operations 27
Resource Manager (RM) 189
ResourceManager 15
RESTful APIs, Spark 102
reverse operation 311
row matrix 286

S

Scala
  download link 71

SchemaRDD 235
semi-supervised learning 285
shared variable 221
Simple Storage Service (S3) 152
Single Abstract Method interfaces (SAM interfaces)
  46
sortByKey() transformation 127, 128
Spark 2.X
  enhancements 33
Spark APIs 25
Spark application, in distributed-mode
  about 178
  Driver program 178
  Executor program 179
Spark application, on standalone cluster
  client mode 186
  cluster mode 186, 187
Spark application
  prerequisites 106, 107, 108, 110, 113, 114
Spark CLI 75
Spark Core 32
Spark Driver program
  functionalities 178
Spark ecosystem 32
Spark Executor program
  functionalities 179
Spark GraphX 32
Spark job
  configuring 96
  executing 83
  submission 96
Spark master
  starting 181
  stopping 184
Spark MLlib
  datatypes 286
Spark REPL
  launching 75
Spark REST APIs 99
Spark shell
  basic exercises 76
Spark slave
  starting 182, 183
  stopping 184
Spark SQL

www.ingramcontent.com/pod-product-compliance
Lightning Source LLC
LaVergne TN
LVHW081332050326
832903LV00024B/1126